THE MISREPRESENTED GOD

EXPOSING THE LIES OF RELIGION, BEHOLDING THE TRUE NATURE, AND CHARACTER OF GOD REVEALED IN CHRIST

...FROM CHANNELS AWARD WINNING AND BESTSELLING AUTHOR

GREAT IGWE

An Imprint of WIGE Publishing House

Virginia- New York- Lagos

Copyright © 2021 Great Igwe.

All rights reserved. No part of this publication may be reproduced, distributed, or transmitted in any form or by any means, including photocopying, recording, or other electronic or mechanical methods, without the prior written permission of the publisher, except in the case of brief quotations embodied in critical reviews and certain other noncommercial uses permitted by copyright law. For permission requests, write to the publisher, addressed "Attention: Permissions Coordinator," at the address below.

Unless otherwise noted, scriptures quotations are from the Holy Bible, King James version (KJV) ©1979-1980-1982-1984 by Thomas Nelson, Inc. used by permission. All rights reserved new international version (NIV), ©1973-1978-1984 by the international Bible Society. Used by permission of Zondervan. Scripture quotations marked (NASB) are taken from New American Standard Bible. Scripture quotation marked (ESV) are taken from the English Standard Version with permission from Good News Publisher.

First Published 2020

ISBN: 978-1-7332803-9-6 (Paperback)

ISBN: 978-1-7332803-8-9 (Hardback)

ISBN: 978-1-7364619-2-1 (eBook)

Library of Congress Control Number: 2021901708

Published and Distributed By

WEGI PUBLISHING HOUSE LLC

6850 Richmond Highway Alexandria

22306 VA.

www.wegipublishing.com

WEGI Publishing House is a Subsidiary of the WEGI Group, Inc. The WEGI Publishing House Name and Logo are trademarks of WEGI Group, Inc. Quantity sales. Special discounts are available on quantity purchases by corporations, associations, and others. For details, contact the publisher at the address above or the author. Email: infor@wegigroup.com. Tel; +1 (240)-688-2092

Table of Contents

INTRODUCTION 1

CHAPTER 1 THIS IS NOT GOD 3

CHAPTER 2 UNDERSTANDING THE SOVEREIGNTY OF GOD & MAN'S INHERENT POWER OF FREE WILL 12

CHAPTER 3 WHO IS GOD REALLY? 19

CHAPTER 4 RE-KNOWING GOD IN CHRIST 34

CHAPTER 5 HOW JESUS' LIFE AND ACTIONS ON EARTH REVEALED THE HEART OF GOD 51

CHAPTER 6 THE PARABLE OF THE LOST SHEEP 67

CHAPTER 7 THE PARABLE OF THE PRODIGAL SON 75

CHAPTER 8 THE PARABLE OF THE GOOD SAMARITAN 88

CHAPTER 9 NO, GOD IS NOT VENGEFUL 98

CHAPTER 10 OLD TESTAMENT ANGRY GOD AND NEW TESTAMENT LOVING GOD. RIGHT OR WRONG? 109

CHAPTER 10 GOD DOES NOT HAVE MOOD SWINGS. 121

CHAPTER 11 THE GOD OF THE OLD TESTAMENT VS. THE FATHER OF THE NEW TESTAMENT 129

CHAPTER 12 GOD IS NOT SCHIZOPHRENNIC? 148

CHAPTER 13 GOD IS NOT JEALOUS LIKE MAN 166

CHAPTER 14 GOD IS NOT ANGRY WITH YOU OR THE WORLD .. 179

CHAPTER 15 GOD ISN'T DISAPOINTED IN YOU 196

CHAPTER 16 THE PURPOSE OF THE LAW 214

CHAPTER 17 COMMON MISCONCEPTIONS IN THE BODY OF CHRIST 235

INTRODUCTION

Throughout history, the knowledge of God – His nature, character, and actions – has been misunderstood and misrepresented by those who are considered leaders in Christendom. This is why the average person, whether Christian or non-Christian, is quick to attribute any major bad events, occurrences, or actions as the will or deeds of God. If there is an earthquake, a global pandemic, a terrorist attack, or a mass shooting, people's first instinct is to believe that God is somehow judging the world or punishing the world for it atrocities, or maybe God is angry at the rise of the LGBTQ in the world.

It's so despairing to think that a child who is so loved, adored, and valued by his father would have such a misinformed perception and mentality that he would believe that all the evil happening around him or to him is the work of his beloved Father. Every parent's greatest fear is for his children to have a wrong impression about him/her. Despite the good works the parent do for the child, as long as that child's mindset, knowledge, or perception towards his father is skewed, every good thing will be seen as undercover evil, and bad events in that child's life will be blamed on the parent.

The Misrepresented God tells the truth about who the Creator is. This book analyzes what religion says about God's heart and personality and measures it up to what God revealed about Himself through his beloved Son Jesus Christ: Love. It simplifies a generation's tangled perceptions of God by taking a journey through the sixteen aspects of love described in one of the most well-known Bible passages in the world, 1 Corinthians 13, also known as "The Love Chapter."

So many Christians have been bombarded with confusing teachings and doctrines that their understanding and knowledge of God describes Satan rather than God. This book takes that twisted mess and replaces it with one soft, warm light of truth that anyone can embrace: God is love. Nothing punctures the heart of every loving father like seeing that his children don't even know him or that they have a misguided view of him to the point they believe that he is the cause of their sickness and pain. They believe they have to pay Him or do one or two things for Him to bless, protect or love them. That is so disheartening. Now, I don't claim to be a psychic reader or some prophet, but I make bold to say that if there is anything that hurts the heart of our Sovereign Father, it is the false knowledge or misrepresentation of His nature and character to His children.

Religion has told so many lies about the nature and character of God that it has destroyed many lives, pushed people away from the Church, or even turned them to atheism, which is on the rise worldwide. The Pew Research Center reckons that atheism and its shadowy second cousin agnosticism, have grown rapidly around the world in the last five years. In 2013, one in five Americans were unable to say that they believed in God, while two in six claimed they no longer believed in God. Social scientists claim there are two main reasons people are embracing "non-belief." First is the religious right's political activism. Second is the blatant hypocrisy in modern Christianity and the misrepresentation and lack of true and uniform teachings and doctrines.

The Orthodox say God is coming back again; the Pentecostals say God is already here; the Old Testament says that Man must keep the Law of Moses to be saved, while the New Testament Grace Preachers say that all man needs to be saved is to accept the finished works of Jesus on the cross. This is enough to confuse even the most intelligent and logical person on earth. There's an urgent need for a re-education in the hearts and minds of Christians and the world at large on the nature and character of God.

It's important that we un-learn and relearn certain views and knowledge we have about God in line with that of the revealed and manifested God in the person of Jesus Christ. One major purpose for Jesus Christ's incarnation was to reveal the Father to His creation again. Therefore, through this book I hope to show you the true nature of God as revealed in Jesus Christ: His character, what He does and will not do. You will learn of the various lies religion and false teachers and prophets have told about God.

CHAPTER 1
THIS IS NOT GOD

Have you ever listened to a preacher talk about God and thought, "That doesn't sound like God"? Millions have become repulsed by the God some churches present. From birth, many Christians have been bombarded with so many contradictory teachings and doctrines that their understanding of God resembles a tightly tangled ball of Christmas tree lights. *The Misunderstood God* throws out that twisted mess and replaces it with the soft, warm light of truth. I have come to realize that the path of truth is a lonely one, and when you choose to walk that path, be prepared to walk it alone. We live in a world that doesn't appreciate fact, but rather appreciates and celebrates lies and corruption. Lies in religion, politics, and business are profitable and bring in fast fame, fans, wealth, and influence.

So, when you resolve to confront the lies and corruption in any of these spheres of life, fasten your seat belt, because they will fight you. Corruption will always fight back; lies will always fight integrity. At some point, in your firm desire to speak truth in boldness and power to those who choose to speak lies in order to enrich themselves, you will lose friends. You might even become enemies with people you once thought were your allies or even family. BUT choose to never surrender! Throughout history, the Truth had always prevailed. It will take time but be comforted in knowing that whatever you lose in your desire to speak the truth to people or institutions of power, you will always gain back a 100-fold over time.

With so many confusing teachings about God and countless contradictions, misunderstandings, outright scams, and simplistic, fear-based teachings, how can we really know who God is for ourselves? *The Misunderstood God* analyzes some of the most common claims about God's heart and personality and measures them against what God has called Himself: perfect love. I believe the only reason you or I haven't loved God more is because He has been misrepresented, and we have misunderstood Him. Through a journey into the sixteen aspects of love from one of the most well-known scriptures around the world, the "love chapter," I'm going to offer step-by-step comparisons and simple, biblical teaching to reveal the profoundly simple truth that God is, indeed, love. He has made it so easy to know His heart that even a child could understand Him.

No educated theologians or credentialed pastors have a corner on the truth about God. He is not locked in a monastery high in the mountains. He's not sitting in church hoping you'll show up. God is not out traveling with the latest super-spiritual faith healer. Finding God is easier than any of us imagined. People who have spent years searching for the truth about Him can finally discover that they have known Him all along. *The Misrepresented God* simplifies a generation's tangled perceptions of God. Finding God is as easy as learning what love means. His character and personality can be known and understood.

There is a God that was explained and interpreted, and there is a God that revealed Himself to the world. When you read about the things that were attributed to God, especially in the Old Testament books of the Bible, and in many of our modern day religious churches, they in no way resemble the God that was revealed in the New Testament books of the Bible.

The actions and nature attributed to God in the Old Testament are also different from the actions and nature of the God that walked this earth in flesh and blood. Many of the pictures we paint of God are more reflective of the Devil than God. This is the reason why devil-centered teachings are more prevalent in today's Sunday services than Christ-centered. Every evil thing is seen as the cause of God's wrath or His vengeance or His will. This is not God. A woman is baren; she feels God is punishing her for all her numerous abortions or evil deeds. That is not my God. A marriage fails; the couple says it's not the will of God for them to be together or have a relationship. That is not God. A man's business collapses; he says God is doing that to him in order to get him to do the work of the ministry or to test his faith. That is not God.

This is why we are so quick to lay curses on people from the pulpit or to ask God to kill our enemies and those who don't agree with us or choose to have a different views on certain subjects in life. Many

Christians see God as a Mafia boss or Cartel leader who requires absolute loyalty and forceful obedience based on intimidation and collects financial dues for his protection and shielding from rival gangs or the cops. But that's not God!! God is not interested in forceful obedience based on fear and intimidation but obedience that flows from love and relationship. You see, such views of God destroy a Christian's relationship with God and distort how the Christian relates with people and sees the world. Any teachings that portray God as a ruler who does both evil and good things – kills people, destroys children, or wipes out those who don't believe in Him or follow His ways – is not true. In as much as certain aspects of the Old Testament tell the story of how people were destroyed when they refused to accept God. Friends, that is not God. God doesn't kill; the wages of sin kill.

God is Love personified. He is Mercy personified. He is Grace personified. This is the core character of God. God is a Father, and His love and mercy towards His children are forever. The Old Testament can seem very contradictory and harmful if not properly studied holistically, in context. The Old Testament scriptures seem to paint God as a merciless God who has some serious temperament issues with His children when they don't get in line. But folks, that's not God. That description of God is totally different from the God who was revealed and manifested in the New Testament. It's different from the God the Apostle Paul taught and spoke of.

It's easy to get caught up with the bloody and horrific scenes of the Old Testament as the handiwork of God but difficult to see the mercy and grace of God at play in so many occasions of the Old Testament. The stories of God asking His people to kill others, wipe out generations, destroy women and children, rape, and other terrible deeds recorded in the Old Testament have been taught and preached in church as God's deeds, and many of us use that as a cover for evil deeds. A majority of the religious wars were fought based on the notion that God had sanctioned them or that God was supporting a race, nation, or people to destroy those who are not like them. Some extremist religious groups and denominations have carried out mass genocide, all based on the belief that they were the chosen ones or that they were God's battle axes. He who believes such is either ignorant or too blind to see the true God in Jesus Christ.

God is not a God of favoritism to love one person more than He loves another or protect one country more than others or bless one nation more than another. That's not God. He loves all equally, He protects and blesses all, regardless of race, background, or origin. His love is universal. He doesn't look at the world and see Muslims or Christians. He sees humanity. His desire is that all will come to know and accept His gift of life and salvation. When we hold an us-versus-them view of the world, we cannot effectively reach out to souls who are perishing. We won't be able to love the way Christ wants us to. We have let our selfishness, traditions, and culture eat into the Word of God to the point that it's of no power in our hearts. We preach the gospel of exclusion instead of love and relationship. The Orthodox are in their corner; the Anglicans are boxed into their own corners; the Baptists are hovering in their own corners and doctrines; the Pentecostals are doing their own thing.

We are busy forming packs like wolfs instead of coming together as one big family, sharing the same word and truth that will edify the body of Christ. We are quick to identify our denomination but slow to help one another. We are quick to condemn those who fall into temptation but terribly slow to actually love in truth. We don't trust our own Christian brothers and sisters and those who are not Christians even less so. We climb the pulpit and preach fire and thunder, but when we go home, we turn a blind eye to our neighbor who needs help or our fellow brethren suffering. That is not God.

Opinion Created God

When you preach about God, which God are you preaching? When you tell someone that God so loved the world that He gave His life for her, what does the word love signify to you? Do you even believe it? Is your knowledge of God in line with that revealed by Jesus Christ or do you just have your own opinion-created God in your heart?

So many zealous conservative Christians wish they could just politely ask God to step down and allow them take over as God for at least a week, so they can deal with the sinful people and clean the world of all the drunkards, smokers, LGBTQ, fornicators, and all liberal folks. If you believe that God is angry at the sinner or hates them, then you don't really know your Father. If you believe that even though a person believes in Jesus Christ he won't enter Heaven or can't be blessed by God because he sins, then you're ignorant of the lethal and volcanic power of the finished work of Jesus Christ at Calvary. We have a lot of opinion-based versions of God which are all influenced by our political affiliations, ideologies, cultural norms, and social identification. But if we must know God in truth and communicate this truth to others, we must subject all that under the lens of Jesus Christ who is the express image of God as recorded in Colossians 1:15 which reads, *"He is the image of the invisible God, the firstborn over all creation"*.

The Prophet Elijah said this about God; the Prophet Zachariah said that about God; Moses said this about God; Your Bishop or Pastor said XYZ about God; Great Igwe said this or that about God. All their statements could be good and worth knowing, but what did God say about Himself? What did Jesus reveal about God? Friend, that's the most important knowledge to behold.

The only reason you or I haven't loved God more

is because He has been misrepresented

and we have misunderstood Him.

Andrew Wommack

It doesn't matter what your Bishop says about God or what any Prophet says about God. If it doesn't agree or corelate perfectly to the gospels, Epistles, and above all Jesus' life, throw it away. There are many antichrist teachings in the church today. They sound good, resonate with our selfish and ignorant minds but are actually making a mockery of the finished works of Jesus Christ on the cross. Many people think the antichrist is a man or group of people with long horns, scaring people with tails and long claws. I guess if you watch too much Hollywood or Nollywood it's expected to have such perceptions about the Antichrist, but folks, that is just funny and false. The antichrist is already here in our midst. It is not some kind of demon or monster we see in children's storybooks or horror movies.

As a matter of fact, the antichrist is not even a person but a teaching and doctrine. Any teaching or doctrine that is against the works of Jesus Christ on the cross is simply ANTI-CHRIST. Many religious people who don't believe in the concept of righteousness through faith in Jesus Christ are just small Anti-Christs ignorantly.

A False Christ & Prophet

Mathew 24:24 reads, "For there shall arise false Christs, and false prophets, and shall shew great signs and wonders; insomuch that, if it were possible, they shall deceive the very elect." Not everyone who has a church building and preaches Christ is preaching Jesus Christ. Any Christ preached that did not finish the work of salvation is a false Christ. Any Christ that needs your works, conduct, good behavior, or fasting to save you from sin is a false Christ.

Mark 13:22 reads, "For false Christs and false prophets shall rise, and shall shew signs and wonders, to seduce, if it were possible, even the elect." A Christ that kills, or a killing Christ is certainly a false Christ. The true Christ is the giver of life and life in abundance. The true Jesus Christ doesn't need your good conduct or good behavior in order to save you from the curse and wages of sin. A Christ that gets angry and cancels or takes away your salvation and blessing if your conduct is not always good is a false Christ. That is not the Christ that incarnated and died for the whole world and declared "It's finished." That is a man-created Christ. A Christ that died for your sins but still requires you to finish the remaining works of salvation is a false Christ.

Any Christ or God preached that needs money or seed faith to bless you or intervene in your situation is a false Christ. That's not God. A God that comes down only when praise goes up is a false God. The true God is already here on earth, residing right inside every believer. He doesn't need praise or worship to come down or manifest. He doesn't need seed faith or offering to bless you or answer your prayers. That's not God.

Any Christ that will keep a record of all your wrongdoings in heaven, any Christ that did not finish salvation and still holds against you all your mistakes, faults, and errors in a book is certainly a false Christ. It doesn't matter the picture the preacher tries to paint. That is certainly a man-created Christ. The true Christ has dealt with sins germanely. He holds no grudge, anger or bitterness against anyone. He has no records of the believer's mistakes or sins. He sees the believer as a totally new creature, righteous in Him.

2 Corinthians 5:19 reads, "To wit, that God was in Christ, reconciling the world unto himself, not imputing their trespasses unto them; and hath committed unto us the word of reconciliation." Did you hear that? God does not impute sin, neither does he hold man accountable for sins anymore. Why? Because Jesus Christ took sin away. He dealt with sin once and forever, so men can receive forgiveness and be declared righteous forever. That's the true Christ. A false Christ will wait for you to be good in conduct before you can be saved. A false Christ can reject your salvation simply because you are not baptized in water by immersion or sprinkling. Salvation is simply confessing with your mouth the lordship of Jesus over your life and you are saved by faith.

God Doesn't Tempt His Children

Friends, temptation does not come from God. God never tempts anyone. Temptation is due to the weakness of our flesh and the product of our desires and lust. James makes this very clear, *"When tempted, no one should say, 'God is tempting me.' For God cannot be tempted by evil, nor does he tempt anyone"* (James 1:13, NIV).

A good thing to know is that God does not tempt us. This may come as a shock to many people, but God does not trick, tempt, or give us opportunities to sin, as has been wrongly preached in the past and is being preached by certain denominations and pastors. This is contrary to His nature. Jesus underwent temptation and testing so we would not have to. After all, the Bible records that Jesus was led by the Spirit into the desert to be tested by the devil (Matthew 4:1; Mark 1:12-13; Luke 4:1-2). In this testing Jesus proved His faithfulness to God, mankind, and the truth. Since this was a victory, we will never be tempted by God. Just as Jesus' temptation had no power and pull with Him, God cannot be tempted by evil and in the same manner would never tempt us with evil.

With this in mind, it is important for us to understand where temptations come from. First, like with Jesus, it can come from the devil. But more likely it comes from our own desires that battle inside us. Immediately after declaring that God would never tempt us, James went on to say, *"Each person is tempted when they are dragged away by their own evil desire and enticed. Then, after desire has conceived, it gives birth to sin; and sin, when it is full-grown, gives birth to death"* (James 1:14-15 NIV).

He made it very clear that our own desires, when focused on and allowed to grow inside, gave birth to sin. Temptation starts in the heart before it is evident in our lives. This is why it is so important to focus on the Spirit and the things of God. Then these things, rather than the desires of the flesh, will be evident in our lives. Paul made this very point in Romans 8. *"Those who live according to the flesh have their minds set on what the flesh desires; but those who live in accordance with the Spirit have their minds set on what the Spirit desires. The mind governed by the flesh is death, but the mind governed by the Spirit is life and peace"* (Romans 8:5-6 NIV). Do you want to experience life and peace? Walk, dwell, and live by the Spirit of God.

It is also important to understand that when temptation comes, God provides the way of escape. *"No temptation has seized you except what is common to man. And God is faithful; he will not let you be tempted beyond what you can bear. But when you are tempted, he will also provide a way out so that you can stand up under it"* (I Corinthians 10:13). This is an amazing truth. No matter how we are tempted, it all falls under the normal human experience. This is not to say that God gives His stamp of approval on every temptation that passes before us, allowing it to happen. But when it does, God does not allow trials or situations to be beyond human resistance. Nothing will be more than you or I can bear. Plus, God is faithful to His Word and compassionate in nature, so He can be trusted not to allow any temptation to exceed our ability to stand against it. If that were not enough, He will always provide a way of escape for us so that we can be removed from temptation, even in the midst of it.

God has given us sure-fire ways to escape the things that can tempt us. First, if we are being tempted by Satan, James tells us, *"Submit yourselves, then, to God. Resist the devil, and he will flee from you"*

(James 4:7 NIV). The truth is that Satan only has power over you if you give it to him. He is a defeated foe (Colossians 2:15). He is afraid of you because, as a believer, you are a co-heir with Christ and seated with Him in the heavenly realm, holding a true position of authority (Romans 8:17; Ephesians 2:6). He must flee. So, in the midst of temptation, if we stop and recognize what is happening, then we will have victory. James gives us the key: submit yourselves to God and resist. What a wonderful combination and sure-fire way to overcome this type of temptation.

Secondly, if our temptation comes from our own desires, then escaping is done through the Spirit. *"So I say, live by the Spirit, and you will not fulfill the desires of the flesh"* (Galatians 5:16 ISV). Living by the Spirit is being consumed with the things of God, planting His Word in your heart, letting His truth and guidance overtake and consume you. We are to live like strangers in this world. When you walk after the Spirit, this world and all its allure have no hold over you. It all pales in comparison to the goodness and glory of God. Lastly, a key to overcoming temptation is understanding God loves you, He died for you, and He will never leave or forsake you (Hebrews 13:5-6). This is so important to know and understand with every fiber of your being. So many times, in life we try to replace our desire to be loved and accepted with material things, alcohol, drugs, or relationships. But this insatiable desire grows from our inherent longing for God. Everyone is born with it, and this need is so great that unless you know the only One who can fill the void, you will try to fill it in other ways, many of which are destructive.

Once you get the revelation of God's love for you, contentment and peace will overtake you. They fill you to overflowing. You will dwell in a state of acceptance, love, forgiveness, and grace, and those things will pour out of you as well. The things of this world become insignificant compared to God's love. Abundant life fills the void until you overflow, and you will no longer look for things to fill that space. You will experience firsthand the goodness of God.

CHAPTER 2
UNDERSTANDING THE SOVEREIGNTY OF GOD & MAN'S INHERENT POWER OF FREE WILL

Many people haven't been Christians very long, and some have read conflicting teachings that make it hard for them to reconcile God's sovereignty with the idea of human responsibility and free will. When it comes to the nature of God, human understanding will only take us so far. Beyond that, we have to walk by faith. We can only move forward by trusting in God's goodness and faithfulness. And we can because He's already persuaded us of His reality and reliability.

The need for faith is particularly true when it comes to the subject we are looking at in this chapter: How do we reconcile what the Bible says about the absolute sovereignty of God with the equally valid scriptural teaching that man has been given free will? If God controls everything, how can we be genuinely responsible for our own choices and actions? God's absolute authority over everything and our freedom to choose—we see evidence of both in Scripture, yet they seem so contradictory. How do these principles work together in our daily life? The Scriptures are teeming with examples of God as the instigating force in our lives.

When God first created man, He established free will in him. He gave Adam and Eve a beautiful garden, animals to tend, plants to cultivate, and one command. Violating that command resulted in a spiritual flatline that became the genetic inheritance of all their offspring, which of course was the result of that inherent power of free-will. When we draw our first breath, we are not spiritually neutral. We are, by nature, children of wrath and must be born again into the family of God by accepting the finished works of Jesus Christ. We need life, freedom, and new birth, none of which we can accomplish for ourselves.

The Meriam Webster Dictionary defines sovereignty as "supreme power; freedom from external control; controlling influence." God is indeed sovereign over all His creation. He knows all, sees all, and is in control of everything, but man's inherent free will or power to make choices is excluded from that sovereignty. God is sovereign, but He doesn't control the choices you make in your life daily. God doesn't control where you go, what you eat, the actions you take or who you marry. If He did, then man would not be a free agent. If God wanted to control the free will of man, He would just force everyone to accept Jesus Christ and make the world a better place with no evil. But you will agree with me that's not the case. Now, it's important we understand that there are consequences for all the choices we make in life, good or bad, and we must be prepared to bear the consequences of our actions or choices.

I think one of the worst doctrines in the body of Christ today is the belief that God controls everything or, as the religious terminology states, "God is sovereign." It's usually presented in one of two ways: One, God originates everything; or two, Satan originates the evil things but has to get God's approval before he can do God's "dirty work." This doctrine seems dominant in the body of Christ today. It's so entrenched that many people will just discount what I have to say before hearing me out. To them, this has become a sacred cow. But this old cow needs to die. They need to kill that sacred cow, or it will kill the power of God's Word in their lives.

Man's inherent free will is excluded in God's Sovereign power

On the surface, it makes perfect sense that God controls everything. After all, He is God. He is all powerful. He can do whatever He wants to do. He is sovereign. I agree that God is sovereign if the word sovereign is used as it's defined in the dictionary. The American Heritage Dictionary defines "sovereign" as "1. Independent. 2. Having supreme rank or power. 3. Paramount; supreme." "Sovereign" comes from a Latin word that means "super, above."

I agree with all of those definitions. God is all of that and more. But religious tradition has redefined "sovereign" to mean God has and exercises "absolute control." I totally disagree with that! At one time,

God was in absolute control of everything, but then He made man and gave him unrestricted power and authority over the earth. Man knowingly gave that power and authority to Satan, and Satan has been messing things up ever since (with our help, I might add). You might say, "God could stop Satan if He wanted to. Therefore, the devil only does what God allows Him to do." That's not true. That's a religious tradition that will render you passive and prey to the devil. When God gave Adam unconditional authority over the earth, He gave him His word (Psalms 89:34). There were no strings attached. He didn't say, "If you blow it, I'll take back My power and authority." No! God had to allow what man allowed. The Lord had given man total control over the earth. It was his to govern as he saw fit. Adam then yielded to Satan the power and authority God intended for man.

God is a good God. If it was only up to Him, we would all be blessed (James 1:17). That can be seen in the life of Job. God blessed Job abundantly. He was the greatest man in wealth and integrity of all the people of his day. But Job didn't have a covenant with God. The Lord didn't really have the legal right to be so good to Job. Job was a sinner and therefore under Satan's control. So, Satan pressed his case, and the Lord had to turn Job over to Satan because he legally came under Satan's jurisdiction. his is why the Lord started making covenants with people like Abraham and, eventually, the whole nation of Israel. If they would comply, then the Lord could legally bless them. This worked, to a degree. The problem was that no one could live up to God's standard for very long. So, instead of the blessing He desired to give, the curse eventually came upon them because "all have sinned" (Romans 3:23).

People have seen many scriptural examples of God's judgment upon man in the Old Testament and have taken from that that judgment is God's way of correcting us. Under the New Covenant, that is no longer the case, and a number of Scriptures will kill that sacred cow. Deuteronomy 28 lists the blessings and curses that would come upon the Israelites depending on their obedience or disobedience to God's commands. Notice the things listed in verses 15-68: sickness, poverty, grief, and every other trouble imaginable. They are curses, not blessings, as many religious people are trying to make them out to be today.

People will say, "This cancer was really a blessing in disguise because it made me turn to the Lord for help." No! It's not a blessing; it's a curse. God didn't put that cancer on them or allow it. The fact that they turned to the Lord is good, but they shouldn't blame God for causing the problem. God never uses evil to correct or draw us to Him. Romans 2:4 says it's the goodness of God that leads us to repentance. Second Timothy 3:16 says that God's Word—not problems—is given to correct and reprove us.

Afflictions are what Satan uses to steal away God's Word (Mark 4:16-17). "But Great, don't all things work together for good?" No! That's not what God's Word says. That's another sacred cow. Look at Paul's actual statement in Romans 8:28. *"And we know that all things work together for good to them that love God, to those who are the called according to his purpose."* Taken in context, that verse says something totally different from what religion has taught us.

The two preceding verses say, *"Likewise the Spirit also helpeth our infirmities: for we know not what we should pray for as we ought: but the Spirit itself maketh intercession for us with groanings which cannot be uttered. And he that searcheth the hearts knoweth what is the mind of the Spirit, because he maketh intercession for the saints according to the will of God."* First, the Greek word for "helpeth" is a compound word that means "to take hold of opposite together, i.e. cooperate" (Strong's Concordance). The Holy Spirit does not intercede for us automatically; we must participate, and as we do, He energizes and quickens and empowers our prayers.

When He takes hold with us, things begin to work together for good. Secondly, in verse 28, there are qualifications that most people ignore. The first is to love God. Did you know that not everybody loves God? Not even all who are born again truly love God. For those who do not, things don't work together for good. The next part says you must be called according to His purpose. What is His purpose? First John 3:8 says that the purpose of Jesus' coming was to destroy the works of the devil. So, if you are functioning according to the purpose of Jesus, you should be out to destroy the works of the devil. Therefore, this passage of Scripture applies to people who are not passive but are interceding and letting the Holy Spirit supernaturally energize them and take their intercession to a level where it's not just human. That eliminates the majority of people right there.

God is not the one who makes our lives a mess.

We have a choice.

Deuteronomy 30:19 says, "I call heaven and earth to record this day against you, that I have set before you life and death, blessing and cursing: therefore choose life, that both thou and thy seed may live." To say we don't have a choice is another way of saying we aren't willing to take personal responsibility for our situations. When we believe we're not responsible, it invalidates the Word of God. The Word tells us to make a choice between life and death, so we do have a choice. God even helped us out by telling us which one to choose: He said to choose life.

The slickest deception Satan has ever employed, primarily through the church, is to get people to embrace his work as the work of God. In my estimation, this is the worst doctrine in the body of Christ. If you really believe God controls everything, why do anything? Why pray? Why study the Word? Why resist? Just eat, drink, and be merry for tomorrow you die, and whatever God wills will happen. James 4:7 says, "Submit yourselves therefore to God. Resist the devil, and he will flee from you." Notice that there are things from God that we submit to and things from the devil that we resist. God does not control everything. Religion has played into the victim mentality because it's the easiest way to explain away failure.

The church has not been effective in helping people overcome things like sickness and financial problems, so they fall into the sacred cow belief that God is allowing this for a reason. God isn't allowing the bad things in your life. The same power that raised Christ from the dead lives on the inside of every believer, and He is waiting on you to resist the devil and utilize what He has already provided through Jesus.

Two Sides of The Same Coin

If we study everything the Bible has to say about divine sovereignty and human free will, we'll find that (in a way we can't fully explain) both are completely valid ideas. Is God completely in charge of everything? Yes. *"For I am God, and there is no other; I am God, and there is none like me, declaring the end from the beginning and from ancient times things not yet done, saying, 'My counsel shall stand, and I will accomplish all my purpose,'"* (Isaiah 46:9b-10, ESV).

Do people have to answer for their choices and actions? Absolutely. *"For whatever one sows, that will he also reap"* (Galatians 6:7b, ESV). So, to be faithful to the testimony of Scripture, we have to acknowledge both sides of the coin. On the one hand, God is absolutely sovereign. On the other hand, human beings have free will and are fully responsible for their own actions.

Consider it this way: We owe everything to God's grace. It's literally by His favor and mercy that we are what we are (1 Corinthians 15:10). But that doesn't mean we're off the hook and can do whatever we want. The choices we make, the words we speak, the things we do … our actions have eternal implications. How can God's sovereignty and human free will be true at the same time? We don't know. But God does. And we can trust that He'll explain it to us when we see Him face to face. Often, human perspective and the mechanics of Christianity eclipse the true nature of God – the God who wants nothing more than to share an intimate friendship with His children.

What makes man different from the angels is the free-will given to man by God at creation. The free will of man cannot be taken away by any supernatural force. God cannot use a man without the permission of the man, neither can Satan. We saw this permission being requested from Mary, the Mother of Jesus. The Angel needed Mary's permission before the supernatural could take over her. The same thing is applicable with salvation. In as much as God would like all men saved by receiving Jesus Christ as Lord and Savior, He cannot force them. He still allowed man the power to exercise his free will.

The truth is contrary to popular belief. Man is the one in charge of the earth, not God or any irrelevant demon. Earth is man's territory and jurisdiction. Whatever man does with it, he will always bear the consequences. So, when you see an earthquake, a global pandemic, mass shootings, or a terrorist attack, that is the result of a combination of several actions of man. It's not God trying to warn man or destroy him, neither is it some demon trying to destroy earth. Folks, the devil has no power against man. The only power the devil has is the one man has ignorantly given to him. If the devil has so much power, why has he not killed you? He should have stopped Neil Armstrong from reaching the Moon, but he can't because he has no such powers. None. The devil is a defeated bastard and fool, only as strong as the ignorance of his victims.

CHAPTER 3
WHO IS GOD REALLY?

There is only one nature that describes God as a sovereign Father, that is LOVE. If you have listened to any of my teachings, you've heard me speak about the love of God. That's what changed my life. I believe a true, experiential understanding of God's love will drastically change anyone's life. That's the point that the Apostle Paul was making in Ephesians 3:19. It reads, *"And to know the love of Christ, which passeth knowledge, that ye might be filled with all the fulness of God."* Knowing God's love experientially surpasses mere head knowledge, and it always results in us being filled with all the fullness of God. I could say it this way: If you aren't experiencing all the fullness of God, then you aren't experiencing God's love.

Many people would argue with that. They would say that they know God loves them but that they are just under their circumstances at the moment. My answer would be, "What are you doing under there!" The Bible says we are to be above only and not beneath (Deuteronomy 28:13). When we are enjoying God's love, everything else pales in comparison. No problem can compare to the unsearchable riches of God's love. It's like the old song says, "Turn your eyes upon Jesus, looking full in His wonderful face. And the things of earth will grow strangely dim in the light of His glory and grace." That is absolutely true.

In one of my weekly podcasts, I taught on the love of God in every season I've had a teaching series available on this subject for years called God's Kind of Love: The Cure for Selfishness and Self-Guilt! Every Christian knows of God's love for them, but because of wrong thinking, it seldom translates into experience. Instead of restating the obvious, I want to specifically counter the wrong thinking that blinds us to His love.

There are things (primarily religious teachings) that dilute and weaken the revelation of God's love. Wrong thinking about the sovereignty of God is one of the biggest hurdles people have to experiencing God's love. Anyone who doesn't get this right will never truly appreciate God's love. It's impossible to feel good about God if you believe the accusers that depict Him as evil. If you believe God is the One causing all the problems in the world, that thinking will definitely affect your relationship with Him.

Let me illustrate it this way: What if you thought I was the one who killed thousands in the September 11 terrorist attacks, caused the tsunamis that devastated Asia, destroyed New Orleans with a hurricane, or caused the recent explosion in Beirut, Lebanon? What if you thought I was so heartless that I would cause babies to be born with birth defects and people to suffer terrible things like murder and rape so I could teach them a lesson? If every evil thing in life were my fault, how would you feel about me? There isn't a civilized nation on the earth that wouldn't have me killed. Yet this is what the Lord is being blamed for every day. It's even written in our contracts—major natural disasters and tragedies are called "acts of God." This isn't a true representation of God. God is not the source of our problems.

Not seeing ourselves "in Christ"

is the root of all unbelief and of the failure?

to experience God's pure love.

Let's discuss God's unconditional love. That is a radical concept. Nearly all of religion links God's love and acceptance of people to their worthiness. In other words, God's love is proportional to their performance. Some Christian groups present salvation as a free gift of God's grace then turn right around and teach new believers that their continuing relationship with the Lord now depends on their performance. If they don't live holy, go to church, read their Bibles, and pay tithes, etc., then the Lord won't bless them or answer their prayers.

That kind of thinking will block a person from receiving the love of God. When their performance falls short – and it always does – their own hearts will condemn them. They just can't believe God could love them. The truth is that God's love for us has nothing to do with our performance. He loves us because He is love (1 John 4:8), not because we are lovely. Understanding that God's love is unconditional will revolutionize your life. It certainly has mine. Another major roadblock to experiencing God's love is this: How can a holy God love unholy people? The answer is that God is a Spirit, and if we are going to truly connect with Him in worship, we have to do it through our new, born-again spirits (John 4:24). When I found out who I was in the Spirit, it forever changed me and allowed me to finally accept God's love.

I am firmly convinced that not seeing ourselves "in Christ" is the root of all unbelief and of the failure to experience God's pure love. This is my life message. It's at the core of all the understanding the Lord has given me, and I believe it has to become a true revelation to every person if they want to experience God's love in its fullness. Much of what people believe about God's rejection of us comes from Scripture. They use Old Testament scriptures as the basis for what they believe, not understanding that Jesus forever changed God's dealings with mankind. They don't understand the difference between the way God dealt with people under the Old Covenant of the Law and the way He now deals with us through Christ. Second Corinthians 5:19 says, *"To wit, that God was in Christ, reconciling the world unto himself, not imputing their trespasses unto them; and hath committed unto us the word of reconciliation."*

Under the New Covenant, God is not imputing our sins unto us. That is the exact opposite of what happened under the Old Covenant. This is explained in detail in the New Testament, and yet members of the body of Christ have missed this truth. The vast majority of Christians are still under sin consciousness, the very thing that Old Testament saints longed to be free from. They saw our covenant by faith and prophesied about the superiority of the New Covenant that God would make with mankind (1 Peter 1:10-12). Yet, modern-day Christians aren't taking advantage of all the benefits of God's love available in that New Covenant. God's people truly are destroyed for lack of knowledge (Hosea 4:6).

> *Once you begin to understand how much God loves you, love will flow out of you toward others like rivers of living water.*

A young man in Ethiopia who follows my teachings wrote me that he had been hearing me teach on this subject via my weekly podcast for 4 months. He said that he thought he had understood, until he heard my series of messages. "Now, I finally get it," he wrote. It brought a revelation of God's love to him that he had never understood before. Many others were experiencing the same thing. God's love was becoming real to them. I want you to have the same opportunity to make this revelation your own.

As I Have Loved You

Imagine the night before Jesus' crucifixion. He has communion with His disciples and washes their feet. He reveals that Judas is the one who will betray Him. He tells the disciples that He is leaving, and they can't come. Then, He speaks these words: *"A new commandment I give unto you, that ye love one another; as I have loved you, that ye also love one another. By this shall all men know that ye are my disciples, if ye have love one to another"* (John 13:34-35). By this would be, in part, His final words to the disciples before His death, they had to be very important. And notice that what He said to them was in the form of a command, not a suggestion. I am sure that you have read or heard this passage many times. But in reality, most do not think that this is something they can actually do. It's a goal that they may strive to reach with gritted teeth, but usually with little success.

It begs the question—would Jesus give His disciples a command He knew they couldn't keep? The answer is obviously no, so why is it so hard for us today to love other people? Could it simply be that we can't give what we don't have? The majority of churches are teaching that God's love for us is conditional. They are misrepresenting His love, and it is one of the main reasons that we as Christians are so judgmental and harsh toward other people. Consciously or not, we tend to treat people the way we believe God is treating us. It's the reason we condemn fellow saints who gave into the desires of their flesh or lust. Many churches in this current dispensation still discipline church members who get divorced or fornicate or fall into adultery. Some of these churches relegate these members to the back seats of the church.

We must understand that God does not love us because we are lovely. He does not love us because we read the Bible, go to church, pay our tithes, or do our best to keep the command to love others as He loved us. The truth is that He loves us without conditions. That's huge!

> *As long as you believe God is judging you according to your performance, you will never fully receive His love.*

I grew up in an Anglican Church where all that was preached was the message of evangelism. They made me feel like I had to pay God back for saving me by leading others to Jesus. It became such a part of me that I used to say this: "The sole purpose for our existence here on this earth is to lead somebody else to Jesus." Then the Lord spoke this to me "If evangelism is the sole purpose for your existence, then what about Adam and Eve? They had no one to lead to the Lord, no Sunday school class to teach, no one to pray for, and no physical need of any kind." The answer can be found in Revelation 4:11, which reads, *"Thou art worthy, O Lord, to receive glory and honor and power; for thou hast created all things, and for thy pleasure they are and were created."*

The original purpose of all creation was to give God pleasure. And that is still God's purpose. Adam and Eve were created for fellowship with God. He wanted someone to love and for them to voluntarily love Him back. God's purpose for creating human beings was all about relationship. But religion has succeeded at turning us from "human beings" into "human doings." When that becomes the focus, we begin to tie God's love for us to something that we do for Him. I did! But that was never His plan. Over the years, I have prayed for many people. The vast majority of those who come forward begin by telling me about their spiritual lives: "I've been praying, fasting, reading the Bible, and attending church, but I'm still not healed." They don't realize it, but they just told me why they weren't healed. They're pointing to what they are doing instead of what Jesus has done.

The same is true about our relationship with the Lord and with other people. We have come to believe that God loves us and acts on our behalf based on our performance. Therefore, we hold others to the same standard—our love for them is in direct proportion to their works, or how they treat us. Romans 5:8 reads, *"But God commendeth his love toward us, in that, while we were yet sinners, Christ died for us."* God's love has never been or ever will be conditional. He loved you at your worst, and most Christian churches would agree with that, initially. They believe you are saved by grace through faith, no matter your history, but that is often where grace stops, and religion starts. And religion always puts the emphasis on the external.

Once you're saved, religion says you must live holy, and the evidence of your holiness will likely be judged by the standards of your church. Do you dress the right way? Do you say the right things? Are you leading people to Jesus? And most importantly, are you tithing? — just to give a few examples. Friend, honestly, that is not how God sees us. God looks at the heart. First Samuel 16:6-7 says this: *"And it came to pass, when they were come, that he looked on Eliab, and said, Surely the* LORD*'s anointed is before him. But the* LORD *said unto Samuel, Look not on his countenance, or on the height of his stature; because I have refused him: for the* LORD *seeth not as man seeth; for man looketh on the outward appearance, but the* LORD *looketh on the heart."*

Samuel was going to choose Eliab to replace King Saul because of the man's outward appearance, but God was not looking on the outside. The church today is judging believers in the same way. You might carouse in secret on Saturday night, but as long as you come to church the next morning well kempt and well dressed with a check in your hand, you're accepted because you have the appearance of holiness.

Under the New Covenant, God is still concerned about your actions and behavior. It's not okay to lie, steal, commit adultery, or any other sin. However, He knows that those are nothing more than the byproduct of a relationship—or the lack of one—with Him. So, He is focused on your heart. As long as you believe God is judging you according to your performance, you will never fully receive His love.

Love is a decision, and God decided to love you even though you don't deserve it. There is nothing you can do to earn it or deserve it, so just receive it as a free gift.

When you understand how much God loves you, it becomes easy to love others. And when you love others as He has loved you, your behavior will change toward them. If you loved your mate the way that Christ loves you—unconditionally—you would never commit adultery. If you loved your neighbor as Christ loves you, you would never steal from them or bear false witness against them. How does the world know that we are disciples of Christ? John 13:35 says, *"By this shall all men know that ye are my disciples, if ye have love one to another."* Did you know that the first-century church evangelized the known world in thirty years? They didn't have television, the internet, smart phones, or texting. But they loved one another, and that love was so evident, it attracted people like honey attracts bees.

A Pharisee, who was a lawyer, asked Jesus this question: *"Which is the great commandment in the law?"* Jesus answered in Matthew 22:37-40 saying, *"Thou shalt love the Lord thy God with all thy heart, and with all thy soul, and with all thy mind. This is the first and great commandment. And the second is like unto it, thou shalt love thy neighbor as thyself. On these two commandments hang all the law and the prophets."*

The Pharisees wanted Jesus to name the most important "Thou shalt not," and instead, Jesus spoke "Thou shalt." Many believers are still living under the Old Testament mentality. They are trying to earn the love of a God who already made the decision to love them unconditionally. Once you begin to understand how much God loves you, love will flow out of you toward others like rivers of living water.

The Day I Fell In Love With People.

In my short years as a pastor and teacher of the Bible, I came to a point in my life seven years ago when I had the sudden realization through the help of the Holy Spirit that I love the message of the gospel more than anything in the world, even more than I love people. But something changed in me after I fell in love with people. I mean, I love my Mother so much, my sister Deborah, my 3 younger brothers and my friends and cousins. I just loved those related to me by blood or by virtue of friendship or how much they had shown me love and care, but I did not love people in general.

One day when I was going out one blessed morning for market evangelism. I reached the market square and was about to pick up my mobile microphone and speaker to start blasting in prayers and asking people to accept Jesus as their Lord and Savior or perish, and the Holy Spirit spoke to me softly. "Listen son, you cannot love My message more than you love My people for whom I sent the message to." I stood still, shocked at the voice in my head. I realized at that moment that I was missing the most important attribute of God. I was more concerned about the "salvation" than I was about the people.

I can remember tears dripping from my eyes because it dawned on me that I was not qualified to speak about Jesus when I didn't even have sincere love in my heart for the very people Jesus died for. I went out to win souls for God, but I returned home broken, in tears because my own heart was won over. I fell in love with people as the message sprang to life in me and became more beautiful and more powerful than ever before. The heart and appearance of my life changed entirely. I could suddenly see that after hundreds of years of preachers putting the message before the people, it had mutated into something so repulsive and terrible that it actually hurt people rather than saving them. But when I finally loved the people more than the message, I could see exactly what the problem was.

In fact, I'm convinced to this day that the only way to know the heart of the pure, unadulterated gospel of salvation is through loving the people the message is for. Loving people unconditionally, without regard for race, ethnicity, national origin, gender, social status, or religion. I fell in love with people after years of preaching the message of salvation, after years of condemnation and exclusion theology, after years of studying the Bible. It was at that market square that I came to fall in love with people.

This one encounter forever changed my views about the world and people, changed my approach to the message of salvation. I've found that when you love people with every part of yourself, you actually see inside their hearts. You become extremely sensitive to every part of their souls as if they were your own. You can see inside them and hear through their ears, see through their eyes, and understand things from their perspective. If someone says something negative to people you love, you can interpret what they heard, how they took it, and what feelings it gave them.

It's not as though you see it from a distance or from the outside looking in. You actually experience it with them. Your heart is woven tightly to theirs. When they become the object of your affection, you suddenly become one with them. Real love takes you outside of yourself and allows you to enter and meld with other people's hearts. When they laugh, your heart laughs because you are one. This is the result of pure love. This is the way to spread the message of salvation.

When you understand how much God loves you,

it becomes easy to love others.

And when you love others as He has loved you,

your behavior will change toward them.

In this new dispensation, our duty as evangelists or reconciliation ministers is not to ask people to repent or to call out their sins. We MUST NEVER do that. Why is this important? Because we are expected to see people as Jesus Christ sees them (i.e., as righteous people who are yet to acknowledge their new state in Christ). Repentance is not a change of conduct or behavior, but rather, a change of mindset. The question then is, mindset of what? The mindset of self-righteousness, mindset of an alien, mindset of a slave, to a mindset that is focused on the finished works of Jesus Christ. A mindset of a son or daughter who is a joint heir with Christ.

We cannot use an Old Testament perspective of evangelism to minister in a New Testament dispensation. Therefore, we must stir from a repentance-based evangelism to a believing (faith) based approach. It's imperative that we do this, bearing in mind that we are not saved because we repented of our conduct. Rather, are saved because we believe in Jesus Christ. Once my eyes were opened to this amazing truth, I suddenly remembered a wedding I attended years before where the pastor read the popular Bible passage that you always hear at weddings. You know the passage from 1 Corinthians 13, the "Love Chapter."

Every person living in Nigeria or America has heard it at least once: *Love is patient, love is kind. It does not envy, it does not boast, it is not proud. It does not dishonor others, it is not self-seeking, it is not easily angered, it keeps no record of wrongs. Love does not delight in evil but rejoices with the truth. It always protects, always trusts, always hopes, and always perseveres.* (1 Corinthians 13:4-7 NIV). When read at a wedding, those verses have a romantic sound. I don't think anyone in the audience at these occasions really believes a word of the passage. It's just something you read at weddings, like you read *The Night before Christmas*-on-Christmas Eve. It sounds so pretty when you hear it, but it's not realistic. At this same wedding, I saw a bumper sticker that read "God is love." That made me laugh out loud. If that were true, I thought, it would mean that the entire Christian religion is wrong. At least everything I grew up hearing. I don't think the outwardly religious could survive such a revelation, much less admit to it. Nevertheless, it did cause me to wonder.

Almost ten years later, I came face-to-face with the revelation of the wedding verse and that bumper sticker. It finally made sense to me. I could suddenly see what the problem was with most of Nigerian and American Christianity. I knew that we had been lied to about God, but now, for the first time in my life, I was beginning to realize with the truth was and how we lost it. People instinctively know that God is love. It's written on their hearts. Something inside every one of us knows the truth about our Creator. We define God by what we think love is. Sadly, this world has altered the true meaning of love in our minds, and in doing so, it has effectively redefined the heart of God to an entire generation.

First Corinthians 13 contains a list of fifteen statements about love. The Bible says, "God is love." This would mean that these fifteen statements are a description of the character and personality of God Himself. You might have even heard this particular passage read with the word *God* replacing the word *love*. If you haven't, I would encourage you to read it that way now because it's very moving. We can also conclude that what we believe in our hearts about love is exactly what we believe in our heart about God. This is precisely where I want to park for a moment. What do you believe about love in your heart? The problem is that the world has taught you that love is the exact opposite of everything written in the passage. Think about it for a moment. I would like to propose to you the idea that you have bought into the world's definition of love, and somewhere in your heart you believe it.

Our passage says that "love is not self-seeking." This is precisely the opposite of everything the world has raised us to believe. How about the phrase "Love keeps no record of wrongs"? Do I need to elaborate on that one? Then our scripture tells us that "love always trusts." We have been taught to look at trusting people as if they were foolish and stupid. How about when it says, "Love always perseveres"? With a divorce rate as high as it is today. I think we can pretty much toss that one aside. We have come to believe that people "just grow apart," and "nothing lasts forever." These excuses even have a ring of wisdom when you hear people use them for their failed marriages.

The point I want to make is that the world has convinced us that love is the exact opposite of everything listed in the passage. Also, I want to make the point that we have bought this lie hook, line, and sinker. Maybe not in our heads, but we have in our hearts. I want you to make a mental list of how many times you have been hurt by love in your past, whether by someone with whom you were in a romantic relationship or by a member of your immediate family. Take a moment and count. If you're like most people, you may have several unforgettable instances that have already surfaced in your mind. Now I have a revelation for you: it wasn't love that hurt you! What you were hurt by was the opposite of love, but in your heart, you believed it was love. Make no mistake about it: love has never hurt you. You were hurt by a deceptive and upside-down definition of love that you swallowed into your heart and believed.

If the Bible says that "God is love," and everything listed in this passage is a description of the character and personality of God, then I have another question: whose description is the *opposite* of everything listed here? The devil. Let's go a step further, if you believe in your heat that "love" is the opposite of what the Bible says, you will inevitably attribute the character and personality of the devil to God. Think about this for a moment, and let it sink in. I believe this is what the vast majority of us believe in our hearts about God. We basically believe He has the character and personality of the devil.

This is precisely the point He was making two thousand years ago. If Jesus Christ were walking the earth today in human form, I believe His message would be the same to us as it was to the Pharisees of His time: "You belong to your father, the devil" (John 8:44 NIV). The Pharisees and religious teachers had painted a picture of God that made Him look like Satan himself. They had made it impossible for the people to have a relationship with God simply because they were terrified and repulsed by Him. We are no different today.

On September 11, 2001, two airplanes loaded with hundreds of innocent passengers were hijacked and flown into the twin towers of the World Trade Center. As millions of Americans watched helplessly in their homes, the towers crumbled to the ground, killing thousands of terrified people. Shortly after this event, several of the nation's most influential Christian leaders appeared on national television and publicly declared that *this was God* sending judgment on America for its many sins. They were not alone in this thinking. Hundreds of other Christians followed them in this belief.

During the beginning of the AIDS epidemic, it was quite common to hear our nation's pastors proclaim that this was a plague sent by God to punish the homosexuals. Many people still hold to this way of thinking today. Every bad thing that happens in this world gets blamed upon God. If we lose our jobs, we think God is at the root of it. If we have a heart attack, God gave it to us. If we lose loved ones, it's because God killed them. If our businesses fail, we immediately suspect that God is punishing us for something we did. Every terrible thing that happens is charged to God's account. We truly believe that God has the character and personality of the devil.

Just listen to the way we talk about our God. It's no wonder Christians have little interest in reading their Bibles. Who would want to read "His" book? People decide beforehand what their interpretation of Scripture will be. If you think God is angry, the Bible will sound *only* angry to you. If you think He is a drill sergeant, the Bible will come across that way. If you have decided He is disappointed with you, you will see only disappointment in the words of the Bible. This is why most Christians never read their Bibles. It is natural for us to avoid contact with someone we don't love. Could you imagine if I had to have a support group of men to keep me accountable in the matter of reading my wife's letters to me? If my wife writes me a love letter, I will plow through an army of men to get to that letter just to see what is says. Then I will read it over and over until the paper literally falls apart in my hands.

Our feelings about God are why most Christians don't pray more than five minutes a week. Who would want to talk to Him? I believe that because of the lies we have been told about the heart of God; it is virtually impossible for us to absolutely love Him. He is terrifying. He turns His face from us. He removes His hand of protection from us. He causes bad things to happen in our lives. He is just not lovable.

Often when we use terms like "committed to Christ" it's proof that we don't love Him. A commitment is a way of forcing ourselves to do what we don't want to do. This is not what love is. God is *not* looking for Christians to make another commitment. If you have to force it, it's not there. Truthfully, I think that many "committed" Christians need to be "committed" to a psychiatric ward. If it were not for the promise of heaven at end of their lives, I honestly think they would have been better off unsaved. Religion has rendered them certifiably insane. It has caused some people to surrender every bit of common sense to a series of jumbled and mixed-up teachings that have no rhyme or reason.

We are terrified of Him, and rightly so, because He is just waiting for us to make a mistake or fall into sin so He can blast us into hell. Most of what we do in our religion is based on fear. We give the offering because we truly believe He won't bless us if we don't. We try our best to witness to others about this wonderful and loving Jesus Christ, but in our hearts, we don't believe a word of what we're saying. We go through every religious ritual we know in an effort to gain His favor. Our prayer lives have been reduced to confessions of "Forgive me" and "I'm sorry" at the end of the day. Something needs to change and soon.

Our problem today is that we subscribe to a theology we can't trust as far as we can throw it. Can you imagine me telling my wife that I love her and will never leave her or forsake her, but if she ever cheats on me, I will proceed to torture her for all eternity? Though she may never cheat on me, she will certainly never get close to me. She will do whatever it takes to survive the relationship, but I will *never* have her heart. This is exactly what many Christians believe about their Father.

When I watch Christians going to "gay pride" parades with megaphones, holding "You're Going to Hell" signs or to hatefully picket abortion clinics and heap truckloads of condemnation on the poor women who go to them, I sit in total amazement. Yet, what's happening is quite natural. These people are being conformed to their image of the Father. It makes perfect sense: if we believe in our hearts that God has the temperament and disposition of Satan, our character will inevitably be conformed to that image.

When you look at it this way, everything begins to make sense. More than anything, it makes sense that our religion keeps dying on us. Christianity has become like the old pickup I used to own. It was a classic, and definitely authentic looking, but it broke down every hundred miles, needing to be revived. The word *revival* is not even in the Bible. It was never the intention of God to have a religion that routinely suffered from heart failure. Sadly, we have become addicted to the electrical shock God has to routinely use to bring our religion back to life every hundred years or so.

I've found that if you take all the clichés in the Christian world that hurt people and hold them up to the light of real love, they prove to be repulsive and untrue. The problem is that most people don't have the guts to hold their belief system up to the light of love. They're not even sure they are allowed to.

They secretly wonder if doing so might make God feel the way we do when the cashier at the convenience store holds our twenty-dollar bill up to the light. It's a feeling of being accused of counterfeiting and undeservingly interrogated. But holding Christian teachings up to the light isn't in any way mistrusting God. He is the light! If you're a lover of people, you may find that many things you hear from the pulpit Sunday morning don't pass the light test. I believe we've been deceived into accepting a lie concerning love. But I also believe there's an even deeper place in our hearts that knows exactly what love is. It's a place that many of us have been afraid to trust most of our lives. This is the place I'm hoping you'll go with me in reading this book. I believe everything you read here will be confirmation of what you already know in our heart.

Could you imagine me holding my nine-month-old son in my arms and telling him that under no circumstances would I share my glory with him? What if I lovingly told him that if he disobeyed me again and again, I would pour gasoline on him and light him on fire? What kind of father would I be if I explained to him that he needed to give me ten percent of everything he had or I would withdraw my hand of protection from his life and allow the fires of hell to swallow him? What if I told one of my younger brothers that he was put here on this earth to be a servant and a slave to me? Could you picture me telling my children that I've written everything about me down in a book and unless they read it every day of their lives, they'll never know me? What parent would purposely inject their child with a terrible disease as a punishment for disobedience? What father would turn his head away from his son or daughter the moment the child made a mistake?

Come with me on a journey – a journey to the heart of God. I would like to take you through this amazing passage. I'd like to show you something that could change everything for you. I want to invite you into your *own* heart and show you what already exists there. You're ready, open your heart and turn the page.

CHAPTER 4
RE-KNOWING GOD IN CHRIST

Friend, who is God to you? What is your perception of His nature and character? What are your views and beliefs about His dealings with mankind? Do you believe He is the angry God? The merciless and unforgiving God? The God who is waiting for you to sin and then curses you or destroys your finances, marriage, or whatever? Do you see Him as the God who enjoys killing His children? The God who commands us to kill our enemies, murder children, women, sons, fathers, brothers simply because they have yet to come to the knowledge of their true identity in Him? Is that your view of God?

Is your view of God tainted by the depiction and presentation of His activities in the Old Testament? Or is it renewed by your knowledge of the revealed God in Jesus Christ? Who is God to you? Do you know Him in truth and spirit? Do you have the sound and revealed knowledge of HIM as the ever-loving and merciful Father who will never kill, tempt, harm, or curse His children? The Father who blesses all and holds nothing back and whose thoughts towards you are thoughts of good and not evil, to bring you to an expected end? A God who is not interested in forceful obedience as portrayed in the Old Testament but rather wants an obedience based on love and relationship? Who is God to you?

A few months ago, I ran into a friend of mine with his six-year-old daughter, Beatrice. Beatrice is such a smart and logical kid for her age, and we always get along so easily. We talk about a lot of things. She tells me all the fun stories from school and about all her friends. She just enjoys talking, especially when she likes you and considers you a friend. You are in for the talk of your life.

I love to listen to kids because I think a majority of the time they say some amazing stuff that we can learn from, and I have learned many wise things by just listening to kids talk, either to me or to their friends. Those who know me will tell you how much I love kids. In fact, if left to me, I would like to have ten of them. Beatrice said something that left me stunned for a minute. "Uncle Great, my teacher in church told me that we should not make fun of people because of how they look, that if we do God will be mad at us and punish us just like He did to the teenagers who laughed at Elisha and were all eaten by two bears."

I explained things in simple terms to my little friend Beatrice, but as I drove away, that statement haunted me. I could not sleep throughout the night because I was worried that such a young child's mindset or knowledge about her sovereign Father had been polluted and skewed by wrong teaching and misrepresentation of the Scriptures on the activities and events of the Old Testament. The truth is that it's not only little Beatrice who has had her view and knowledge about God tainted. The majority of today's Christians are in the same situation. There are Christians who sincerely believe that God is a tempter, that sometimes God can use bad things to tempt us to find out if we are faithful to Him or not. Some have been taught that God can allow an accident, barrenness, or terrible diseases or sickness to afflict us just so we can change our ways and turn to Him or to get us to be obedient to Him.

I once had such a mindset about God. But is that God? Is that the true nature of our Father? There are some Christians who think that God still punishes them if they sin or give in to the desires of their flesh. They believe that God doesn't bless all His children but only the obedient ones or those who live in a certain way, dress in a certain way, pray in a certain way, talk in a certain way or act in a certain way, and those who do the opposite are cursed or rebels and thus not bona-fide children of God.

Ask yourself: Does that sound or look like God? Does this representation of God correlate to what was revealed to us in Jesus? This wrong view and perception of God is because of wrong teachings on the nature and character of God by some ministers in the body of Christ who misinterpreted the Old Testament. Folks, it's important that we re-educate ourselves on the nature and character of God. It's important that we unlearn certain views and knowledge about God and re-learn or re-know God in light of Jesus Christ, who is the express revelation and image of the invisible God. Why is it paramount that we have a sound knowledge of the revealed God? It's important because knowledge is power. It's important because ignorance of the nature of God is the devil's greatest tool against any child of God. Show me a Christian who is ignorant about the nature and character of God, and I will show you a believer who is a play toy in the hands of the enemy.

There are Christians who still believe that they are cursed or under satanic oppression and need deliverance. Why would a believer who has been washed and redeemed by the blood need deliverance? Or need to run to the church podium to be delivered? What are you going to be delivered from I ask you? Is it the Holy Spirit in you that you want to be delivered from or what? Don't you know you are a new creature?

The reason why many Christians have a very false perception about God is because they are seeing God through the lens of the Old Testament prophets, kings, and events. You cannot have a sound relationship with God if your knowledge of Him is so clouded by Old Testament writings and descriptions of His nature and character. The Old Testament was written by people who never saw God or had the kind of revelation of Him as did the New Testament people (us included). Thus, in their interpretation of God, they depicted a God who is totally different from the God manifested through Jesus.

Have you noticed that the Old Testament is filled with lots of blood, killings, plagues, famine, rape, all kinds of violence that is able to cause one to just dislike God? And many preachers and even Christians believe those are the actions of God. The killing, murder, rape of women, and killing of children. Lots of preachers and Christians believes that these things where done by God to punish man or the rebellious people of the past. Friend, that is a lie, and I will prove this to you. Some of the characteristics we portray as belonging to God are much more like Satan than God, honestly. The Old Testament is filled with personal opinions that are not God's words or instructions but just people's opinion about God. For example, the book of Job is such text in the Old Testament that is filled with opinions about God.

Let's take a look at few activities or events in the Old Testament that we have attributed to God. First is Deuteronomy 20:16-17 which reads, *"But the cities of these peoples which the LORD your God gives you as an inheritance, you shall let nothing that breathes remain alive, but you shall utterly destroy them: the Hittite and the Amorite and the*

Canaanite and the Perizzite and the Hivite and the Jebusite, just as the LORD your God has commanded you, lest they teach you to do according to all their abominations which they have done for their gods, and you sin against the LORD your God".

Let's look at Acts 5:1-11. It reads, *"But a certain man named Ananias, with Sapphira his wife, sold a possession. And he kept back part of the proceeds, his wife also being aware of it, and brought a certain part and laid it at the apostles' feet. But Peter said, 'Ananias, why has Satan filled your heart to lie to the Holy Spirit and keep back part of the price of the land for yourself? While it remained, was it not your own? And after it was sold, was it not in your own control? Why have you conceived this thing in your heart? You have not lied to men but to God.'* "Then Ananias, hearing these words, fell down and breathed his last. So great fear came upon all those who heard these things. And the young men arose and wrapped him up, carried him out, and buried him. "Now it was about three hours later when his wife came in, not knowing what had happened. And Peter answered her, 'Tell me whether you sold the land for so much?'" *She said, 'Yes, for so much.'* "Then Peter said to her, 'How is it that you have agreed together to test the Spirit of the Lord? Look, the feet of those who have buried your husband are at the door, and they will carry you out.' Then immediately she fell down at his feet and breathed her last. And the young men came in and found her dead, and carrying her out, buried her by her husband. So great fear came upon all the church and upon all who heard these things".

Let's also look at 2 Kings 2:23-24. It reads, *"And he went up from thence unto Beth-el: and as he was going up by the way, there came forth little children out of the city, and mocked him, and said unto him, Go up, thou bald head; go up, thou bald head. And he turned back, and looked on them, and cursed them in the name of the LORD. And there came forth two she bears out of the wood, and tare forty and two children of them."* When we read these events, a majority of us believed that was God because we have been told so, and by the way, it's in the Bible and mentions the name of God. Yes, people who sinned died in the Old Testament but not of God. They were killed by the wages of sin. They were under the law of Moses, and the law of Moses has in place punishment for those who are unable to keep it. But it was not God who was killing them.

Ask yourself this question; if it was God, why did Jesus, who is the express image and revelation of God (Hebrews 1:3), not kill people who sinned while He was on earth before His crucifixion? Or did God just suddenly change? You and I know God is unchangeable. He is consistent. He is the same yesterday, today, and forever. It's our views, knowledge, and description of Him that keep changing due to lack of knowledge or renewed knowledge of Him. If you believe that God killed Ananias and his wife Sapphira for lying about their wealth, then my question to you is this: Why has God not killed you for all the lies you have told? Some may argue that well, God can choose who to kill and who not to. As much as that reasoning might resonate with your mind, that is not God. He is not a God of favoritism.

You might also say, well grace is covering you. But I'd like you to remember that at the time of the death of this man and his wife, Jesus had already resurrected and ascended, so the new covenant was already in place. Forgiveness of sin was already released.

Elisha, Little Children, and the Bears

Another text of the Old Testament that has been used to describe God – and many pastors have used it as a fall back for cursing the children of God or showcasing how dreadful and angry God can be if His children cross the line or insult or challenge a pastor – is the story of Elisha, the children, and the bears. The question to ask is this, why would God allow two bears to maul little children for insulting Elisha? Were they God's actions? Many years ago, an atheist questioned me on the event where some little kids taunted Elisha, and he cursed them, and two bears came out of the woods and ate them all. I've sought answers to that one for a long time and could never find a satisfactory response until a few years ago when I got a better contextual understanding of this passage.

Both non-Christians and Christians struggle with difficult passages in Scripture, just as they do with difficult situations in life, often asking, "Why would God allow/cause/do that?" It just doesn't get the job done to say, "We're sure He had a good reason." Nor does such a glib answer fulfill the command God gives us in 1 Peter 3:15 to be always ready to give an answer. Of course, we cannot see into the hearts of people or see the future as God sees it, so we generally need to avoid dogmatic pronouncements about the hard whys of an individual's life (as the disciples did in John 9 when they saw a man born blind).

But, as I stressed in the previous chapter, to understand events or activities in the Old Testament, we must examine Scripture in context and compare Scripture with Scripture to answer these hard questions. In so doing, paying careful attention to the whole of Scripture and to the context should keep us from either expunging the parts we don't personally like or falsely accusing God of characteristics He doesn't have.

In 2 Kings 2:23-24, the prophet Elisha, God's new messenger to the corrupt nation of Israel (the Northern Kingdom), had just returned from bidding Elijah, his predecessor, farewell. God had taken Elijah up to heaven in a whirlwind right before Elisha's eyes and promised to give him a double portion of Elijah's "spirit." This spiritual power that Elisha sought was important because Israel was rife with idolatry. This idolatry caused much suffering in this world, idolatry that would eventually cause God's judgment to fall on the whole nation at the hands of the vicious Assyrians. Elisha's job—to call the people to return to the true God and worship Him alone, to put away idolatry and all the vile practices associated with it—was important for the spiritual and physical well-being of the thousands of individuals in the nation and for the nation as a whole. He needed credibility with the king, with his fellow prophets, and with the people. He was taking on Elijah's job now.

This odd incident recorded in verses 23–24 occurred near Bethel. Bethel was notable as one of the two centers for idolatrous worship in the Northern Kingdom. Israel's first king, Jeroboam, had instituted idolatrous worship as a political maneuver to keep his citizens from visiting Jerusalem. Jeroboam set up golden calves at Dan and Bethel and ordained a program of counterfeit worship (1 Kings 12:26-33).

Eight kings and several dynasties later, Bethel had undoubtedly become a prosperous city, thriving on the commerce enjoyed by being a worship/tourist center. But there remained at Bethel a remnant of God-fearing people, represented by the "sons of the prophets" described in verse 3 of the same chapter. Elisha would need the same credibility that Elijah once had in order to lead them and the people of Israel, yet they were already somewhat doubtful of him. Their concerns about this not-quite-proven prophet are seen in their distrust of his account of Elijah's trip to heaven (2 Kings 2:16-18). As Elisha approached Bethel, no less than 42 *"little children" came "out of the city, and mocked him, and said unto him, Go up, thou bald head; go up, thou bald head"* (verse 23). Elisha *"turned back, and looked on them, and cursed them in the name of the Lord."* Then *"there came forth two she bears out of the wood, and tare forty and two children of them"* (verse 24).

One vital point of concern to most here is the age of these "little children." We recoil in horror at the idea of bears mauling a gaggle of preschoolers. Of course, most don't quibble when they see a Sunday school picture of a little boy David flinging a rock at the big, bad giant, but that image of David is quite incorrect. David was already "a mighty valiant man" and "a man of war" who was "prudent in matters" and had already slain a bear and a lion himself (*see* 1 Samuel 16:18, 17:34-36) before anybody ever heard of Goliath.

The Hebrew words used for Elisha's detractors include the Hebrew words qatan, na'ar, and yeled, (here translated "little", the "children" of verse 23, and the "children" of verse 24), respectively. Qatan means small in quantity, size, number, age, status, or importance. Thus, we see it used to describe a cake, a cloud, a room, a city, and a finger, as well as the younger daughter of marriageable age in Laban's household and the youngest son of Jacob, Benjamin, who was a grown man. This word even describes Saul (a very tall man, but low in status) at the time God anointed him king of Israel (1 Samuel 9:2; 15:17)!

Na'ar means a boy or girl, servant, or young man. It is a word that can cover a range of ages from infant to young adult. "Yeled" likewise means a boy, child, son, or young man—essentially, someone's offspring. In seeing how these words are used throughout the Old Testament, we see that "little child" (qatan na'ar) is used to describe the young rebel Hadad the Edomite (1 Kings 11:14, 17) who fled Solomon's kingdom and married pharaoh's sister-in-law. The combination is also used by Solomon to refer to himself when he prayed for wisdom after becoming king (1 Kings 3:7). Thus, we can already see the phrase "little child" being used by the King James translators to refer to the relative youth or immaturity of grown men.

Na'ar is also used to refer to David—the mighty man of valor described above—and all his brothers, as well as David's son Absalom as he led a civil war, the field hands in Boaz's fields, and a number of soldiers throughout the Old Testament. The word describes Joseph at age 17 (Genesis 37), Isaac at about 25 to 28 on Mount Moriah (Genesis 22), spies in Joshua, and (along with yeled) the young men who gave Rehoboam such lousy advice in 1 Kings 12.

Thus, as we ponder the translators' word choice as well as God's judgment, we see plenty of precedent for using "little children" to emphasize the relative youth or immaturity of the subjects. The reference to his baldness was likely an ordinary sort of insult: baldness on the back of the head, historically, "was considered a blemish among the Israelites as well as among the Romans." However, when we consider the rest of the taunt these "little children" hurled at the prophet, we see evidence that they possessed a certain amount of theological understanding.

Their taunt to "go up" was a reference to Elijah's recent ride to heaven. By shouting this challenge to Elisha, they were challenging his right to follow in Elijah's footsteps as God's designated representative to Israel—and declaring their intention that they wanted him to meet his Maker as well. Yet if the people were to be called back to God, Elisha had to have credibility as God's designated representative. Another question to ask is this, did they die? The Strong's meaning for tare is (baqa'). This word variously refers to the breaking open of mountains and city walls, dividing the Red Sea, splitting wood, breaking bottles, making a way through a line of soldiers, getting a group of citizens to disavow their nation, and—in a prophetic metaphor for the destruction of a nation in Hosea 13:8—tearing by wild beasts.

When we look at information on modern day bear attacks, we see that some attacks are fatal, and some are not. The language of the Bible here is not specific regarding the fate of the 42. As Wilmington's Guide to the Bible puts it, "forty-two of these arrogant rebels were clawed as a divine punishment." Maybe there were 42 funerals, maybe not. We simply cannot say. But one thing is sure: everyone watching and everyone who survived learned a lesson that day: God's message is serious, and Elisha is His new messenger.

The false gods popular in the nation publicly failed to protect these hoodlums from the God whose messenger they challenged. In summary, we have plenty of internally consistent biblical evidence that the events of that day in Bethel involved an unprovoked, verbal assault by a group of young hoodlums. The most important question to answer therefore is this, was it God that killed those teenagers? The answer is NO. God has given us great power and what we do with that power is left on us. We can use it to bless or to curse people. Whatever we choose to do with that power, God often allows for reasons we just sometimes can't understand or comprehend with our physical brains and minds. One of my professors in college always said that the present is key to understanding the past.

Today many of us make mockery of some Pastors and clergy men. Comedians do that. We laugh at the fashion and speech patterns of some of the religious leaders in our communities, or their poor vocabulary or grammar, but God has not killed us. So, if he has not killed anyone for laughing or making fun of a church leader, why do we believe that the same God did kill those 42 teenagers in 2 Kings? This belief is something we must correct in our minds.

Who is God? This is the central question of our day, and many believers do not have an adequate answer for it. Simply knowing about God is not enough for life with God; we must know Him personally in truth as revealed in Christ. Thus, we need to ask, how can I know God?

If I were to ask a group of people what's the greatest thing in life, I would probably get as many answers as there were people. Certainly, many things contribute to a full and happy life, but I hope all believers would agree that knowing God is absolutely the greatest and most important of all. Without that, everything else loses meaning. The Apostle Paul put it this way in Philippians 3:8: *"Yea doubtless, and I count all things but loss for the excellency of the knowledge of Christ Jesus my Lord: for whom I have suffered the loss of all things, and do count them but dung, that I may win Christ."* Think of this: Paul wasn't a loser. He hadn't hit rock bottom with nowhere else to go. He wasn't turning from a life of failure and counting that as "dung." He was one of the most educated and accomplished men of his day. He was the elite of the religious class. People knew of him, and they wanted to be like him.

Paul wasn't writing just about the time before he was born again. He had been a Christian for decades at the time he wrote this. He had traveled the world and been used of God as few men ever had or ever will be. Yet here he was still seeking to know God more (Philippians 3:10). Paul was saying that the best life had to offer and the greatest accomplishments and pursuits of any man, when compared to knowing God, ranked in the same category as manure. He was admitting that he hadn't arrived but that he had left and was pressing toward that goal of knowing God more (Philippians 3:12-14).

What does it say when the man who wrote half of the New Testament was still pursuing knowing God decades after his conversion? Certainly, there has to be a depth of knowing God that goes far beyond just getting saved. Paul spoke of this in Ephesians when he prayed that the Ephesian Christians would come to know the height, length, depth, and breadth of God's love (Ephesians 3:18-19). He said something very interesting in Ephesians 3:19: *"And to know the love of Christ, which passeth knowledge, that ye might be filled with all the fulness of God."* At first glance this seems confusing. How can we know something if it passes knowledge? Paul is speaking about experiencing God's love in a way that is infinitely greater than mere intellectual knowledge. And notice that when we experience God's love in this way, we will be filled with all the fullness of God. What a statement!

All we have to do is recognize that we aren't experiencing God's fullness in order to realize we don't know God's love the way Paul described it. If we did, we would be filled with all His fullness. Therefore, there is a dimension to knowing God that the average Christian hasn't experienced. How do we get there? First of all, we have to realize that there is more to knowing God than just becoming a Christian. Multitudes of people have received salvation, and if they were to die, they would go straight into the presence of the Lord. But they don't know God. They don't know that He loves them because He is love and not because they are lovely. They think they have to earn God's favor, and they are needlessly suffering condemnation and lack of fellowship with Him because they feel unworthy. They don't know Him as a loving heavenly Father but see Him as a harsh taskmaster.

Many Christians think our Father is the source of all their troubles and suffering. They think He uses those problems as tools to teach them something or change their behavior, even though the Word clearly proves the opposite (James 1:13). They don't know their God as Healer or Provider or in any of the other ways He manifests Himself to them. Truly, God's people are destroyed for a lack of knowledge about Him (Hosea 4:6).

Much of the blame for this, falls on the church. The Bible says in Romans 10:17, *"So then faith cometh by hearing, and hearing by the word of God."* The church, as a whole, has proclaimed that Jesus died for us to keep us from going to hell. Now, that's true and quite a benefit. If that's all there was to salvation, that's more than we deserve. I would preach that message if that was all there was, but that's not what the Scripture teaches. *"For God so loved the world, that he gave his only begotten Son, that whosoever believeth in him should not perish, but have everlasting life"* (John 3:16). That verse specifically says the goal of salvation is "everlasting life." And everlasting life was defined by Jesus in John 17:3, which says, *"And this is life eternal, that they might know thee the only true God, and Jesus Christ, whom thou hast sent."*

Knowing God, the Father and Jesus Christ is eternal life. That doesn't start when we go to heaven. Knowing God (eternal life) is something we can have right now (John 3:36). The word "know" is used in Scripture to describe the relationship between a man and his wife that produces a child (example: Genesis 4:1). It is speaking of intimacy. So "knowing God" is speaking of intimacy with Him. To receive salvation and then stumble through life without experiencing intimacy with the Lord is to miss or ignore the most important part of what Jesus provided. Let me put it this way: if you received forgiveness through the sacrifice of Jesus and then continued on without an intimate, personal, close relationship with God, then according to John 3:16, you are missing the real purpose of salvation. This is where the vast majority of Christians live.

People believe they need to get saved because that's the message they've heard. So, they get saved, and then they get stuck. They aren't hearing that knowing God is the real goal or that it's even attainable. They are waiting on the sweet by and by but struggling in the rough here and now. Knowing God in the way I'm discussing isn't even on the radar screen of most Christians. They aren't pursuing it, and they aren't experiencing it. It begs the question: how do we get started in our pursuit of intimacy with the Lord? We can begin by spending time getting to know Him through His Word. The Apostle Peter said in 2 Peter 1:3-4, *"According as his divine power hath given unto us all things that pertain unto life and godliness, through the knowledge of him that hath called us to glory and virtue: Whereby are given unto us exceeding great and precious promises: that by these ye might be partakers of the divine nature, having escaped the corruption that is in the world through lust."*

It's through the knowledge of God that we are able to receive all things that pertain to life and godliness. He has already given them, but it's knowing Him that allows us to partake of His divine nature, to receive all His great and precious promises, and to escape the corruption of this world. What a deal! Knowing the Word is knowing God.

The Call to Re-Know God In Christ

When I speak of knowing God, it is important to understand that we are not talking about abstract or speculative thought concerning God or mystical experiences but about coming alive to God through Jesus Christ and surrendering ourselves to Him in grateful love (Romans 12:1). As John says, "Whoever has the Son has life; whoever does not have the Son of God does not have life" (1 John 5:12). We must also understand that knowing God is not an optional part of the Christian life; it is the Christian life. Jesus said, "And this is eternal life, that they know you, the only true God, and Jesus Christ whom you have sent" (John 17:3). The English word know in this verse is a translation of the Greek word *ginosko*, which, in this context, means an experiential knowing, not simply an intellectual understanding of facts about God or Jesus or the Bible. In other words, it refers to an "I-Thou" relationship.

> *Show me a Christian who is ignorant about the nature and character of God, and I will show you a believer who is a play toy in the hands of the enemy.*

This relationship begins when we come alive to God -- that is, when, by grace, we are awakened from the state of spiritual death into which everyone is born and receive the eternal life Jesus offers to those who trust in Him for salvation. The first part, recognizing and turning from our sins, is repentance. The second part, trusting in Jesus and His atoning death on the cross to forgive our sins, is faith. Coming alive to God requires both. Jesus described this as being born from above or born of the Holy Spirit. It means birth into God's family and entrance into His kingdom (John 3:3-8). Without rebirth by the Holy Spirit, a person cannot see, perceive, understand, or know God in truth. As vitally important as the new birth is, that is not the focus of this book. Here I will address what is involved in growing to know God more deeply after the new birth. This is a major and pervasive need in the American church today.

The metaphor of birth provides a helpful way of understanding fuller implications of what it means to know God and to grow in that relationship. Just as a human being is physically born into the world and moves through a developmental cycle from infant to child to adolescent to adult, so a child of God is born spiritually and is called to move through a similar developmental cycle. These stages are mentioned in the New Testament. Paul, for example, makes a distinction between "the mature" and "infants in Christ" (1 Corinthians 2:6, 3:1), and the writer of Hebrews does the same (Hebrews 5:11-14). John distinguishes between "little children," "fathers," and "young men" (1 John 2:12-14). What does this mean? Spiritually the newest infant in Christ knows God, but not very well. As this baby grows in grace, he or she will progress toward maturity and, in doing so, will come to know God better and better.

You may have seen this if you have been a believer for a while. What a joy it is to encounter an infant in Christ, a new convert, eager and zealous for the knowledge and relationship with God. But what a blessing to meet a father or mother in Christ, a mature believer who has faithfully walked with God for decades and whose life is characterized by a degree of love, joy, peace, patience, kindness, goodness, faithfulness, gentleness, and self-control that is truly Christlike! This kind of mature relationship with God is what every believer is called to demonstrate and live by in his or her community.

The opening chapters of Genesis paint a beautiful picture of Adam and Eve enjoying a personal relationship with God. The story of God and Abraham does the same. But Moses and David open a window into their hunger to know God more intimately. On Mount Sinai, Moses cried out to God, "If I have found favor in your sight, please show me now your ways, that I may know you," and God responded with an extraordinary revelation of Himself (Exodus 33:13; 34:7-9). Though he was by no means perfect, King David's life (1 & 2 Samuel) and his many psalms reveal a deeply personal relationship with God and a longing for Him: "O God, you are my God; earnestly I seek you; my soul thirsts for you; my flesh faints for you, as in a dry and weary land where there is no water" (Psalms 63:1). Their hunger for God is an example given to encourage our desire for God (Romans 15:4).

Knowing God more deeply was not the privilege of only a few luminaries in the Old Testament or for the Bishops, Pastors and Prophets of our time. God wants all His people to know Him personally and love Him supremely with heartfelt devotion. He called Israel to "love the Lord your God with all your heart, with all your soul, and with all your strength" (Deuteronomy 6:5). And through Jeremiah we hear, *"Thus says the LORD: 'Let not the wise man boast in his wisdom, let not the mighty man boast in his might, let not the rich man boast in his riches, but let him who boasts boast in this, that he understands and knows me, that I am the LORD who practices steadfast love, justice, and righteousness in the earth. For in these things I delight, declares the LORD"* (Jeremiah 9:23-24 ESV).

God delights when His people truly know Him, love Him, and enjoy the blessings of His faithful love, justice, and free gift of righteousness. A notable New Testament example of hunger for God is the apostle Paul. Near the end of his life, Paul said that his greatest passion was "that I may know him and the power of his resurrection and may share his sufferings" (Philippians 3:10 ESV). Paul had had a dramatic encounter with Christ thirty years earlier on the road to

Damascus, and he had had several other experiences with Him afterward. But he longed to know Him more deeply. Paul's example shows us that no matter how long or how well we have known the Lord, there is always more.

Paul's longing to know Christ points the way for us as we seek to know God today. We see God most clearly and know Him most nearly through His Son, Jesus Christ. Jesus said, "Whoever has seen me has seen the Father" (John 14:9 ESV), and Paul says, "He is the image of the invisible God," and "in him all the fullness of God was pleased to dwell" (Colossians 1:15, 19 ESV). Getting to know God more deeply doesn't happen overnight; it takes time. Paul had known Christ for many years when he said his passion was to know Christ better. He went on to say, "Not that I have already obtained this or am already perfect, but I press on to make it my own" (Philippians 3:12a ESV). Nor is getting to know Christ better an automatic process; it takes real effort. Is effort contrary to grace? No.

Grace is opposed to earning (law) but not to effort. Effort is a vital part of how grace operates in sanctification. Thus Paul, the apostle of grace, went on to say to the Philippians: *"Not that I have already obtained this or am already perfect, but I press on to make it my own, because Christ Jesus has made me his own. Brothers, I do not consider that I have made it my own. But one thing I do: forgetting what lies behind and straining forward to what lies ahead, I press on toward the goal for the prize of the upward call of God in Christ Jesus. Let those of us who are mature think this way, and if in anything you think otherwise, God will reveal that also to you"* (Philippians 3:12-15 ESV).

But (lest we fall into law and self-generated-works righteousness) we must note well and always remember that this "straining and pressing on" is not merely unaided human willpower. Rather, it is rooted in the deep work of God in our hearts, arousing hunger and desire and drawing us to engage our wills and strength to seek Him, as Paul had earlier said when he urged the Philippians to "work out your own salvation with fear and trembling, for it is God who works in you, both to will and to work for his good pleasure" (Philippians 2:12-13 ESV).

Doing this, of course, is utterly dependent upon our being filled with the Holy Spirit daily, for He alone can supply the power we need (which Paul emphasizes in Romans 8, Galatians 5, and Ephesians 5). And the rewards of our Spirit-empowered efforts far transcend the greatest earthly pleasures! Paul's words reinforce the idea that a person is as close to God as he or she really wants to be.

But it is not just Paul who urges us onward. God told Israel, "You will seek me and find me, when you seek me with all your heart" (Jeremiah 29:13 ESV). Jesus told His disciples, "Ask, and it will be given to you; seek, and you will find; knock, and it will be opened to you" (Matthew 7:7 ESV). In each case, those who seek are the ones who find. And if we don't seek, we will not find.

How do we press on? God offers everything we need to grow into deeper fellowship with Him and His Son, but we must embrace it. He gives the milk, but we must drink it. This is what Peter meant when he said, "Like newborn infants, long for the pure spiritual milk, that by it you may grow up into salvation—if indeed you have tasted that the Lord is good" (1 Peter 2:2-3 ESV). You owe it to yourself to seek to know God in Christ by teachings, studying the Bible, and just seeing God in everything around you. God is not far away, neither is He a mystical concept. God is all around you. The trees, the clouds, and all the beauty of the earth testify of His presence and love.

What is the spiritual milk we should long for? Peter is using the image of "newborn infants" to say that just as babies need their mother's milk to grow up physically, so believers need spiritual milk to grow up spiritually. Considering 1 Peter 1:23-25, it's likely that the milk Peter has in mind is the Scriptures, but the way he describes it, he may well mean all the resources necessary for healthy spiritual growth. Therefore, it's important that every believer find a church that teaches the undiluted principles of God: His nature, character, and personality. When you are attending a church that focuses more on prophecies of doom, prosperity teaching, or daily deliverance services or prayer and fasting programs than on your relationship with God, you are not helping yourself. Prophecies, fasting, and prayer don't grow you spiritually. What you need to grow in the knowledge of God is sound teaching.

Great Igwe

CHAPTER 5
HOW JESUS' LIFE AND ACTIONS ON EARTH REVEALED THE HEART OF GOD

If we want the most accurate picture of God, we don't need to look any further than Jesus Christ. In Jesus we meet God as God really is. Jesus said, *"Anyone who has seen me has seen the Father"* (John 14:9, NIV). Jesus Christ is the perfect revelation of the Father. *"No one has ever seen God, but the one and only Son [Jesus]...has made him known"* (John 1:18, NIV). Through Jesus' words and actions, we hear and see what matters most to every human being—that God the Father loves us unconditionally. *"God so loved the world that he gave his one and only Son, that whoever believes in him shall not perish but have eternal life"* (John 3:16 NIV). The Old Testament prophets did their best to explain God to us. The kings and all the amazing people of the Old Testament did wonderful jobs describing God, but in Jesus, God the Father revealed himself to humanity.

Jesus is God's self-revelation to the world. God has broken through to us by sending his eternal Son into our world. Jesus upheld the understanding that the one God is the object of our love and worship (Mark 12:29-31). Jesus emphasized that God (Father, Son, and Holy Spirit) was reconciling humanity to Himself. That is why He instructed His followers to welcome people into right relationship with God by baptizing them in the name of the Father and of the Son and of the Holy Spirit (Matthew 28:19).

The God we worship through Jesus Christ is the Triune God. The doctrine of the Trinity is central to how we understand the Bible and all points of theology that flow from it. That theology begins with an essential "who" question: "Who is the God made known in Jesus Christ, and who are we in relation to Him?" Jesus is the center of our faith and of our devotion to God. Jesus reveals to us what God is like (John 6:37). *"No one knows the Father except the Son and those to whom the Son chooses to reveal him"* (Matthew 11:27b, NIV).

Trinitarian theology is first and foremost Christ-centered. Jesus is the unique Word of God to humanity and the unique Word of humanity to God (John 1:1-14). As the representative of all humanity, Jesus responded to God perfectly.

Jesus indicates that He is the key to understanding Scripture. He said to a group of Jewish religious leaders in John 5:39-40, *"You study the Scriptures diligently because you think that in them you have eternal life. These are the very Scriptures that testify about me, yet you refuse to come to me to have life"* (NIV). Jesus, who is the focus of Scripture, is our source of salvation. So, we seek to understand the Bible through the lens of who Jesus is. He is the basis and logic of our faith—for He alone is the self-revelation of God.

Relationship-Focused

Trinitarian faith is relational. Even before creation, there was a relationship of love between the Father and the Son (John 17:24). And in Jesus, that relationship of love is extended to all humanity. Jesus Christ, the only Son of God, has become one with us in our humanity to represent us as His brothers and sisters in the very presence of the Father (*see* John 1:14; Ephesians 1:9-10, 20-23; Hebrews 2:11, 14).

Human beings turned away from God and broke the bonds of communion with God. But because of Jesus, God has reconciled us and renewed our relationship with Him! Not only that, as we respond to His call to us to share in that restored relationship, He comes to live in us by the Holy Spirit (Romans 8:9-11). In Jesus and through the Holy Spirit, we become God's treasured children, adopted by grace (Romans 8:15-16). This means that Christian life and faith are primarily about four kinds of personal relationship: (1) The relationship of perfect love shared by the Father, the Son, and the Holy Spirit for all eternity; (2) The relationship of the eternal Son with humanity, established when the Son became human in the person of Jesus; (3) The relationship of humanity with the Father through the Son and by the Spirit, done through faith; and (4) The relationship of humans with one another, in the Spirit, as children of the Father.

Who is Jesus?

"Who are you, Lord?" was Paul's anguished question on the Damascus Road where he was confronted by the resurrected Jesus (Acts 9:5). He spent the rest of his life answering this question and then sharing the answer with all who would listen. The answer, revealed to us in his writings and elsewhere in Scripture, is the heart of the gospel and the focus of Trinitarian theology.

The Son of God, who is eternally united to the Father and the Spirit, is now also joined to humanity because of His incarnation—His becoming a real flesh-and-blood human being (John 1:14). We summarize this by saying that Jesus is both fully God and fully human. That fact will never change because he remains, in His divine nature and His human nature, the one mediator between God and humanity for all time (1 Timothy 2:5).

If you carefully study the actions and descriptions of God in the Old Testament and compare them with the life and actions of Jesus in the New Testament, you will see a huge difference. The Old Testament paints a picture of a truly angry and vengeful God. Genesis 6:6 says the Lord regretted creating Man. The Old Testament paints a picture of a nepotistic God, a God who hates sin and can't look at the poor man in his times of weakness. But that was totally different from the actions of Jesus. We are going to examine the life of Jesus Christ while on earth, His actions and statements, and through this examination we will see the true nature and character of God and His heart towards humanity. Is He the angry God that the Old Testament and some of our ministers paint Him to be? Is He the scary and sin-hating God the Old Testament portrayed Him as, who keeps a list of all our wrongdoings and expects us to act right at all times or else face his fury?

His incarnation did not end with His death or with His ascension. It continues forever. He was resurrected bodily, and He ascended bodily. He will return bodily, the same as He departed. So, when we say Jesus Christ, we are referring to God, and we are also referring to humanity. As the One who is uniquely God (Creator and Sustainer of all) and fully human, Jesus is the unique meeting place of God and humanity.

Through the life, death, resurrection, and ascension of Jesus, God and humanity were reconciled, and human nature was regenerated—made new (2 Corinthians 5:17-18). In Jesus Christ, all humans are reconciled to God (Colossians 1:19-20). As the Lord and Savior of all humanity, He has opened the way for all to enter an eternal union and communion with God.

The miracle of the incarnation is not something that happened "once upon a time," now long past and simply affecting one person, Jesus. What He accomplished changed human nature itself, changed history, changed how the entire cosmos is "wired"—it is a new creation (2 Corinthians 5:17). The spiritual reality is, for now, hidden in Christ, and we still experience the effects of evil that occurs in this world. The incarnation of the eternal Son of God, entering time and space and taking on our human nature changed everything forever, reaching back through all human history and reaching forward to encompass all time.

He has now become our Lord and Savior, not as an external agent, but from the inside, in His humanity. As Paul teaches, God was, in Christ, reconciling the world to Himself (2 Corinthians 5:19). Paul speaks of this transformation in Romans 7:4, where he says that even while we are alive, we are already dead to the law by the body of Christ. Jesus' death in human flesh for us, though a historical event, is a present reality that applies to all humanity (past, present, and future). *"You died,"* Paul says to the Colossians, *"and your life is now hidden with Christ in God"* (Colossians 3:3 NIV). Even before we die physically, we are given new life—made alive with Jesus in His resurrection.

Christ's incarnation and atoning work accomplished the renewal of our human nature. In Him, God has reconciled to Himself every human being, even those who lived before Jesus came. In Ephesians 2:5-6, we read that those who trust in Christ share in His life, death, resurrection and ascension. Here, Paul asserts that just as we are dead already in Jesus' substitutionary death, we have also already been "made alive together with him" and we are "raised up together with him" and "seated together with him in the heavenly realms." All this comes from God's grace and is experienced through faith—the faith of Jesus that He shares with us by the Spirit.

In Romans 5, Paul addresses believers, but he also explains what Christ accomplished on behalf of all humanity even before anyone came to faith in God through Christ. Jesus Christ died for people who were still: "powerless" and "ungodly" (verse 6), "sinners" (verse 8), "God's enemies" (verse 10). God accomplished His great work for us out of His "love for us" even while "we were still sinners" (verse 8). The result was that even "while we were God's enemies in our minds, we were reconciled to Him through the death of His Son" (verse 10). Paul goes on to explain that what Jesus Christ accomplished as the second Adam counteracts what the first Adam did. Through Christ, as the new head of all humanity, *"God's grace and the gift that came by the grace of that one man Jesus Christ abounded for the many"* (verse 15).

Paul continues: The gift "brought justification" rather than condemnation (verse 16 of Romans 5). *"Those who receive God's abundant provision of grace and of the gift of righteousness reign in life through the one man, Jesus Christ! ...One righteous act resulted in justification and life for all people. ...Through the obedience of the one man the many will be made righteous"* (verses 17-19). *"Grace increased all the more"* so that *"grace might reign through righteousness to bring eternal life through Jesus Christ our Lord"* (verses 20-21).

God did all this for us before we were even born. The benefit of what Jesus did so long ago extend to the past, to the present, and into the future. Paul says, *"How much more, having been reconciled, shall we be saved through his life!"* (verse 10). This shows that salvation is not a one-time event, but an enduring relationship that God has with all humanity—a relationship formed within the person of Jesus Christ, who has brought God and humanity together in peace. Jesus has not simply done something for us, He has done something with us by including us in His life, death, resurrection, and ascension. Paul explains this in Ephesians 2:4-6. When Jesus died, we, in our sinful human nature, died with Him. When Jesus rose, we, in our reconciled human nature, rose with Him. When Jesus ascended, we, in our redeemed human nature, ascended and became seated with Him at the Father's side.

Everything God has done in Christ shows us the mind, heart, and character of the Father, the Son, and the Holy Spirit. God is on the side of His people and all His creation. God is for us, even before we respond to Him (verse 5). He has provided reconciliation and eternal life in communion with Himself for every human being. Our good or bad acts or conduct do not determine God's response towards us or in any way influence His perception, love, blessings, or protection in our lives.

Fully God and Fully Man

Jesus is in our place and on our behalf. Throughout the book of Hebrews, Jesus is depicted as our great High Priest, representing all humanity, providing a perfect response to God on our behalf. He is the one who stands among us, in the midst of the congregation, and who leads us in worship (Hebrews 2:12-13). He represents us as our older brother. He has become one of us, sharing our very nature, learning obedience, being tempted as we are, but overcoming that temptation perfectly (Hebrews 2:14-18; 4:15). Theologian Thomas Torrance explained it this way: "Jesus steps into the actual situation where we are summoned to have faith in God, to believe and trust in him, and he acts in our place and in our stead from within the depths of our unfaithfulness and provides us freely with a faithfulness in which we may share." That is to say, if we think of belief, trust, or faith as forms of human activity before God, then we must think of Jesus Christ as believing, trusting, or having faith in God the Father on our behalf and in our place.

Jesus is the one who, as we respond, perfects our faith and makes us holy (Hebrews 12:2; 2:11; 10:10,14). He acted as one of us "in our place" or "on our behalf" (Hebrews 2:9; 5:1; 6:20; 7:25, 27; 9:7). So how do we personally share in all that Christ has graciously done for us? How can we personally participate and be in communion with God who has already reconciled us to Himself? We do so by trusting in Him—by having faith that He, by grace, has accomplished for us all that is needed for our salvation. In short, we say we are saved by grace through faith (Ephesians 2:8). Does this mean that we are saved by a faith that we work up? Does our salvation depend upon how great and sincere our repentance or our faith is? No, for salvation would then be dependent on something we do rather than dependent upon grace alone.

The good news is that our salvation does not depend on what we do. It does not depend on the strength of our faith or our repentance. It depends on the strength of our Savior; it depends on His faithfulness. He died for us. The gift has been given; our repentance and faith are simply responses to what God has given us. They are the way we accept and receive the gift. Jesus has done everything necessary for our salvation from start to finish, so even our responses of repentance and faith are gifts of sharing in Jesus' perfect responses for us as our faithful mediator.

As Thomas Torrance explained, "If we want to think of faith as a human activity, then we must think of Jesus as having done that for us as well. Just as he died for us, he lived righteously for us." As our representative, He presents to God a perfect response on behalf of all humanity. We are saved by His obedience (Romans 5:19)—and that includes His faith. Our salvation rests on Jesus—the perfect foundation. As our High Priest, Jesus takes our responses, perfects them and gives them to the Father, all in the Spirit. As our mediator (1 Timothy 2:5), He ministers both from God to us and represents us in our relationship to God. So, we join Him in His response. What God has done in Christ to reconcile us to Himself calls for a response. We are urged to accept Him, to welcome and receive Him. We do so by trusting in Him and what He has accomplished for us. The Holy Spirit enables us to freely welcome the truth and walk in it. But God does not force us to accept the truth of His love for us. A love that forced a responding love would not be loving. God's love calls for our decision to freely receive and freely love God in return.

Our choice is to either affirm or deny the reality that God loves us and has made every provision for us to be His children. Denial of this truth has consequences, but it will not change the reality of what God has done for us in Christ and thus who we are in Christ. Human beings choose to accept who Christ is or attempt to live in denial of who He is. Real freedom is found in God, as theologian Karl Barth reminds us: "The real freedom of man is decided by the fact that God is his God. In freedom he can only choose to be the man of God, i.e., to be thankful to God. With any other choice he would simply be groping in the void, betraying and destroying his true humanity. Instead of choosing freedom, he would be choosing enslavement."

So, what is our place in all of this? We choose to accept Jesus and all He has to offer or to reject Him. Through the Spirit, God the Father is calling all people to place their trust in Jesus with a thankful and hopeful heart and to share with other believers in the Body of Christ, which is the church. As we celebrate together in communities of faith and worship, our lives are transformed. Jesus called people to repent and believe (Mark 1:15). The early church continued this message, calling people to repent and be baptized and to be changed (Acts 2:38; 3:19). Our response is important. The apostle Paul writes in Romans 5:17 that *"those who receive God's abundant provision of grace and of the free gift of righteousness [will] reign in life through the one man, Jesus Christ"* (NIV). Abundant and freely given grace calls for us to receive it in faith.

In Romans 5 Paul weaves together elements of the reality accomplished by Christ on behalf of all humanity and our response and participation in that relationship and reality. We must take care not to confuse what is true in Jesus for all humanity with each person's response to that truth. God's gift is offered to all to be received by all. It is received by having faith in what God in Christ through the Holy Spirit has done for us. It is by faith in the grace of God that we begin participating in the relationship Jesus has restored and start receiving the benefits included in that relationship. We do not "decide for Christ" in the sense that our personal decision causes our salvation. Rather, we accept what is ours already in Christ, placing our trust in Jesus, who has already perfectly trusted for us in our place. When we accept the grace of Jesus Christ, we begin to participate in God's love for us. We begin to live according to who we really are, as the new creation that God made us to be in Christ prior to our belief.

Some people find it helpful to explain this using the terms objective and subjective. An objective truth is a reality, whereas our understanding of and response to that reality is subjective. There is a universal, or objective, truth about all humanity in Jesus, based on the fact that He has joined Himself to our human nature and turned it around. But there is also the personal, or subjective, experience of this truth that comes as we surrender to the promptings of the Holy Spirit and join with Jesus Christ.

These categories of objective (universal) and subjective (personal) truth are found in Scripture. In 2 Corinthians chapter 5, Paul starts with the objective nature of salvation: *"All this is from God, who reconciled [past tense] us to himself through Christ and gave us the ministry of reconciliation: that God was reconciling the world to himself in Christ, not counting people's sins against them. And he has committed to us the message of reconciliation"* (verses 18-19). Here we find an objective truth that applies to all—God has already reconciled all to himself through Jesus, the incarnate Son of God. Paul then goes on to address the subjective truth: *"We are therefore Christ's ambassadors, as though God were making his appeal through us. We implore you on Christ's behalf: Be reconciled to God"*.

How can all be "reconciled" already and yet some need to "be reconciled"? The answer is that both are true. All are already reconciled in Christ—this is the universal/objective truth. Yet, not all embrace it and personally experience their reconciliation with God—that is the personal/subjective truth. God has a gracious attitude toward all people, but not everyone has responded to His grace. No one benefits, even from a freely given gift, if that gift is refused, especially the gift of coming under the grace of God in Jesus Christ in the power of the Spirit. A second example of objective/subjective truth is found in the book of Hebrews, where the author states in a straightforward manner, *"For good news came to us just as to them, but the message they heard did not benefit them, because they were not united by faith with those who listened"* (Hebrews 4:2, ESV) The benefits of a relational reality such as salvation can only be subjectively (personally) experienced when received by faith.

So, while Christ is Lord and Savior of all, has died for all, and has reconciled all to God, not all will necessarily be saved. Not all will receive Christ, who is their salvation. Not all will enter into their salvation, which is eternal union and communion with God as His beloved children. Some may somehow "deny the Savior who bought them" (2 Peter 2:1). While Scripture teaches the unlimited scope of Christ's atoning work, taking away the sins of the whole cosmos, it does not offer us a guarantee that all will receive the free gift of grace.

No explanation is given as to why or how this rejection of grace could happen. But rejection is presented as a real possibility, one that God has done everything to prevent. If there are those who reject Christ and their salvation, it will not be due to any lack or limit of God's grace.

If you've committed your life to Christ, you have a relationship with Him. That's a great beginning! Developing that relationship involves getting to know Him better. The best way to learn about Jesus is to read His claims concerning His identity in the Gospels. The Gospels are the first four books in the New Testament and tell the "good news" (which is what gospel means) of Jesus Christ. They were written in the first century A.D. and based upon eyewitness accounts of Jesus' life. Jesus was born about 4 or 5 B.C. (Our calendars are a little off.) The nation of Israel was under Roman occupation, and the Jews fought to maintain their national identity. Every faithful Jew kindled the hope that one day the Messiah would appear and provide salvation for the nation by overthrowing Roman rule. Messiah is a Hebrew word meaning "the anointed one."

The bulk of the Gospel accounts is devoted to the three years that Jesus spent ministering around the Sea of Galilee in northern Israel. They tell us of the life and teachings of a unique person. Jesus, the Gospels explain, demonstrated His divine powers by healing the sick, blind, and lame, by raising the dead, by walking on water, and by calming a storm at sea. Jesus' teaching lacked the exacting legalism and piousness that characterized so much of contemporary Judaism. He became tremendously popular among the masses in Galilee.

Throughout His ministry Jesus kept pointing the people to Himself. The masses wanted a political liberator. The religious establishment wanted their positions of power and piety recognized. Jesus pandered to neither group. Let us examine four incidents in the Gospel of John to determine what Jesus claimed about Himself. In the Gospel of John, chapter 5, Jesus was accosted by Jewish religious leaders for healing an invalid on the Sabbath (the Jewish "Day of Rest"). They considered any expenditure of effort on the Sabbath a violation of God's command to maintain it as a day of rest. Over the centuries they had meticulously codified what was permissible, and Jesus' action flaunted their strict rules. Jesus defended His action of healing on the Sabbath by explaining that God, as the sustainer of the universe, never rests but continually keeps working. And God is always doing good in human history and cannot stop His work. He told them, "My Father constantly does good, and I'm following his example."

At that point, the Jewish leaders were all the more eager to kill Him because in addition to disobeying their Sabbath laws, He had spoken of God as His Father, thereby making Himself equal with God (John 5:17-18). The Jews saw Jesus' claim to deity as a virulent blasphemy. During the centuries of occupation by foreign nations, many Jews had endured terrible sufferings to remain faithful to the worship of Jehovah, the one true God. How could Jesus, a good Jew, ever think of saying that He was equal with God? John 8: Jesus Teaching that He has always existed. Three chapters later in John's Gospel, Jesus is conversing again with the Jewish leaders. He was in Jerusalem for the Feast of the Tabernacles, a celebration commemorating God's direction to Moses and the nation of Israel during their journey from Egypt to the Promised Land.

In this conversation, Jesus made several claims. He said that He was the Light of the World, that He could free men from sin and that anyone who believed in Him would not die. The Jewish leaders were again incensed by His seemingly preposterous claims but apparently decided to humor Him, hoping to reveal His inconsistencies. Not even Abraham, venerated founder of Judaism, had claimed to be immortal, so how could Jesus claim this? Jesus replied: *"'Your father Abraham rejoiced at the thought of seeing my day; he saw it and was glad. You are not yet fifty years old," [the Jews] said to Him, "and you have seen Abraham! Very truly I tell you,' Jesus answered, "before Abraham was born, I am!' At this, they picked up stones to stone Him"* (John 8:56-59, NIV). Hahahahahaha!!!!! I can only imagine their anger and look, like… What?!!!

His remarks were even more inflammatory because of His use of the words "I am." In the Old Testament, Moses saw a burning bush as he was tending sheep in the desert. Approaching the bush, God suddenly spoke to Moses and told him to return to Egypt and lead the Israelites out of bondage. God assured Moses that He would be with him.

Moses asked God who he should say sent him. God replied: *"I AM WHO I AM. This is what you are to say to the Israelites: 'I AM has sent me to you"* (Exodus 3:14, NIV). I AM was not so much a label for God as it was an indication of God's complete ability to deliver the Israelites from bondage. Jesus ascribed this same name and power to Himself. John 10: His third claim. At the Feast of Dedication, or Hanukkah, Jesus is again in Jerusalem, and there is considerable speculation among the crowds and religious leaders. Will Jesus announce that He is the Messiah? Tradition had always taught that the Messiah would be revealed at one such feast.

The Jewish leaders gathered around Jesus and asked Him if He was the Messiah. It may have been genuine curiosity, but more likely they intended to set a trap for Jesus, forcing Him to say something that would warrant His arrest and execution. Instead of giving them a direct answer, Jesus said that He had already told them who He was and that they had not believed Him: 'My sheep recognize my voice, and I know them, and they follow me…my Father has given them to me…I and the Father are one.' Then again, the Jewish leaders picked up stones to kill Him. Jesus said, 'At God's direction I have done many a miracle to help the people. For which one are you killing me?' They replied, 'Not for any good work, but for blasphemy; you, a mere man, have declared yourself to be God'" (John 10:27-33).

John 11: Jesus Teaching that He Offers Life Eternal. Lazarus, a close friend of Jesus, lived in Bethany, less than two miles east of Jerusalem. He became ill while Jesus was many miles to the east, ministering along the Jordan River. After He heard of Lazarus' illness, Jesus waited two days before departing. By the time He arrived in Bethany, Lazarus was already dead and buried. Martha, Lazarus' sister, went out to meet Jesus and exclaimed that her brother would still be alive if Jesus had arrived sooner. Then follows this exchange: "Jesus said to her, 'Your brother will rise again.' Martha answered, 'I know he will rise again in the resurrection at the last day.' Jesus said to her, 'I am the resurrection and the life. The one who believes in me will live, even though they die; and whoever lives by believing in me will never die.

Do you believe this?' 'Yes, Lord,' she replied, "I believe that you are the Messiah, the Son of God, who was to come into the world'"

(John 11:23-27, NIV). Jesus moved near the cave-like tomb where Lazarus was buried. Praying aloud, He thanked His Father for hearing Him: "I knew that you always hear me, but I said this for the benefit of the people standing here, that they may believe that you sent me" (John 11:42, NIV). His prayer finished, Jesus commanded Lazarus to leave the tomb, and the dead man came out, still wrapped in grave clothes. Jesus made what seemed to be extravagant claims about Himself: equality and oneness with God, eternal pre-existence, and the source of everlasting life. These are not the statements of a mere mortal (at least a sane one). Jesus also declared that He had final authority over all the earth, that He would one day return and judge the earth, that He could forgive sin, and that He was the only way to God. He said He could give life and fill man's greatest hunger. He called Himself the Son of Man, an Old Testament prophetic term for the Messiah. He allowed others to worship Him even though Jews were to worship God alone.

> *Jesus was killed not for what He did but for who He said He was*

During the trial preceding the crucifixion, the Jewish leaders said this to the Roman governor Pilate: "We have a law, and according to that law He must die, because He claimed to be the Son of God" (John 19:7, NIV). Jesus of Nazareth was killed not for what He did but for who He claimed to be. C.S. Lewis once remarked: "I am trying to prevent anyone saying the really foolish thing that people often say about Him: 'I'm ready to accept Jesus as a great moral teacher, but I don't accept his claim to be God.' That is the one thing we must not say.

"A man who was merely a man and said the sort of things Jesus said would not be a great moral teacher. He would either be a lunatic—on a level with the man who says he is a poached egg—or else he would be the Devil of Hell. You must make your choice, either this man was, and is, the Son of God: or else a madman or something worse." Jesus' Life and Teaching are unique. Of all the founders of major world religions, Christ alone claimed to be God! Abraham, Mohammed, Confucius, Buddha—none claimed to be God. Buddha, for example, told his disciples near the end of his life not to worry about remembering him, but to remember his teaching about the way of enlightenment.

Each of these founders of world religions can be divorced from his teaching without a total and irreparable loss to that religion. But Christianity is built upon Christ: who He claimed to be and what He did. His teaching is almost embarrassingly self-centered. What else can be said of someone who declares: "I am the way and the truth and the life. No one comes to the Father except through me" (John 14:6, NIV)? But if Jesus' claims are true, then His statements are full of hope. We can know God because Jesus is God. Jesus Christ is not only fully God, but He is also fully man. He experienced hunger and thirst, loneliness, and the pain of betrayal and rejection. He suffered the humiliation of hanging naked upon a cross. He experienced temptations. He ate real food, cried real tears at the death of a friend, and lost real blood during His crucifixion. Even His resurrection was physical. Jesus Christ was fully man.

What does it mean to us that Jesus Christ is fully God and fully man?

1. Because Jesus is God, He is worthy of our worship. We should treat Him as God, with reverence and respect. Jesus is not our buddy; He is our Lord. The Lordship of Jesus means allowing Him direction over every area of our life: not only our religious worship and our private devotions, but our career, our family, our finances, our attitudes. Knowing Christ should affect our relationship with others and what we watch on television. Giving Christ control of these areas isn't what gets us into heaven. Giving Christ control is a response to our eternal relationship with Him. He is your powerful Lord. Love Him. Worship Him.

2. Because Jesus is God, He can handle all our problems. There is nothing we face that God cannot overcome. Jesus is the "I AM" who can do all things. Jesus claims that He is able to make all things work for good in our life (Romans 8:28). In fact, He is "able to do immeasurably more than all we ask or imagine" (Ephesians 3:20, NIV). As you get to know Jesus better, I hope you will see that He has the power to do in your life what He promises.

3. Because Jesus is God, He was able to reconcile us to God. Jesus is more than a friend. He is our Savior.

4. Because Jesus is fully man, He identifies with all our needs and problems. There is nothing we go through that He cannot understand. *"Because He Himself suffered when He was tempted, He is able to help those who are being tempted"* (Hebrews 2:18, NIV). By living among us, Jesus perfectly understood all that we feel.

5. Jesus' identity as fully man affirms our humanity. We do not become more Christian by becoming less human. God created us in His image and wants us to enjoy life with all of its possibilities. He gave each of us talents and abilities that He wants us to develop. This does not mean that following Christ will make you healthy and wealthy (though it will make you wise!). Jesus is the one who reveals the Father to us. If we want to know what the Father is like, all we have to do is look at Jesus.

If we want to know how the Father cares for people, we can look at how Jesus ministered to them. If we want to know the Father's will for our lives, we can listen to Jesus' words and know they reveal the Father's truth. Jesus revealed the nature of the Father in His actions and His words, and Jesus continues to reveal the Father to us. He is the One through whom the fullest revelation of the Father comes. We look to Jesus if we really want to know the Father. Why is God so angry in the Old Testament and so loving in the New? A non-Christian friend argued that the scriptural picture of the Lord's nature and character is inconsistent and self-contradictory, but Christians always say that God never changes. The Bible is very clear about the unchanging nature of God, but our views and explanations have never been consistent. Consider two passages that assure us there has not been (and never could be) any shift in God's character: *"Every good gift and every perfect gift is from above, coming down from the Father of lights, with whom there is no variation or shadow due to change"* (James 1:17, ESV). *"Jesus Christ is the same yesterday and today and forever"* (Hebrews 13:8, ESV).

However, my friend isn't the only one who questions these claims. Many people read the Old Testament and see a God of violence. They see this God as an absolute contrast to the loving Heavenly Father of the New Testament, which is true to a large extent if the scriptures are not properly interpreted contextually. But the problem of supposed differences between the Old Testament God and the New Testament God is far more complex than it first appears. To say that the God of the Old Testament is wrathful and punishing while the God of the New is loving and kind distorts the issue. Let us take a closer look at what the Bible really says. God's nature is consistent. The God of the New Testament is clearly a God of love (1 John 4:8). No doubt about it. But does that mean He's only a kind, permissive, doting, grandfatherly figure? Hardly. He is also a God of justice, which means He alone is the universal sovereign arbiter of the entire planet. The author of Hebrews agrees: *"It is a fearful thing to fall into the hands of the living God"* (Hebrews 10:31, ESV). Why? Because "our God is a consuming fire" (Hebrews 12:29, ESV).

On the other hand, the God of the old covenant isn't the relentlessly bad-tempered taskmaster many gospel preachers make Him out to be. The Old Testament describes Him more than once as "merciful and gracious, slow to anger, and abounding in steadfast love," a God who "does not deal with us according to our sins, nor repay us according to our iniquities" (Psalm 103:8-10 and Exodus 34:6-7, ESV). Paul's emphasis on grace and faith in the New Testament (as opposed to works of the law) didn't start with him. This central biblical theme can be traced all the way back to Genesis. Abraham "believed in the Lord, and He accounted it to him for righteousness" (Genesis 15:6; Romans 4:3; and Galatians 3:6). The same idea appears in Habakkuk 2:4, where the prophet writes, *"Behold, his soul is puffed up; it is not upright within him, but the righteous shall live by his faith"* (ESV). In other words, grace isn't just a New Testament idea; it's a biblical idea. It's been in place but only finally fulfilled in the New Testament. In the next three chapters we will see how Jesus' parables revealed the heart of the Father to all.

CHAPTER 6
THE PARABLE OF THE LOST SHEEP

Jesus often taught in parables, an ancient Eastern literary genre. The prophet Ezekiel, for example, wrote in parables, such as the eagles and the vine (17:1-24) and the parable of the pot (24:1-14). When people talk about the ministry of Jesus, it's easy to focus on His miracles. Jesus performed some amazing feats that the world had never seen (and hasn't seen since). But one of the most exciting things about His ministry was His teaching style.

Jesus taught using parables—simple stories intended to impart a spiritual lesson. He's so identified with this teaching style that Mark's gospel tells us that *"He did not say anything to them without using a parable"* (Mark 4:34a, NIV). Jesus spoke the word to them with many parables, as much as they could understand. The word parable in Hebrew is *mashal*. The root meaning of the word means placing side by side for the sake of comparison. By simple definition, parables aren't doctrine. They are illustrations used alongside a teaching. Both Greek and Hebrew words agree they are figurative. Consequently, all parables must be viewed in context.

The parables of Jesus are recorded in the Synoptic Gospels of Matthew, Mark, and Luke. Some parables are common to all three Synoptic Gospels, such as the Parable of the Sower (Matthew 13:3-23, Mark 4:2-20, and Luke 8:4-15). Matthew relates ten parables on the Kingdom of Heaven, seven of which occur in Matthew 13 and are central to that gospel. All parables contain fiction which will have facts the audience can relate to, all to convey a lesson. Parables need no epic explanation or a line by line exegesis on the characters used. What does the parable tell us about Jesus (the visible display of God)? Let's look at some of these parables.

Luke 15:3-7 (NIV) reads, *"Then Jesus told them this parable: 'Suppose one of you has a hundred sheep and loses one of them. Doesn't he leave the ninety-nine in the open country and go after the lost sheep until he finds it? And when he finds it, he joyfully puts it on his shoulders and goes home. Then he calls his friends and neighbors together and says, "Rejoice with me; I have found my lost sheep." I tell you that in the same way there will be more rejoicing in heaven over one sinner who repents than over ninety-nine righteous persons who do not need to repent.'"* The parable of the lost sheep is one of the teachings that reveals the heart of God and the extent He is willing to go for His creation. It also shows that no one is less significant in the eyes of God, unlike the religion of exclusion we have these days tends to portray Him to be.

Who was Jesus' audience when he told this parable? It was a large crowd of tax collectors, sinners, Pharisees, and teachers of the law. As Jesus spoke to the crowd, the Pharisees began grumbling about the low moral quality of the people Jesus associated with. When Jesus overheard Pharisees disparaging Him for associating with sinners, He began instructing them about God's passion for the lost. In God's economy, a shepherd leaves his flock to find a single lost sheep—and upon finding it, he rejoices. But noticing the grumbling among these religious people, Jesus offered another parable called the parable of the lost coin, as recorded in Luke 15:8-10. This was intended to communicate the same truth. God is like a woman who loses one of her 10 silver coins, and she overturned the house until she found it. Once it was found, she called all her friends to celebrate the recovery of the coin.

These parables demonstrate the incredible sincerity of God's wish to save mankind. Every time we encounter setbacks and sink into temptation, when our faith falters, we can encourage ourselves with these parables. At no time will God's desire to save us ever change.

If God is compassionate, then certainly those who love God should be compassionate as well.

The way Jesus expressed metaphor utilized something within the scope of human knowledge. If God had said something similar in the Age of Law, people would have felt that it wasn't really consistent with who God was, but when the Son of Man delivered this passage in the Age of Grace, it felt comforting, warm, and intimate to people. When God became flesh, when He appeared in the form of a man, He used a very appropriate metaphor to express the voice of His heart in humanity. This voice represented God's own voice and the work He wanted to do in that age. It also represented an attitude that God had toward people in the Age of Grace.

Looking from the perspective of God's attitude toward people, He compared each person to a sheep. If a sheep is lost, He will do whatever it takes to find it. This represents a principle of God's work among mankind, this time in the flesh. God used this parable to describe His resolve and attitude in that work. This was the advantage of God becoming flesh: He could take advantage of mankind's knowledge and use human language to speak to people, to express His will. He explained or 'translated' to man His profound, divine language that people struggled to understand in human language, in a human way. This helped people understand His will and know what He wanted to do.

He could also have conversations with people from the human perspective, using human language, and communicate with people in a way they understood. He could even speak and work using human language and knowledge so that people could feel God's kindness and closeness, so that they could see His heart. Through the parable of the lost sheep, not only can we realize how real God's love and salvation for us are and see how much responsibility He takes for our lives, but we can also see one advantage of God becoming flesh. If He had done this work in His spirit form, appearing to people through thunder, clouds, and pillars of fire, we would have no way of drawing close to God, nor would we be able to understand His will.

When God incarnated as the Son of Man to work in our midst, the Lord Jesus used human language as well as things we often see and encounter in our lives, things we can easily understand, to create parables. This includes the parable of the sower (Matthew 13:1-9), the parable of the tares (Matthew 13:24-30), the parable of the mustard seed (Matthew 13:31-32), and the parable of the net (Matthew 13:47-50). We can gain a better understanding of God's will through these parables, know what He requires of us, plus understand what He has and is and His disposition.

When we read the parable of the lost sheep, we can see God's resolve and attitude toward saving mankind and that He'll save a lost sheep at any cost and will not rest until He's done. We also gain true understanding of the Lord Jesus' merciful and loving disposition, and we feel how kind and approachable God is—the distance between us and God grows smaller. If it weren't for God becoming flesh and using human language to come up with these parables, to create these examples, it would be so hard for us to understand God's will, and this is something that we'd never realize.

God personally became flesh and came to walk among us to work and speak. He used commonplace, easily understandable language to guide us to understand His will and requirements so that we have a path of practice. This shows how important it is that God incarnated to work and speak on earth – for our understanding of the truth and of God. We just know to enjoy God's grace and blessings, but we've never thought about God's will behind His every word and deed. We don't realize that God became flesh and spoke to us with human language so that we could better understand the truth, be redeemed by the Lord, and understand God's disposition. God is so attentive in His considerations for our salvation!

Let's take another look at the last sentence in this passage: "Even so it is not the will of your Father which is in heaven, that one of these little ones should perish." Was this the Lord Jesus' own words, or the words of His Father in heaven? On the surface, it looks like it's the Lord Jesus who is speaking, but His will represents the will of God Himself, which is why He said: "Even so it is not the will of your Father which is in heaven, that one of these little ones should perish."

People at that time only acknowledged the Father in heaven as God, and this person that they saw in front of their eyes was merely sent by Him, and He could not represent the Father in heaven. That's why the Lord Jesus had to say that as well, so that they could really feel God's will for mankind and feel the authenticity and the accuracy of what He said. Even though this was a simple thing to say, it was very caring, and it revealed the Lord Jesus' humility and hiddenness. No matter whether God became flesh, or He worked in the spiritual realm, He knew the human heart best and best understood what people needed, knew what people worried about, and what confused them, so He added this one line. This line highlighted a problem hidden in mankind: People were skeptical of what the Son of Man said, which is to say, when the Lord Jesus was speaking He had to add: "Even so it is not the will of your Father which is in heaven, that one of these little ones should perish."

> *When you try to know or describe God outside of Jesus Christ, you will only end up misrepresenting the true nature and character of God.*

Only on this premise could His words bear fruit, to make people believe their accuracy and improve their credibility. This shows that when God became the Son of Man, God and mankind had a very awkward relationship, and the Son of Man's situation was very embarrassing. It also shows how insignificant the Lord Jesus' status among humans was at that time. When He said this, it was actually to tell people: You can rest assured this doesn't represent what's in My own heart, but it is the will of the God who is in your hearts.

For mankind, wasn't this an ironic thing? Even though God working in the flesh had many advantages, He had to withstand their doubts and rejection as well as their numbness and dullness. These words really point to the true state of people at that time: They only believed in a God up in heaven, in a God they imagined as vague within their hearts, and they had absolutely no true understanding of or faith in God incarnate. It's just like what Philip said to the Lord Jesus: "Lord, show us the Father, and it suffices us" (John 14:8). Philip's words show that he didn't treat the Lord Jesus as God at all. The Lord knew that even though people followed Him, they didn't understand the essence of Christ, instead treating Him as a regular person.

That's why He followed the parable of the lost sheep by saying 'Even so it is not the will of your Father which is in heaven.' It was so we would believe that those words had come from our Father in heaven and thus better accept the Lord Jesus' words, believe that the Lord's love for humanity is genuine, and not doubt His salvation of mankind. All of us remember that the Lord Jesus responded to Philip by saying, "Believes you not that I am in the Father, and the Father in Me? The words that I speak to you I speak not of Myself: but the Father that dwelleth in Me, He does the works" (John 14:10).

We can see here that the Lord Jesus is God Himself—His work and words were entirely governed by the Spirit of God, and what He did was God's own work. However, the Lord Jesus knew that people didn't understand His essence, so recognizing mankind's immaturity and ignorance, He didn't directly state that He was God, but instead quietly performed His work, expressing God's will to save mankind from the perspective of the Son of Man so that people would be more able to believe and follow Him and thus gain salvation. We can see from this how humble the Lord Jesus was, and how sincere His desire to save mankind is!

The Lord Jesus knew that we didn't have an understanding of the incarnation and wouldn't be able to worship Christ as God, so He spoke of it in a way that we'd be better able to accept His words. The Lord understands our shortcomings so well! Even though they didn't realize that the Lord Jesus was God Himself and didn't worship Him as God, He was forgiving of our ignorance and used His words to strengthen our faith so that we could better accept the Lord's words. From the Lord's words we can also get an understanding of God's will to save mankind. This is an advantage of God personally coming to earth to speak! Thanks be to the Lord for His enlightenment and guidance!

Now we understand that every word uttered, and every deed done by God in the flesh contained truth we can seek. God's will, His requirements of us, and His love for us are hidden within all of this. This is why we must maintain a heart of reverence toward God incarnate's work and words. We have to seek and ponder these things more—this is the only way we'll be able to understand the deeper meaning with God's words.

Through this parable we come to learn that even at our worst, God loves us. John continues, "For God did not send his Son into the world to condemn the world, but in order that the world might be saved through him." The Father sent Jesus to us out of His love and His commitment to save us. Why is it imperative that we look at the life and actions of Jesus to see the pure heart and nature of God? Because like I said in chapter 1, Jesus is the express image and revelation of the

Father. He is the visible display of the invincible God (Colossians 1:15). The Bible says in Colossians 2:9, *"For in Him [Christ] dwells all the fullness of the Godhead bodily"*. Did you see that? It means that one can't know God outside Jesus Christ.

When you try to know or describe God outside of Jesus Christ, you will only end up misrepresenting the true nature and character of God. The New Testament is the revelation of the Old Testament (Scriptures). One gross error I have seen among many ministers of the gospel is that they pick Old Testament scriptures and just preach on it or ask people to abide by what the scripture is commanding or requesting, especially the dealings of God with the Israelites. When the Scriptures are interpreted outside of the New Testament, without carefully subjecting that Scripture to the interpretation of the Gospels, the Epistles (which are the climax of revelations), and most importantly through the lens of Jesus Christ, that Scripture loses it power. God was concealed in the Old Testament but was revealed in the New Testament. This knowledge is key to understanding the Bible.

Through various parables, statements, and actions, Jesus communicated the nature of God to us. The parable of the prodigal son, the parable of the lost sheep, the parable of the good Samaritan, the parable of the wheat and weeds, and other great parables mentioned in the synoptic Gospels, if carefully understood, will give one a good view of God's intents and desires for humanity. Jesus said, "I know my sheep and my sheep know me." The question then is, do you know God in truth? What are your views about Him? What is your perception about the nature and personality of God? God desires to know you—and for you to know Him. "I will live with them and walk among them, and I will be their God, and they will be my people," He said in 2 Corinthians 6:16 (NIV). And again, in Hebrews 8:10, "This is the new covenant I will make with the people of Israel on that day, says the Lord: I will put my laws in their minds, and I will write them on their hearts. I will be their God, and they will be my people."

In fact, this is a recurring theme—starting in Genesis—that appears dozens of times throughout Scripture. God wants to know you and for you to know Him! This deep desire from the Father is fulfilled in Jesus. It's through Him that we can get to know the Father personally. We've been invited to know Jesus and, by extension, our

Father God. What a privilege! Jesus confirmed, "My Father has entrusted everything to me. No one truly knows the Son except the Father, and no one truly knows the Father except the Son and those to whom the Son chooses to reveal him" (Matthew 11:27). The connection is so strong, when the Pharisees asked Jesus about the Father, He sharply answered, "Since you don't know who I am, you don't know who my Father is. If you knew me, you would also know my Father" (John 8:19).

There's nothing quite like knowing Jesus! When you become a Christian, Jesus spiritually bonds with you. He comes into you, and you enter into Him. As you get to know Him more and more each day, you draw closer and find life more and more fulfilling and rich.

You get to know Jesus through His Word, His works, prayer, and even other believers. Knowing God and obeying His voice don't stop with reading His Word and spending time in prayer. If we want to truly know God, we must choose to love our brothers and sisters in Christ. We must love one another—just as He has loved us. Loving one another means walking in love in all we do (1 Corinthians 13). It means being patient and kind, not jealous, boastful, proud or rude. It means not being irritable, demanding our own way or rejoicing over injustice. "Love never gives up, never loses faith, is always hopeful, and endures through every circumstance" (1 Corinthians 13:7). If you want to know God, get to know Jesus today through the Word and prayer, and by loving others. As you do, you'll find your relationship with Him skyrocket to new heights. And the Lord will love that…because He wants to know you and have you know Him!

CHAPTER 7
THE PARABLE OF THE PRODIGAL SON

The parable of the prodigal son is one of my most cherished metaphoric illustrations of Jesus. It's so simple and filled with lots of love and awesomeness. Let look at this parable! *"I will set out and go back to my father and say to him: Father, I have sinned against heaven and against you. I am no longer worthy to be called your son; make me like one of your hired servants.' So he got up and went to his father. But while he was still a long way off, his father saw him and was filled with compassion for him; he ran to his son, threw his arms around him and kissed him"* (Luke 15:18-20 NIV).

Let's review the account. A man had two sons. One day the younger came to him with a demand. He wanted an early disbursement of his inheritance. Despite the likely hardship that would come from taking this money from the estate, the father gave the son his portion. So, off the young man went into another life. He traveled to a far country. Distance in a relationship is not always measured in miles. It would seem the distance in this relationship had grown to become quite vast long before he left the family home. The son no longer wanted to live under his father's roof. Did he no longer respect his father? Had some longstanding, unresolved tension between the two led to a severing of relations to where they could no longer "walk together".

Two alternative names for this parable could have been "The Parable of the Angry Elder Brother" (the attitude of much of the church today) or "The Parable of the Loving Father." Note that the son was a "SON" first before he became the "prodigal son." This implies that Jesus was not talking about an unbeliever that receives salvation for the first time but about a born-again believer that went out from his father's house to live according to the desires of his flesh. Then, when the son beat himself up and groveled in self-pity and guilt about how unworthy he was, thinking his father was going to punish or reject him because of the sins he had committed (does this sound familiar?), his father did not love him anymore or any less. In fact, when the son returned home, his father didn't even want to listen to his confession, but simply overwhelmed him with kisses and affection flowing from his heart of love.

We sometimes forget that God has already forgiven all our sins (past, present, and future). 2 Corinthians 5:19 says that God was in Christ reconciling the world to Himself, not imputing their trespasses to them. He is always on the edge of ambushing us with another wave of His goodness. It is not our confession of mistakes that "restores" God's approval of us – we were already reconciled with Him over 2000 years ago when Jesus took our punishment on Himself, and He has been pleased with us ever since. By putting our faith in God's grace, we become partakers of all the benefits of the New Covenant, including a new, born-again nature, having the person of the Holy Spirit living inside us, as well as healing, deliverance, blessings, life, wealth, and much, much more! This parable also illustrates that born-again believers can live subject to the laws of this world if they live in disbelief of God's promises. It is possible to live like a pauper in the house of a King! Yes, God has given us precious promises in His Word, but we have to believe in them to receive them. Bad choices and our refusal to believe in God's goodness and His attitude of favor towards us may have dire consequences for us in our lives here on earth

Galatians 6:8 declares: "For he who sows to his flesh will of the flesh reap corruption, but he who sows to the Spirit will of the Spirit reap everlasting life". This corruption refers to suffering loss in the natural realm. If we sow to the flesh, we will not have our minds renewed, not walk in the promises of God (because we will persist in unbelief), and not live life to its fullest in our Father's house.

Galatians 4:1-10 reads, *"Now I say that the heir, as long as he is a child, does not differ at all from a slave, though he is master of all, but is under guardians and stewards until the time appointed by the father. Even so we, when we were children, were in bondage under the elements of the world. But when the fullness of the time had come, God sent forth His Son, born of a woman, born under the law, to redeem those who were under the law, that we might receive the adoption as sons. And because you are sons, God has sent forth the Spirit of His Son into your hearts, crying out, 'Abba, Father!' Therefore, you are no longer a slave but a son, and if a son, then an heir of God through Christ. But then, indeed, when you did not know God, you served those which by nature are not gods. But now after you have known God, or rather are known by God, how is it that you turn again to the weak and beggarly elements, to which you desire again to be in bondage? You observe days and months and seasons and years".*

As he did every day, the father in the parable walked from his home to the small hill where he could look down the road and see for several miles. He always thought and hoped that he would see a familiar figure heading his way. His thoughts were always the same—a mixture of longing, of hope, and of regret. When he failed to see what he'd hoped to, he would turn and go about the business of the day. There was always work to be done, but there was also the empty place created by the one who, a long while back, had chosen to leave and go far away from his home.

The father remembered the day his son left the family. The young man wanted his portion of inheritance to go out on his own and make an independent life. It would create a hardship to divide off his portion earlier than planned. But the father did it, with regret, knowing it was the only thing that could be done. His son would learn life's hardest lesson no other way. Watching him go was the most difficult moment of the father's life, knowing that his son wasn't prepared for life and that he wouldn't listen to him for instruction or wisdom. When would he return? And when he did, could the family environment be the same? The story Jesus Christ told recounts a son's departure from his father's home, the lessons he learns, and his return, wiser for the experience. It is also the story of a family's journey to reconciliation.

Families are the foundation of life. The biblical family is the model on which God is building a spiritual family of glorified sons and daughters. This parable tells of a son who was lost and then found. While it shows many details about a family, in the end one truth stands out—a father's patient endurance for the son he loves. For this boy's father to have seen him "a great way off" would imply that the Father had been eagerly awaiting his son's return. Certainly, in the spiritual application of this parable, our Heavenly Father is longing to cleanse and receive the sinner, if the sinner would just repent and come to Him for forgiveness. Jesus was using this parable to rebuke the Pharisees for their harsh, self-righteous, unforgiving attitude towards sinners.

The older brother in this parable was symbolic of the Pharisees. Like the brother, the Pharisees had not lived an outward life of rebellion, and they thought that others who didn't measure up to their standards were surely hated by God. But "God so loved the world," and "Christ Jesus came into the world to save sinners." When believers begin to see that they have been truly set free from the law (including observing the Sabbath and all the other commandments), it will not only stop them living like beggars in bondage to the elements of this world, but also bring about a divine sense of royalty – not an arrogant and prideful "I am better than others" attitude – but an inner realization of their true identity: "I am a citizen of heaven, and my Father is the King of the universe."

However, even if we do stumble into what the world sees as some huge sin (the prodigal son spent half of all the money his father had on sleeping with prostitutes and consuming everything on his fleshly lusts), there is still grace upon grace for us from God.

Older Brother Syndrome

Like the older brother, fellow believers may choose to judge a backslidden Christian for the things he/she has done, but God will never judge His children nor be angry with them ever again according to the covenant He made. Just like many Christians today, the older brother, when he saw his Father showering love on a person that didn't deserve it, became angry and resentful. This is what being under the law does to a person.

The legalists work and work their backsides off for God and think that He owes it to them to bless, love, and approve them in return. Look at the elder brother's words in Luke 15:29b. *"Lo, these many years I have been serving you; I never transgressed your commandment at any time"*. Just as this older brother was self-centered and jealous, the Pharisees were not operating in the love of God towards sinners because they were so in love with themselves. They resented Jesus giving the sinners what the Pharisees thought they themselves deserved. If relationship with his father had been the real desire of the older brother, he would have rejoiced to see his father's joy at the return of his brother. The repentant prodigal son had learned the vanity of things and he had come home to a relationship with his father that neither he nor his older brother had known before.

The scribes and Pharisees, like the older brother, had gotten caught up in serving self through their religious actions. The publicans and sinners who repented were supplying their Father with what He really wanted: relationship. Relationship with the Father was always available to the scribes and Pharisees, but they chose the temporal praise of men rather than relationship with God.

Just like many people today grade their relationship with God by how well they manage to obey the law, the older brother thought He could earn his Father's approval through his own level of obedience. And then, when God blesses someone that didn't deserve it ("grace" is giving someone what they don't deserve), the legalists become angry and jealous and hate that person. Instead, they should realize that none of us deserve any of it anyway and just get over it and get happy!

God is looking into the distance for you,

trying to find you, and longing to bring you home.

The older son was in the field, and as he drew near to the house, he heard music and dancing. Right now, this is what's happening in heaven. There is music and dancing in our Father's house! It should make us wonder how so many churches can be so dull, introspective, reserved, conservative, and religious on Sunday mornings… The parable allows almost anything to be read into it to provide an explanation. Father-son relations are beautiful to behold but at times complex. Could it be that the younger son had emotionally left the home long before he physically walked out the door? In time, the son burned through his money and found himself penniless. High living beyond his means reduced him to doing manual labor for a daily wage.

Using all the material enticements available to us today, it's easy to imagine how his money could have easily disappeared. A new car. An expensive motorcycle. Costly meals. Entertaining and spending money on people whose friendship was dependent on his ample bank account—their friendship lasting only as long as he had money. After working at a job that paid little and gave no satisfaction, he began to re-evaluate his situation. He was barely making enough money to buy food. It seems the animals that he fed ate better than he. No money. No friends. No good prospects.

All the Good Reasons

> *"And he was angry, and would not go in: therefore, came his father out and entreated him." Luke 15:28*

If this elder son had considered his brother, he would have rejoiced at his return even as his father did. Rather, he was totally self-centered (that's pride) and became angry. This illustrates Proverbs 13:10: *"Only by pride cometh contention."* How can we esteem others better than ourselves when in truth we think we are better than others? First, we need to recognize that our accomplishments don't make us better than others. Some people are better athletes than others. Some are better businessmen than others. Some are better speakers than others, and so forth. However, there is a difference between what we do and who we are. Better performance does not make a better person. A person's character can be severely wanting even though his performance is good. A classic example of this is found in the Pharisees of Jesus' day. They did the right things for all the wrong reasons. Inside they were corrupt. So, our evaluation of others needs to change. God judges by looking on the inside, not the outside (1 Samuel 16:7).

Secondly, to esteem someone better than ourselves simply means to value them more than we value ourselves. To some that may seem impossible, but it isn't. It is exactly what Jesus did. If Jesus, who was God in the flesh (1 Timothy 3:16), could humble Himself and value our good above His own welfare, then we should certainly be able to do the same. It can happen when we die to self and live for God.

For most of my life I struggled to find God, to know God, to love God. I tried hard to follow the guidelines of the spiritual life—pray always, work for others, read the Scriptures—and to avoid the many temptations to dissipate myself. I have failed many times but always tried again, even when I was close to despair. Now I wonder whether I have sufficiently realized that during all that time God had been trying

The Misrepresented God

to find me, to know me, and to love me. The question is not "How am I to find God?" but "How am I to let myself be found by Him?" The question is not "How am I to know God?" but "How am I to let myself be known by God?" And, finally, the question is not "How am I to love God?" but "How am I to let myself be loved by God?" God is looking into the distance for me, trying to find me, and longing to bring me home.

Did you know that if a person really knew God and understood God as the wonderful father He is, there would be no trouble believing Him and His words? There has been a great emphasis in the body of Christ in recent years on teaching faith and confessing His word to bring faith. I believe in speaking what God's word says, and believers need to have faith in God. But I also believe many of us have missed an important key. Having faith in others means developing relationship with them to the point where you know them so well, you just completely trust them.

A Pastor friend of mine once said that as he carries his little girl around, she never has to say, "I confess with my mouth and believe with my heart that my dad will not drop me. And I confess with mouth and believe with my heart that my dad's going to feed me." There is no striving to believe her father is going to be good to her. She just rests and relaxes in her loving relationship with him. She knows he is going to take care of her, because she knows him and his character. In the same way, Christians will find it easy to have faith in God to provide their needs by simply getting to know Him better. And since everything we receive from God comes through faith in Him (including our salvation), knowing Him intimately becomes especially important! Really, everything we receive from God comes out of knowing Him.

One reason the Christian life has been so hard for a lot of people – and I'm including people who have heard teachings about faith and confession – is because they haven't really developed personal relationship with God. They don't know Him intimately. When you really know a person is trustworthy, it's not hard to believe him or her. I personally believe that faith is a direct result of knowing God better. It's not hard for those who really know Him to believe Him and His word. And when they believe God's word, it's not hard for them to receive from Him. But if they don't know God very well, Satan can discredit Him and say all kinds of false things about Him because they don't know any better.

Before I get into more of this subject, I have to admit to you that I tend to minister by shock technique. One of the hardest things to get people to do is to pay attention, to really *hear* what you have to say. So, to get their attention, I say things that paint me in to such a corner that they are interested to find out how I'm going to get out of it. They get the point I am trying to make. The Word of God is simple. A preacher I know says it's so simple, you've got to have somebody help you to misunderstand it. There's nothing hard about the Word of God. The biggest problem is that people don't get to hear it. People are thinking of what they had for breakfast, where they are going to eat lunch, or about this or that. So, before I explain what I believe is the nature of God, I'm sharing with you that some of my points may seem somewhat dramatic.

For example, I was teaching at a Bible conference in Maryland two years ago that God is not the one who puts problems on believers. A man was there with his twelve-year-old daughter, who was paraplegic in diapers, paralyzed and confined to a wheelchair. She was in such bad condition that she couldn't even relate to what was going on around her. Because I had said God was not the one who put that affliction on his daughter, this man got upset. The people who brought him to the meeting said to him, "You at least do the young pastor the courtesy of talking to him after the service and letting him explain himself." Afterwards, the man came up to me and said, "God did this to my daughter. She was born this way. This is God's will for her, and He's getting glory out of this."

I answered him, "No, God didn't do this. It is not God's will that a girl be in a wheelchair and not be able to function normally. That is not the way God made people." I started sharing scriptures with him, and he started sharing scripture right back. I thought he was misusing his scriptures, and he thought I was misusing mine. It was getting to be a theological standoff, with nobody getting anywhere. What finally broke the standoff was when I looked at him and said, "What's the matter? Don't you love your daughter? What kind of father are you? Don't you care if your daughter ever comes out of the wheelchair or not? Don't you care if she is ever normal and can run and play?"

Well, if he was mad at me before, he really got mad at me after I said that! I think he was at the point of punching me in the nose. He shot back, "I love my daughter! I would do anything for her. I don't have much money, but I would sell anything for her. I would borrow, I would do whatever I had to do to come up with the money if it was within my power to produce healing in my daughter." At a point I felt like he might even give me a dirty slap or yell, "Get the hell out of my face you crazy immigrant!" Lol.

The parable provides no happy ending. Instead, it leaves us face to face with one of life's hardest spiritual choices: to trust or not to trust in God's all-forgiving love.

At this point, I said, "And you think God loves her less? You think God, with all His power, is just going to sit back and withhold His healing from her because He wants to afflict her to teach somebody something?" You see, that man could argue with my doctrine, but when I presented God as a father to him, he saw that God is a good, heavenly father who doesn't want His daughter paralyzed. It wiped out all his anger. Understanding that God is a good God and that He loves us takes away the effectiveness of Satan's weapons against our faith. You may have been believing and praying for healing, and you know that the Word says, *"by whose stripes ye were healed"* (1 Peter 2:24). You probably know all about faith teaching, how to confess the Word, and all the related principles; yet you've got this nagging doubt that you can't overcome. It is a fear inside that makes you wonder, "Is God really going to heal me?"

Did you know fear can be totally cast out of people's thinking if they understood the perfect love of God for them? First John 4:18 says that *"perfect love casteth out fear."* If people become fearful, wondering if God's will for their life is going to come to pass, then they don't really understand and know God and His immense love. If God loves us enough to send His only Son to die for us, then doesn't He love us enough to bring about His will in our lives if we are being obedient to Him? We may know some things *about* God, but if we really *knew*

God's love for us, we would not doubt Him so easily or question His willingness to help us. He couldn't be discredited so easily if we really understood how much He cared for us. Can you see that?

Our human relationships are imperfect, so they aren't an exact parallel to our relationship with God. I have good enough relationship with some people that if you came to me and told me they were criticizing me and saying negative things about me, I wouldn't believe it. That's because I know them. We have such a good relationship established that if they were upset with me, they would come talk to me about it. I know they would do that, so you just couldn't lie to me about them.

If people told me that my fiancée, Ashley, had been unfaithful to me while I was travelling in ministry, they would just be barking up the wrong tree. I know my Ashley so well. I trust my fiancée with my liver, lungs and heart. Somebody may think, "Well, Mr. Great, you just can't be sure; you never know." Well if that's your reaction, it just shows the lack of relationship you have with your mate. It is possible to come into relationship with others to the point that you know what they would be like and what they would do in any set of circumstances. Our relationship with God is no different. He wants us to be assured that we can trust Him to act in our best interest no matter what the situation. And that is what this book is all about: getting to know God so well that no one can talk you out of His goodness towards us.

It's Never Too Late

How many of you are waiting for a child to return to you and your home—back to a relationship that may have been severed long ago? You think back over the long months and years—lost time that cannot be regained. Yet you haven't lost hope. You wait for a letter, an e-mail, a call, or to hear footsteps on the path to your house. You know that someday it will happen, you just don't know when. A day doesn't go by that you don't think about your child.

The news recently carried a story about an 87-year-old man who was reunited with his daughter after 40 years. He had divorced her mother when the daughter was four, and he last saw her when she was 12. For more than 40 years he didn't see his child. She grew up, married, had children and grandchildren. One day she called him on the phone and said, "This is Victoria, your daughter." The man discovered he had a family he knew nothing about. He quickly agreed to meet and began making up for lost time, knowing time could not be regained but determined not to allow any more to be lost. That is how it will be one day for those who decide to see Jesus instead of religion and dead works. That is what this parable is talking about. The prodigals will return. They will come to a moment of clarity and say: "I want a relationship once again with those who love me and pray for me. I need to go home!"

A Message About Deep Love

This parable encourages families. God's great plan of salvation is based on the family structure of a father and mother and children born within the love of a relationship based on His laws governing the family. And the basis of that law is love—the love of a parent for a child. This parable shows the deep love of a father for his lost son. I can imagine him praying each day for his son's return, requesting God to guard him from harm, asking God to help the son even when the son's behavior didn't honor God. During these prayers, the understanding that God wouldn't suspend the law of consequences didn't keep him from asking for God's mercy and goodness on the lad.

The home is not complete

until the prodigal son comes back

This parable is also about each of us. God the Father stands waiting for the time when each of His children will at last realize the need for a lasting and satisfying relationship with Him. The image of family reconciliation and turning of hearts is quoted in one of the great prophetic messages of the Old Testament, Malachi 4:6 *"He will turn the hearts of the parents to their children, and the hearts of the children to their parents; or else I will come and strike the land with total destruction."* (NIV).

The parable of the lost son combined with this prophecy helps us to understand God's deep desire to bring reconciliation within His creation. Together these form a promise that you can take to His throne of grace and claim in full faith. When hearts turn to God, they will also return to those human relationships that have been broken through the years. You can count on it.

Holding Out Hope

The parable of the lost son is a parable for today. It offers hope for all who long for reconciliation. Whether it be with a child, a parent, or a friend from the past, this story points to hope. It teaches that even when hope is deferred and the heart is sick, there is the promise that hope will blossom into a tree of life (Proverbs 13:12). Imagine for a moment the day the father goes out to the hill and at last sees his son coming up the road. What joy and elation he feels! His heart immediately reaches out to his returning son, his feet quickly propelling him forward to the exuberant embrace. Father and son are together again, the distance bridged, and the time apart forgotten.

His years of hope and longing are summed in the declaration, "This my son was dead, and is alive again; he was lost, and is found" (Luke 15:24). You may think this is a good place to end. But the story goes on. There is the reaction of the older son. Remember him—the one who stayed and honored his father and worked to build the family business? At first, he wasn't that happy over the return of his brother. When he came home that day and heard the noise from the celebration, he wondered what it was all about. When he heard his brother had returned home and a banquet was being held in his honor, it was more than he could handle.

He refused to join in the celebration. On hearing of his son's anger, the father pleaded with him to join in welcoming his brother home. But he couldn't because, as he put it: "These many years I have been serving you; I never transgressed your commandment at any time; and yet you never gave me a young goat, that I might make merry with my friends. But as soon as this son of yours came, who has devoured your livelihood with harlots, you killed the fatted calf for him" (Luke 15:29-30).

Once again, the father showed his wisdom: "Son, you are always with me, and all that I have is yours. It was right that we should make merry and be glad, for your brother was dead and is alive again, and was lost and is found" (Luke 15:31-32, NKJV). The bond forged between the father and the older son could never be broken. The loyalty and dependability of the son here had been proven beyond doubt. Such relationships need no party or grand demonstration. Trust was simply there. I like to imagine the two brothers reconciling and their healed relationship becoming stronger and enduring through the years. The father lives on to see grandchildren run through his home with shouts of joy and fun. In his later years he thanks God for all his family, and in time he dies, full of years and giving thanks to God with his last breath for His goodness and grace.

CHAPTER 8
THE PARABLE OF THE GOOD SAMARITAN

Each Jew knew the command: "Love your neighbor as yourself." When a man asked Jesus who exactly was meant by "neighbor" he was trying to get out of his responsibility. By telling the parable of a Samaritan who helped a stranger, Jesus made it plain that any person who is in need is our neighbor. This also shows us that loving people and just being kind to those around us is a great virtue for the believer.

In the book of Matthew, Jesus referred to loving God as the "greatest command" and loving your neighbor as the command like it. He even said that all the Law and the Prophets hang on these two commandments (Matthew 22:34-40). Being an expert in the law (a lawyer), the man asking Jesus questions would have been familiar with these commands. He also would have been familiar with the many additions to the law that the Pharisees had made. He would rather debate the law than think about his own personal obedience. He tries to test Jesus or trap Him in His own words. Jesus takes this potentially volatile situation and turns it into a teaching moment.

Again, Jesus speaks in a parable in Luke 10:25-37 saying: *"On one occasion an expert in the law stood up to test Jesus. 'Teacher,' he asked, 'what must I do to inherit eternal life?' What is written in the Law?' he replied. 'How do you read it?' He answered, Love the Lord your God with all your heart and with all your soul and with all your strength and with all your mind; and, Love your neighbor as yourself. You have answered correctly,' Jesus replied. 'Do this and you will live.*

But he wanted to justify himself, so he asked Jesus, 'And who is my neighbor?' In reply Jesus said: *'A man was going down from Jerusalem to Jericho, when he was attacked by robbers. They stripped him of his clothes, beat him and went away, leaving him half dead. A priest happened to be going down the same road, and when he saw the man, he passed by on the other side. So too, a Levite, when he came to the place and saw him, passed by on the other side. But a Samaritan, as he traveled, came where the man was; and when he saw him, he took pity on him. He went to him and bandaged his wounds, pouring on oil and wine. Then he put the man on his own donkey, brought him to an inn and took care of him. The next day he took out two denarii and gave them to the innkeeper. "Look after him," he said, "and when I return, I will reimburse you for any extra expense you may have." Which of these three do you think was a neighbor to the man who fell into the hands of robbers?'*

The expert in the law replied, 'The one who had mercy on him.' Jesus as a response told him, *'Go and do likewise'"* (NIV). This was not an actual event but one that was believable because it could easily have happened. The distance from Jerusalem to Jericho is about 25 kilometers. This familiar road ran through rocky, desert country that provided places for robbers to hide and make surprise attacks on people. The people listening to this parable would have been able to relate to the trouble that the man in the parable was in. It would have been a relief for the injured man to see a good Jewish priest come along. How must he have felt to see the priest pass by without helping? Another Jew, a Levite, should have also stopped, but he did not.

This Jewish audience would have expected other Jews to help a Jew in obvious need. What they did not expect was the next thing that Jesus said. It was not a Jew that finally helped this man, but a Samaritan! The Samaritans were looked down on by Jews. They were considered half-breeds and not true Jews. This goes back to 2 Kings 17:24-41 when the Jews of the northern kingdom were taken into Assyrian captivity and the King of Assyria made an attempt to resettle Samaria with his own people. Samaritans were the descendants of the Jews who returned and of the Samarians

In this parable, the Samaritan went to extraordinary measures to help the man. He not only helped him in the moment of need, he got personally involved in the man's situation. He spent the night taking care of him and then paid an inn keeper so that the man would be taken care of until he was well. Two silver coins would have been equal to two days' wages, which would have been enough for up to two months' stay in an inn.

We are to love our neighbor as we love ourselves. Neighbors are not just the people who live near us or that are in our circle of friends and family. Neighbors are not even just the people who attend church with us or even just those who believe in God. Neighbors are anyone who is in need. Sometimes helping our neighbor is very difficult and inconvenient. Sometimes it means getting out of our comfort zone or even facing some ethical dilemmas. When Jesus challenged the lawyer with this parable, even this expert in the law knew that the Samaritan had obeyed God's command while the priest and Levite had not.

"A Good Samaritan is not simply one whose heart is touched in an immediate act of care and charity, but one who provides a system of sustained care." James A. Forbes

---

If you were to make a list of Jesus' most beloved and well-known parables, the Good Samaritan would top the list. It's a powerful and evocative story that reveals a fundamental truth about the heart of God and His expectations of us. To grasp the meaning of Jesus' story, we need to look at the context in which He told it. It all started when an expert of Mosaic law came to Jesus with a question.

When it comes to examining parables, people often get lost in the weeds. They spend so much time trying to attach significance to every detail that they misunderstand the story. But the details are a vehicle to communicate a central point. So, what's the gist of this story? The teacher of the law intended to trap Jesus, but Jesus turned the conversation back around. When eternal life comes down to loving God and loving your neighbor, the man wanted to justify himself. So, he asked Jesus a question, intending to quibble about identifying neighbors. Jesus answered the question by telling a story about a man beaten, robbed, and left to die on the side of the road.

Both a Jewish priest and a Levite (assistant to a priest) passed him by. This would have shocked the man listening to the story. Of all the people likely to show compassion to a fallen Jewish traveler, it would be one of these fellows. Both go out of their way to avoid the injured man. Jesus intentionally chooses the Samaritan to be the hero because he's the most unlikely candidate. The Jews and Samaritans were mortal enemies. In fact, Samaritans were so hated that when traveling from

Judea to Galilee, Jews would travel twice the distance in order to avoid Samaria entirely.

By making the Samaritan the good guy, Jesus cuts to the heart of the man's question. Our neighborhood is as wide as the love of God. It's not enough to hold religious titles or positions like the priest and the Levite. It's not enough to feel a pang of remorse or sadness at someone's ill fortune. Loving your neighbor means acting on behalf of others, regardless of who they are or where they're from.

Who Is My Neighbor?

Most of us, when we think of a neighbor, imagine the person who lives next door that's always having a party and leaving their trash outside our home the next morning. But a neighbor is more than that. You probably know this story as the story of the Good Samaritan. But do you know the meaning behind it? No, not just helping people in need. Do you know what it really means to be a good Samaritan?

The expert in the law asked, "Who is my neighbor" with the intention of excusing himself. His question was more about defining who wasn't his neighbor. Jesus' response was that even our enemies are our neighbors. The kingdom question is never "Who is my neighbor," it's always "How can I become a better neighbor?" Being a neighbor is not restricted to relation or proximity. It is merely the demonstration of the love and mercy of God to all in need, whomever and wherever they may be, regardless of race, denomination, or belief.

Jesus teaches us that love is an action, not just a feeling or a theory, and that it sometimes requires the shouldering of others' burdens, an often-uncomfortable process. The priest and the Levite were religious men, and yet they acted inhumanely, and the Samaritan demonstrated just the opposite. Religious vocation or affiliation is empty without the actions to back it up. To be a neighbor, according to Jesus, means to come alongside someone. We instinctively tend to limit for whom we exert ourselves. We do it for people like us, and for people whom we like. Jesus will have none of that. By depicting a Samaritan helping a Jew, Jesus could not have found a more forceful way to say that anyone at all in need – regardless of race, politics, class, and religion – is your neighbor. Not everyone is your brother or sister in faith, but everyone is your neighbor, and you must love your neighbor.

As Nigerians, Americans, white, black, or brown, we must remember that we are Christians first. Our nationality should never surpass our faith and its duties. This is what we must keep in mind when we consider our "neighbor." A neighbor doesn't just entail our geographical placement in relation to another human being but how we treat those we don't even know. Being a neighbor requires that we be kind to others, even if we don't particularly like that person.

And though it's hard to do, it's something especially we as Christians need to work on. But how? In a time when there is so much tension between races, political leaders, and countries, it's hard to show anything short of disdain for one another. Everyone is at odds, everyone is at each other's throats, from the poor to the rich, from the powerless to those who hold offices of power and influence. Why can't we all get along? Why can't we be neighbors? It's easy to get along with someone who is kind to you. If someone were to hold the door for you, it's easy to grab the next door for them in return. But what about when that person doesn't hold the door? When the tables are turned, will you repay them in the same manner? Or could you somehow find the strength to be a neighbor to them regardless of what they did in the past?

For many of us, this is a challenge even when we face a situation as simple as holding the door. But a much harder task is to love them in spite of what they did to us. It's even harder when we as Christians are called by God to love our enemies. Not like them, love them. That means regardless of what a person does to you, you should still love them. No matter how much they get on your nerves you should still love them. Why? Because it's easy to love those who love you. But as Christians we are to do the hard thing; as Christians, we are to love our enemies. Having the intent to help is good, but acting on that intent is much better. The Samaritan's intent didn't save the wounded man from death. His actions ultimately saved the man's life. He didn't walk away, unlike the two men before him. He decided to do something.

At times we feel outnumbered in our attempts to improve the world—to brighten and beautify, to preserve and heal, and do what's best for humanity. Selfless efforts can start to feel beleaguering, discouraging, even pointless with so little support. At these times I remind myself that I would rather be the last Good Samaritan standing than join the ranks of selfish multitudes creating misery. In our time, that half-dead man's photos would end up on social media before he even got to the hospital. Everybody would take pictures, but very few would actually dare to help. We would feel sorry for that person but not enough to get involved. Now, are we the good Samaritan or are we the men who walked away? What makes this story very compelling is that Jews and Samaritans are historical enemies. Jews didn't talk to Samaritans as they considered them renegades, and this enmity was returned by the Samaritans.

But what has two-thousand-year-old story to do with us? Like any parable, Jesus used this story to teach us lessons about life and, most importantly, about God. Xenophobia and racial prejudice have always been a great divider among nations. Since ancient times, we have distrusted those who don't look like us or sound like us, but the Samaritan didn't care about race. He showed us that racism has no place in charity and that we should help others, regardless of where they came from or what they believe in. After all, we are all created equal. No one race is superior nor inferior to the other. And at the end of the day, we all belong to the same race: humanity. Have you ever wished ill of your enemy? Admit it or not, at some point in our lives we've all done it. Sometimes, the temptation to take revenge on our enemies is just so strong and difficult to resist.

In the story, the injured traveler most likely hated the Samaritan. And the Samaritan knew that the dying man may still hate him after he recovered. Yet, he helped him. The civil rights activist Martin Luther King Jr. famously said: "On the parable of the Good Samaritan: I imagine that the first question the priest and Levite asked was: 'If I stop to help this man, what will happen to me?' But by the very nature of his concern, the good Samaritan reversed the question: 'If I do not stop to help this man, what will happen to him?'" It's easy to assume no one in modern society would pass by someone ailing on the side of the road. But we can all recall a time when we witnessed someone pulled off to the side of the freeway … alone. We so often don't pull over to help. Sometimes, out of a healthy fear of very real and opportunistic evil in the world. Other times, we choose not to put ourselves in danger on account of another. Further still, we are all consumed by the amount of time we have in each of our days.

The story of the Good Samaritan reminds us to take time to notice and to inconvenience ourselves to stop and sacrifice our precious minutes and resources to love our neighbor the way we're called to as Christians. God has purposed us to love one another. Resist the cultural urge to frame those struggling as soft or weak. Suffering from the consequence of their own decisions doesn't afford us a license to love someone any less. We've all made bad decisions, suffered through our own consequences, or been hurt at the hands of another. Let gratitude for the people God had in place to pull us through fuel our love for them now.

Remembering keeps us humble, reminds us to be grateful, and spurs us to pass it on. Instead of convincing ourselves we don't have the time or the means to help, focus prayerfully on allowing God to show us how He wants us to love those suffering around us. John Bloom wrote, "If our restlessness is due to the disillusionment of having to deal with difficult, different people and defective programs, then perhaps the change we need is not in the church community but in our willingness to love our neighbors, the ones God has given us." The parable of the Good Samaritan provides an example of risk-taking love. Jesus does not specify the victim who was attacked and abandoned. He is anyone. He is everyone. Christ wants us to be moved by a love that pays no attention to racial, religious, or socioeconomic categories. The parable of the Good Samaritan raises many questions.

In the story of the Good Samaritan, everybody knows the robber is bad, but doesn't Jesus also imply an indictment on the priest and Levite? . . . They are 'righteous' in a superficial way. They don't rob anybody. They're not like that lousy criminal who is over there, on the bad side of the line. Do you see it? That's the line we modern Christians try to live on the right side of. The Samaritan traveler lives on a higher level, altogether. The issue isn't who is wrong or righteous; that's obvious. The issue is who is profoundly good. Deep wounds are not easily healed. But the Good Samaritan poured oil and wine into the wounds of the stranger who lay helpless on the road to Jericho and set him on the road to recovery. Each one of us can go and do likewise

How do we relate to people who are different from us? What is our responsibility towards the many hurting people in our world? Who is our neighbor? Christ's message was that if we wish to be reconciled to the Father, we must demonstrate love towards all people, regardless of race, religion, or social position. Love is active, inconvenient, risky, and might not be reciprocated. What if, in Jesus' parable of the Good Samaritan, the wounded traveler had died or was unable to repay the Samaritan? This parable foreshadows Christ's sacrifice on the cross and the free gift of grace He offers to repentant sinners. Jesus took a risk: "While we were still sinners, Christ died for us" (Romans 5:8 NIV). He paid everything so that those who believed in Him for salvation would be saved, knowing many would reject the gift. God asks that we meet lost people in their painful messes and lead them to the cross, risking rejection but hoping to witness their salvation.

Natural Enemies, Unnatural Love

Jesus Christ in His parable did not specify that the victim "attacked by robbers" and abandoned "half-dead" was Jewish, Samaritan, or otherwise. So I assume he could be anyone. He is everyone. Jesus wants us to be moved by exceptional compassion; love that pays no attention to racial, religious, or socioeconomic categories. The original Greek says that the Samaritan did more than "[take] care of" this man but offered "care and devotion" such as the kind "shown by parents and nurses to children." The man's emotional and financial investment in a stranger's care, his generosity, was staggering. What the Samaritan paid to the innkeeper was the equivalent of over $1500, or enough for slightly more than three weeks lodging. His love was extravagant.

He did not preach compassion to the innkeeper or return for payment from the beaten man. The Samaritan took responsibility financially and personally and lived out a belief: Your neighbor is the person who needs saving. The word *splagma* used in the original Greek means "pity from your deepest soul." The Samaritan's heart was broken, reflecting a heart for God and the heart we receive from God for others when we embrace salvation through the mercy of Christ. God invites us to see beyond the exterior of lifestyle, color, and even religious affiliation to the Imago Dei in everyone. He reminds us that we were once the same as that broken, bleeding man. "Once you were alienated from God" and were even His "enemy" but you have been "reconciled [...] by Christ's physical body through death" and are now "without blemish and free from accusation" (Colossians 1:21-22 NIV).

Our sin nailed Christ to the cross, and the Father has every right to despise us, yet He has made us "heirs with Christ" (Romans 8:17). This extravagant love should inspire us to love others extravagantly. His radical grace gives us a new identity. In this new identity, the Father also gives us dignity. Like the man who had been beaten and robbed in Jesus' parable, we were once naked, in need of covering. The Father clothed us in the blood of His Son. God rescued us from death for eternity, but He also restored us to communion with others and with Him today. He bestows value and dignity onto all who love Him, including those who are rejected by the world.

"True compassion is more than flinging a coin to a beggar. It comes to see that a system that produces beggars needs to be repaved. We are called to be the Good Samaritan."

Martin Luther King, Jr.

In the story of the Good Samaritan, Jesus not only teaches us to help people in need. More deeply, He teaches us that we cannot identify who "has it," who is "in" with God, or who is "blessed" by looking at the exterior. It is a matter of the heart. There, the kingdom of the heavens and human kingdoms great and small are knit together. Draw any cultural or social line you wish, and God will find His way beyond it.

True compassion like Martin Luther rightly pointed out, is indeed more than "flinging a coin to a beggar". It comes to see that a system that produces beggars needs to be repaved. We are called to be the Good Samaritan, but after you lift so many people out of the ditch you start to ask, maybe the whole road to Jericho needs to be repaved. And you know, it's possible that the priest and the Levite looked over that man on the ground and wondered if the robbers were still around. Or it's possible that they felt that the man on the ground was merely faking.

And he was acting like he had been robbed and hurt in order to seize them over there, lure them there for quick and easy seizure.

And so, the first question that the Levite asked was, "If I stop to help this man, what will happen to me?" But then the Good Samaritan came by, and he reversed the question: "If I do not stop to help this man, what will happen to him?" Psychologists tested the story of the Good Samaritan. What they learned gives us reason to pause. The greatest determinant of who stopped to help the stranger in need was not compassion, morality, or religious creed. It was those who had the time. Makes me wonder if I have time to do good.

CHAPTER 9
NO, GOD IS NOT VENGEFUL

Beloved brothers and sisters in Christ, it's pertinent that we address the various doctrinal inconsistencies regarding the nature and character of God that religion has preached versus the person of Jesus Christ. If we don't want a monstrous God who occasionally commands genocide, and if we don't want a malleable God who is slowly mutating away from a violent past, how do we view the Old Testament?

The Old Testament is the inspired telling of the story of Israel coming to know their God. It's a process. God doesn't evolve, but Israel's understanding of God obviously did. If the revelation of God is perfectly depicted in the Pentateuch, why follow the storyline of Scripture into the Prophets, Gospels and Epistles? It seems obvious that we should accept that as Israel was in the process of receiving the revelation of Yahweh, some unavoidable assumptions were made. One of the assumptions was that Yahweh shared the violent attributes of other deities worshipped in the ancient Near East. These assumptions were inevitable, but they were wrong. For example, the Torah assumed that Yahweh, like all the other gods, required ritual blood sacrifice, but eventually the psalmists and prophets take the sacred text beyond this earlier assumption.

Even a casual reader of the Bible notices that between the alleged divine endorsement of genocide in the conquest of Canaan and Jesus's call for love of enemies in His Sermon on the Mount, something had clearly changed! What changed was not God but the degree to which humanity attained an understanding of the true nature of God. The Bible is not the perfect revelation of God: Jesus is. Jesus is the only perfect theology.

Perfect theology is not a system of theology; perfect theology is a Person. Perfect theology is not found in abstract thought; perfect theology is found in the Incarnation. Perfect theology is not a book; perfect theology is the life that Jesus lived. What the Bible does infallibly and inerrantly is point us to Jesus, just like John the Baptist did. The Old Testament tells the story of Israel coming to know the living God, but the story doesn't stop until we arrive at Jesus! It isn't Joshua, the son of Nun, who gives us the full revelation of God but Yeshua of Nazareth. It's not the warrior-poet David who gives us the full revelation of God but the greater Son of David, Jesus Christ. We understand Joshua and David as men of their time, but we understand Jesus Christ as "the exact imprint of God's very being" (Hebrews 1:3).

> *That the Scriptures are inspired by God doesn't mean that violence and genocides in it were sanctioned or commanded by God.*

Once we realize that Jesus is the perfect icon of the living God, we are forever prohibited from using the Old Testament to justify revenge, the use of violence, or the use of curses on people. Using Scripture as a divine license for the implementation of violence is a dangerous practice that must be abandoned by us who walk in the light of Christ. If we hold to the bad habit of citing the Old Testament to sanction our own violence, how do we know that we won't use those texts to justify a new genocide?

This isn't inflammatory rhetoric but a legitimate question. It's a legitimate question because the Old Testament has been used by Christians to justify genocidal violence, hate, slavery, and just pure evil. This was the justification used by European and American Christians during the American Indian genocide in North America. The majority of the transatlantic slave traders were Christians, and these Christians used scriptures to justify the inhuman treatment of their fellow human beings. Here is an example of such scripture, and I will explain this scripture in context. Ephesians 6:5-6 reads: *"Slaves, obey your earthly masters with respect and fear, and with sincerity of heart, just as you would obey Christ. Obey them not only to win their favor when their eye is on you, but as slaves of Christ, doing the will of God from your heart"* (NIV).

In 1637, the English colonial leadership in Connecticut sought to launch a war of aggression against the Pequot tribe for the sole purpose of acquiring their cultivated land. A war party of 90 settlers was raised and placed under the command of John Mason. When some of the colonists expressed moral qualms about launching an unprovoked attack on their peaceful neighbors, the matter was referred to their chaplain, the Reverend John Stone. After spending the night in prayer, Reverend Stone "was 'fully satisfied' with Mason's proposal."

At dawn on May 26, 1637, the armed colonists attacked the main Pequot village at Mystic Lake on the central Connecticut River, killing an estimated 400 to 700 Native Americans. Most of the dead were women and children—often historically the victims of ethnic cleansing—burned to death in their wigwams as the English slaughtered those who ran. Captain Mason describes the slaughter in these words: "Thus was God seen in the Mount, Crushing his proud Enemies and the Enemies of his People ... burning them up in the Fire of his Wrath, and dunging the Ground with their Flesh: It was the LORD's Doings, and it is marvelous in our Eyes!"

Notice how John Mason attributes the massacre of Pequot Indians to the actions of God. What followed over the next few months was the virtual extinction of the Pequot tribe. But apparently not all the colonists were comfortable with a Christian-led genocide. In his critically acclaimed history of Native America, *The Earth Shall Weep*, James Wilson writes, "There also seem to have been colonists with misgivings about what had happened." Captain Underhill was clearly replying to criticism when he wrote: "It may be demanded, why should you be so furious? (as some have said). Should not Christians have more mercy and compassion?" He echoes Mason by taking his defense from the Old Testament, presenting the English—typically—as the put-upon underdog in a crusade against evil. "I refer you to David's war. When a people are grown to such a height of blood and sin against God and man ... Sometimes the Scripture declareth women and children must perish with their parents ... We had sufficient light from the Word of God for our proceedings."

There you have it. The Bible used to bless barbarism. Genocide justified in the name of God. (This kind of biblical justification of genocidal violence against the native peoples of North America continued throughout the 17th, 18th, and 19th centuries.) There is a sad and twisted logic to evoking God's will as the rationale for ethnic cleansing. If Captain Joshua can claim God commanded the Israelites to kill Canaanite women and children, why can't Captain Mason and Captain Underhill claim God commanded English colonists to kill Pequot women and children?

My point is, if you leave the door open to justify the Canaanite genocide, don't be surprised if modern crusaders try to push their way through that same door and then cite the Bible in their defense. We need to say something more responsible about the depiction of God-endorsed violence in the Old Testament. We should acknowledge that in the late Bronze Age, Israel made certain assumptions about the nature of God, assumptions that now must be abandoned in the light of Christ. It is abundantly clear from the Gospels that Jesus has closed the door on genocide, just like He has closed the book on vengeance.

God's Depicted Violence In The Old Testament

Among the questions I'm most often asked about the Bible is this: "Why does God seem so loving in the New Testament but angry, harsh, and vengeful in the Old Testament?" These violent passages not only trouble thoughtful Christians but give fodder to atheists who assert, sometimes rightly, that religion is the source of much of the violence in the world.

> *Since we believe that Jesus Christ is the only and express image and revelation of God, it's fair to conclude that much of the violence in the Scriptures attributed to God are the perception of the writers and not a true representation of God's nature and character.*

Let's consider three categories of Old Testament texts that are morally problematic and go against the character of Jesus Christ who is the revealed God to humanity.

1. The "crimes" for which God prescribes the death penalty
2. God's anger and wrath in punishing His people
3. God's command to the Israelites to commit genocide.

The death penalty. There are numerous "crimes" for which God, through the Law of Moses, requires the death penalty. Among these are sacrificing to a god other than Yahweh (Exodus 22:20), persistent rebelliousness on the part of a child (Deuteronomy 21:18–21), a child who hits or curses his or her parents (Exodus 21:15 and 17), working on the Sabbath (Exodus 35:2), premarital sexual intercourse (Deuteronomy 22:13–21), and the requirement for a priest to burn his daughter alive if she became a prostitute (Leviticus 21:9).

God's anger and wrath. In the Old Testament, God's anger repeatedly burns against His people for their disobedience. At times, the punishment He dispenses seems particularly harsh, unjust, and disproportionate. Let's consider just one example.

In 2 Samuel 24, we find that King David decided to take a census of the men of fighting age. The prophet Gad was sent to David to announce God's displeasure with the taking of the census. The punishment for David's sin: "The Lord sent a pestilence upon Israel from the morning until the appointed time; and seventy thousand of the people…died" (2 Samuel 24:15, NASB). David makes a decision that does not please God, and God kills 70,000 Israelites for it? How could this action ever be reconciled with a God of mercy, compassion, justice, and love?

Genocide in the name of God. I'll mention one last category of scriptures related to the violence of God: those that describe the conquest of Canaan. At the time the Israelites entered the land to conquer it, Canaan was populated with small city-states or kingdoms made up of various ethnic groups speaking similar languages. God promised Israel that he would give them this land, but to do so these people had to be displaced.

This is problematic enough, but God wasn't asking the Israelites to forcibly relocate them to other lands. God instructed the Israelites to kill every man, woman, and child among these Canaanites. In Deuteronomy 20:16-18, Moses gives these instructions: "As for the towns of these peoples that the Lord your God is giving you as an inheritance, you must not let anything that breathes remain alive. You shall annihilate them—the Hittites and the Amorites, the Canaanites and the Perizzites, the Hivites and the Jebusites—just as the Lord your

God has commanded". The Hebrew word for "annihilate" has as its root *herem* (also transliterated as *cherem* or sometimes *charam*). The classic Brown-Driver-Briggs Hebrew and English Lexicon notes the meaning of the word in English is "to exterminate." It also has the sense of devoting something to God by completely destroying it. This is sometimes translated as "ban"—a word that in this context means "given to God by complete destruction."

In Joshua 6:20b–21, you can read about what this looked like as the Israelite army entered the town of Jericho: the Israelites "charged straight ahead into the city and captured it. Then they devoted to destruction by the edge of the sword all in the city, both men and women, young and old, oxen, sheep, and donkeys". After the destruction of Jericho, next came the people of Ai, then the people of Makkedah and Libnah and Lachish and Eglon and Debir—every man, woman, and child slaughtered and dedicated to God. In the end, the entire population of thirty-one city-states was utterly destroyed.

I suspect that most people who read the Bible either don't think about this, gloss over these sections, or skip them altogether. I was fourteen years old when I first read the Book of Joshua. The stories didn't trouble me at that time. They were epic battles with great story lines and heroic figures. Who doesn't enjoy reading about how the walls of Jericho "came tumbling down"? Behind each story was the idea that God was fighting on behalf of His people. I suspect that's how most people read these stories today.

But when I grew up, I reread these stories and began to think about the humanity of the Canaanites. These were human beings who lived, loved, and had families. Among them were babies and toddlers, mothers and fathers. Yet they were all put to the sword by "the Lord's army." Thirty-one cities slaughtered with no terms of surrender offered and no chance to relocate to another land. I came to see the moral and theological dilemmas posed by these stories. How do we resolve the moral and theological dilemmas presented by these and other texts like them? It's paramount that we reconcile this false depiction of the nature and character of God with the person of Jesus Christ, since we have seen from scriptures and agreed that only Jesus has seen God, was in the beginning, and is the only express image of God.

Since we believe that Jesus Christ is the only and express image and revelation of God, then it's fair to conclude that much of the violence in the Scriptures attributed to God is the perception of the writers and not a true representation of God's nature and character. That the scriptures are inspired by God doesn't mean that the violence in them was sanctioned or commanded by God.

How do we come to terms with all this violence and the evil acts attributed to God in the Old Testament? How can we effectively explain these events and acts spiritually, logically, and above all, in subjection to the revelation of the revealed God in Christ? A possible first way of making sense of the violence of the Old Testament, particularly related to war, is to recognize that Moses, Joshua, and David were Israel's heroes. They were warrior-saints. These stories were written down long after their time to inspire others to courage and absolute commitment to God. An analogy would be the story of William Wallace of Scotland.

Wallace died in 1305, but to this day he is a legendary hero in Scotland. He fought against the English in the wars for Scottish independence. Every Scottish child is taught about William Wallace. Memorials to him are found throughout the country. Sir Walter Scott expanded the legend with his writings. And Wallace's story was told in the 1995 Oscar-winning film Braveheart, with Mel Gibson playing the part of Wallace. Only the English criticized Wallace's methods in war, accusing him of killing civilians. In Scotland, he's remembered for his heroism.

Here's what I'm suggesting: Perhaps the stories of the conquest of Canaan were to ancient Israelites what the stories of William Wallace are to the Scots. Written long after the time of these heroes, they were meant to demonstrate courage, resolve, and faith and to inspire later generations still struggling against their own enemies. These stories were written from the theological perspective of the ancient Near East, where gods sent heroes into battle and fought alongside them. No one reads Sir Walter Scott's book on William Wallace to find a model for the ethics of war. They read it to be inspired by a national hero. The same was true of the book of Joshua.

There's a lot more about this topic that should be said, entire books have been devoted to addressing the issue of violence in the Bible. My goal is to point you toward some possible ways of making sense of this violence without justifying it. The answers that make the most sense to me require that we recognize the humanity of the Bible's authors, their intent in writing, and the culture that shaped them. This approach also invites us to question those parts of Scripture where God is portrayed in a way inconsistent with Jesus's life and message. Where a particular teaching in Scripture is at odds with what Jesus said, we are right to consider that the passage may reflect the culture, the worldview, or the perspectives of the human author of Scripture rather than the timeless heart, character, and will of God.

It would be easy to decide never to read difficult sections of Scripture like Joshua, but that would be a tragic mistake. There are a great many ways in which God speaks through these biblical texts. There are a handful of passages in Joshua that are moving and powerful, including its dramatic conclusion, when Joshua calls the Israelites to "choose this day whom you will serve, whether the gods your fathers served in the region beyond the River, or the gods of the Amorites in whose land you dwell. But as for me and my house, we will serve the LORD" (Joshua 24:15, ESV).

But perhaps the most important reason for reading Joshua is to remind us of how easy it is for people of faith to invoke God's name in pursuit of violence, bloodshed, and war. The Crusaders marched into battle in Jerusalem in the name of Christ. Colonists from the Old World arrived in the New World, Bibles and weapons in hand, to claim America for Christ. Nazi belt buckles proclaimed, "Gott Mit Uns"— God is with us—as they sought the extermination of Jews and other "undesirables." "Christian" nations have often gone to war invoking God in their efforts. When America marches to war, patriotism and faith are quickly melded so that to be a good Christian is to support the war effort.

Some of those war efforts might have been morally justified (if one holds to the theory of just war), but others were "pre-emptive wars" that did not meet the criteria of the just war. Regardless of whether the war effort was morally justified or not, our troops marched off to battle to the tune of "God Bless America." If this is the case today, it should not surprise us that people who lived 3,500 years ago also invoked God as they marched off to war.

If every word of the Bible was chosen by God, then our conclusion must be that, at least in the Old Testament period, God was a violent God, burning people alive, stoning them to death for anything that brought Him offense, killing tens of thousands for the sin of their king, and commanding His own people to wipe out entire cities and peoples. But if we take the Bible's humanity seriously, we find the possibility that the violence of Scripture is a reflection of the values and the theological and moral vision of some of its human authors, not of the God they sought to serve.

I've repeatedly suggested that we judge all other words of Scripture in light of God's definitive Word, Jesus Christ. He taught that His followers were to love their neighbors, turn the other cheek, forgive those who wronged them, and pray for those who persecuted them. This Word stands in direct opposition to encouraging slaughter in the name of God. Ultimately the violence-affirming passages of the Old Testament serve as a reminder of how easily we might still be led to invoke God's name as a justification of violence in our world. To the degree that we see Jesus as the definitive Word of God and that we listen carefully to His words, we are able to free ourselves from this tragic dimension of our human condition. Second—and the only option for those who hold to verbal, plenary inspiration—is to accept that these commands and stories accurately capture what God said, what God did, and what God commanded His people to do. Then the task is to explain how the character of God revealed in these seemingly harsh and violent texts is consistent with the character of God revealed by Jesus Christ.

To make this case, advocates usually speak of God's authority to give and take life at will and of the need for God to demonstrate a firm hand to the Israelites in order to lead them to walk in His path. In the process, they downplay God's attributes of love, kindness, mercy, compassion, and justice. To explain the total and merciless destruction of the Canaanites, they point out the Canaanites' wickedness, surmising that they were more wicked than other peoples in the ancient Near East. They argue that the Canaanites deserved their extermination. One author describes it as a form of collective capital punishment for the evil every Canaanite had committed. In response, it's been pointed out that this is the same argument that has often been made throughout history to justify genocide. Think back to the arguments Hitler made concerning the Jews.

Many of us read these justifications for why God prescribed horrible and seemingly immoral acts of violence but find it impossible to reconcile these acts with the character of God Christianity proclaims. Jesus broke bread with sinners. He ministered to prostitutes and adulterers. He hung on the cross and prayed for His accusers and executors, "Father, forgive them for they know not what they do." "God so loved the world that he gave his only begotten Son." This is far from the God who, with little compunction, destroys tens of thousands of people.

So, what is the alternative? The Bible says these things. If the Bible says it, are we not required to accept it? The point of the first half of this book was to recognize the complexity of the Bible and to help you see its humanity. If we understand the Bible as having been essentially dictated by God, then yes, we have no choice but to accept what is written as accurately describing God's actions and God's will.

But if we recognize the Bible's humanity—that it was written by human beings whose understanding and experience of God was shaped by their culture, their theological assumptions, and the time in which they lived—then we might be able to say, "In this case, the biblical authors were representing what they believed about God rather than what God actually inspired them to say." If we use Jesus's words, and His great commandments, as a colander, we'll see that these violent passages in the Hebrew Bible contradict not only these great commands, but the very life and ministry of Jesus who was God's unmitigated Word. As humans, regardless of how anointed we are or how spiritually inspired we maybe, we are bound to make mistakes. We are bound to add or subtract from words said to us in ways that may seem to favor us, drive our point home, or maybe just simply err due to lack of understanding.

The impulse to kill, to destroy the enemy, and to put to death those who violate social norms is a continuing part of our world today. For those who believe in God, this violence is often perpetrated while asking for God's blessing and help, and at times it is even committed in the name of God. But violence is an equal-opportunity illness in the human condition. Atheist regimes sought to impose their view of utopia by slaughtering millions of people in the last century. The human story is that throughout history, we have tragically supported the use of violence to enforce the will of dictators, kings, and even the majority in democratic societies. What is true today was true in the ancient Near East, only without the terrifying weaponry that can destroy entire cities with a single bomb.

In August 1868, a stone was found in a field in Jordan, commonly called the Moabite Stone or the Mesha Stele. It dates to around 840 BC, and it describes the victory of King Mesha of Moab over Israel. Mesha and the people of Moab worshipped the Canaanite god Chemosh. Listen to King Mesha's account in this selection from the Moabite Stone: "And Chemosh said to me, 'Go, take Nebo from Israel!' so I went by night and fought against it from the break of dawn until noon, taking it and slaying all, seven thousand men, boys, women, girls and maid-servants, for I had devoted them to destruction for (the god) Ashtar-Chemosh."

What we see in this text is that Mesha believed his god had urged him to go to war, and as an expression of devotion (or possibly as a means of justifying genocide), the people of the town were "devoted to destruction" (others translate this as "put to the ban"). The idea that a god had directed the king to go to war and that the king was leading his people in battle on behalf of, at the will of, and with the help of a god seems to have been a common way of justifying war and rallying the people to fight.

So, one possible resolution to the moral and theological dilemma raised by the texts we've been studying is that Moses, Joshua, and David were warriors living in times when violence was seen as a means for God to accomplish His purposes. They attributed to God words, commands, and deeds that they believed God would have authorized or done. Old Testament passages about violence and war thus tell us more about the people who wrote them and the times they were living in than about the God in whose name they claimed authority to do these things.

CHAPTER 10
OLD TESTAMENT ANGRY GOD AND NEW TESTAMENT LOVING GOD. RIGHT OR WRONG?

If you're reading through the Old Testament, you may be in for a shock. There's blood. There's gore. There's more violence than a lot of movies. How can a loving God call for so much killing and violence? It can seem like there's a divide between the violent "God of the Old Testament" and the loving "God of the New Testament." But God is the same yesterday, today, and tomorrow. So, what's the deal with the blood and gore we read about in Scripture?

A covenant perspective on the Bible can help us understand the seeming divide. The God who made a covenant with Abraham to bless all nations in the Old Testament (Genesis 22:14-18) is the same God who fulfills that covenant in the New Testament through His divine Son, Jesus Christ, and His catholic Church (Acts 3:25; Galatians 3:16; Matthew 28:18-20). How are we to interpret these passages? One way is to see them not as commandments or actions from God, but as human projections on God. It is easy to claim that God wants the same things for us that we passionately wish for ourselves. How much more so would that be true for a people who believed themselves to be chosen as God's especially favored nation! If we accept the notion that God commanded the genocide in Canaan, then we should not have any issues if the present nation of Israel decided to invade Cameroon tomorrow and say God instructed them to do so.

The tendency to attribute human emotions and actions to God exists in all nations and religions. The Crusaders went to war saying *Deus Vult!* or "God wills it!" European settlers in North America often took Native American lands and lives, believing it was their divinely given Manifest Destiny. In the Middle East today there are fanatics who give their lives to wreak destruction in the name of Allah. Another possible response to these passages is to say that religious understanding evolved through the centuries the Bible was written. It is widely believed that the earliest parts of the Old Testament were developed when folks were more primitive in their thinking. By this theory, Jesus most fully reveals a corrected understanding of God as compassionate and forgiving.

Both of these theories have some validity, but there are also problems. One, of course, is the tendency to pick and choose those Biblical passages with which we are most comfortable and dismiss the rest. Another problem is that we may be committing the same error, imposing our desired picture of God onto the Divine Mystery. Perhaps God is much greater than our imaginations. Through the ministry of Jesus, we see completely unmerited forgiveness for a woman caught in the act of adultery (and presumably the man who was not dragged before Jesus as well). Jesus ministers to Romans and Samaritans, who should have been destroyed according to the commands God gave Israel. Instead of destroying and killing, Jesus served others and even sacrificed Himself.

Around the New Year, many of us jump in on a Bible reading plan. Reading through the Bible in one year is a great goal. It's challenging, but not impossible. It builds a positive habit and gives you a deeper understanding of faith and church history. But once the exciting days of Genesis and Exodus are behind you, you'll find yourself moving on to Leviticus, Numbers, and Deuteronomy. "Oh man," you might start thinking. "I don't know if this was such a good idea." As you thumb through passages detailing everything from animal sacrifices to genocide to prophets' warning of doom and gloom, you might start to wonder if there's any value in reading this content.

In his famous book *The God Delusion*, noted anti-theist Richard Dawkins says, "The God of the Old Testament is arguably the most unpleasant character in all fiction: jealous and proud of it; a petty, unjust, unforgiving control-freak; a vindictive, bloodthirsty ethnic cleanser; a misogynistic, homophobic, racist, infanticidal, genocidal, filicidal, pestilential, megalomaniacal, sadomasochistic, capriciously malevolent bully."

If we accept the notion that God commanded the genocide in Canaan, then we should not have any issues if the present nation of Israel decided to invade and annihilate the entire

> *country of Cameroon tomorrow and say God instructed them to do so.*

When we read those parts of the Old Testament that we don't tend to cover in Sunday school, we might start wondering how we got from the God who was demanding bloody animal sacrifices to Jesus, who is all about love and hope and peace.

What Dawkins said seems harsh, and certainly should not be taken seriously by any believer. But there are definitely parts of the Old Testament that make me cringe. In light of that, what are we supposed to do with the first two-thirds of the Bible? Do we have to read it? Do we have to like it? Are we supposed to follow the rules and regulations in it? The author of the book of Hebrews wrote, "Jesus Christ is the same yesterday, today and forever." Based on this, it seems clear that we must pay attention to what the Old Testament says, for when we ignore it, we ignore the God we worship and call Father. But we also need to better understand the purpose of the Old Testament so we can allow it to be part of our faith, rather than treating it like a crazy uncle we try to ignore.

An important aspect of God's work of creation is that He put things in order and in relationship with one another. The divine mandate to humans, therefore, is to "tend the garden;" that is, to help things grow together. There may be times when destruction is part of the task, but it is for the sake of pruning – improving the garden – rather than simply wreaking violence. Apparently, this stewardship involves even non-violence toward animals. The man and woman are given permission to eat the fruit of the ground and trees – except for the tree of the knowledge of good and evil. There is no mention of eating meat, even by animals. Humans and animals were meant to be vegetarian.

The second story of creation (Genesis 2:4) has significant differences from the first story but continues the vision that humans are created to continue God's work. For instance, they were instructed to name the animals, which involved using words and reasoning, as God did when He created the universe in the first place. And when God punished Adam and Eve for their transgression, He did so not in anger but to protect the divine order of things. Many examples of God's involvement in violence – throughout the Old Testament in particular

– are not done to destroy so much as to restore the original vision of a just and whole creation. God's acts are restorative, not retributive.

For example, when God sent plagues upon Egypt as part of the campaign to free the Hebrews in captivity and later destroyed the Egyptian army in the Red Sea, the divine violence is aimed to achieve justice and wholeness, not simply to cause bloodshed and heartache for the Egyptians, who were also God's children. A primary example of God's vision for the universe is found in the Ten Commandments (Exodus 20:1-17), These are basic rules for building and maintaining community, as relevant today as they were thousands of years ago – and as difficult to apply, especially as we now live in an interdependent global community. The Commandments begin with a unifying vision: recognizing God as the center of life. They then go on to insist on mutual respect as the necessary ingredient for living together: respect for the ties of marriage, for family relationships, for integrity and for the property of others.

In the middle of the Commandments, however, is a seemingly simple rule: "Thou shalt not kill." The problem is, the Old Testament is full of other commands from God to kill. Numerous portions of the Law prescribe capital punishment for a number of sins, ranging from adultery to children talking back to their parents. Furthermore, various passages tell of God's command to totally wipe out communities and nations that resist the "Chosen People."

Most scholars today, particularly Jewish scholars, agree that the commandment's word translated "kill" in the King James Version should more properly be translated "murder." Therefore, many modern versions translate this verse as "You shall do no murder." This would exclude legal executions, self-defense, and acts of war. It would apply primarily to criminal acts against another in one's own tribe or nation. Christian thought, however, has extended that circle to include all humanity, since all human beings are considered children of God and therefore persons of sacred worth.

Jesus, in fact, offered an even more stringent understanding of the commandment against murder: to hate another person is tantamount to murder in God's eyes. One's inner attitude can therefore be as dangerous to one's own soul as a violent act would be harmful to one's

The Misrepresented God

victim. This same Christ died for all sins past and future, including the Original Sin of Adam and Eve (Romans 5:6-21), as promised by His eternal Father in the Old Testament (see also the Suffering Servant passage in Isaiah 52-53). In the Old Testament, God – whose names include Elohim, Yahweh, Adonai, and El Shaddai – is active, angry, and violent. He talked to Moses, defeated armies, guided by pillars of smoke and of fire, and threatened those who disobeyed. But in the New Testament, God seems to be more relaxed – a voice at Jesus' baptism and not much else – while Jesus, and later the Spirit, take center stage. Is this a fair picture, a caricature, or totally wrong? What should we Christians think about the Old Testament picture of God, especially the violence He seems to sometimes initiate?

God in the Old Testament

There is no doubt that God is portrayed in the Old Testament as commanding and doing some things we would regard as barbaric today. Perhaps the classic example is 1 Samuel 15:3. *"Now go, attack the Amalekites and totally destroy all that belongs to them. Do not spare them; put to death men and women, children and infants, cattle and sheep, camels and donkeys"* NIV).

But this isn't the whole story. God is also portrayed as loving and patient, and there are many commands to love and be merciful and care for the poor and the defenseless (Deuteronomy 24:14-15), even refugees (Deuteronomy 10:18-19), and provide opportunities for justice rather than revenge (Exodus 24:13). The prophets revised the picture we got from the earlier parts of the Old Testament, showing vividly that God cares about compassion for the poor and justice and honesty for all. Despite what critics say, the loving nature of God is more on display than the violent. Many years ago, I did a genuinely random selection of 100 Old Testament verses, and found that there were twice as many positive portrayals of God as there were ones we would find negative now (although they almost certainly wouldn't have been understood as negative back then).

God in the New Testament

Of course, we know the picture looks very different in the New Testament. 1 John 4:8 says God is love. Jesus said if we've seen Him we've seen the Father (John 14:9), and we see Him caring for the female victims of a male-dominated society (John 8:10-11), outcast lepers (Matthew 8:2-3), and hated tax collectors (Luke 19:5). And Jesus is very strongly opposed to violence, saying, *"But I tell you, love your enemies and pray for those who persecute you, that you may be children of your Father in heaven"* (Matthew 5:44-45, NIV).

We've noted that the words of Jesus seem to contradict passages in the Old Testament that depict God as sanctioning and even commanding violence. Indeed, much of the New Testament seems determinedly anti-violent. But that may not convey the whole message of the New Testament. A key passage for discussion is Matthew 5:38-48. *"You have heard that it was said, 'An eye for an eye and a tooth for a tooth.' But I say to you, do not resist an evildoer. But if anyone strikes you on the right cheek, turn the other also; and if anyone wants to sue you and take your coat, give your cloak as well; and if anyone forces you to go one mile, go also the second mile. Give to everyone who begs from you, and do not refuse anyone who wants to borrow from you.*

"You have heard that it was said, 'You shall love your neighbor and hate your enemy.' But I say to you, Love your enemies and pray for those who persecute you, so that you may be children of your Father in heaven; for he makes his sun rise on the evil and on the good, and sends rain on the righteous and on the unrighteous. For if you love those who love you, what reward do you have? Do not even the tax collectors do the same? And if you greet only your brothers and sisters, what more are you doing than others? Do not even the Gentiles do the same? Be perfect, therefore, as your heavenly Father is perfect."

Jesus modeled this instruction in His own life, even to the point of death on the cross. He based this notion of non-violence on God's nature. This form of living marks us as God's children. Jesus presented the ultimate truth about violence: it is an affront to God's sovereignty, an act of rebellion as serious as Adam and Eve's sin of disobedience.

The Old Testament certainly sanctioned some violence as legitimate, such as self-defense. As the saying goes, "The only thing that can stop a bad man with a gun is a good man with a gun." Jesus' commandment seems to challenge this idea. His followers are to break the circle of violence by refusing to participate in it. Jesus reiterated this idea in a number of ways, for instance saying that following Him means to take up a cross (Matthew 16:24). This was all too vivid a metaphor for a conquered people for whom death by crucifixion was a public spectacle. In fact, in 6 A.D., when Jesus was a child, the Romans crucified 2000 rebels at one time in Sepphoris, Galilee.

Why would Jesus offer such a radical idea? Some authors point out that the inhabitants of Judea and Galilee in Christ's time lived under the harsh authoritarian rule of Rome. They were, for the most part peasant farmers and townspeople, untrained in the ways of war and lacking the weapons of the Roman legions. They were certainly outnumbered; resistance to Rome would unquestionably end in disaster, as every rebellion proved to be. Perhaps, then, Jesus' counsel for non-violence was simply prudent: "You can't win, so don't start the fight. And if the fight comes your way, duck and cover – don't try to resist."

Here are some questions people have asked me several times on this issue of God's character.

1. Does Jesus' emphasis on non-resistance to evil means that one cannot protect himself? How about protecting others, such as one's family?
2. Are there ways of resistance that do not involve violent actions?

Jesus certainly didn't shrink from a fight. By entering Jerusalem as He did on Palm Sunday and cleansing the Temple, He was posing a challenge which the Sanhedrin couldn't ignore. And, since the Jewish legal system couldn't impose the death penalty, Roman military power would inevitably be called in. Jesus was no fool; He was raising a red flag which could only end in death. Yet He also calmly refused to retaliate against those who tormented Him. In fact, when Simon Peter tried to protect Him the night of His arrest, Jesus rebuked him, told him to put his sword away, and restored the severed ear Peter had cut off (Luke 22:49-51).

Interestingly, Matthew, Mark, and Luke report that at His trial Jesus did not complain over His mistreatment, but John tells us that when one of the Sanhedrin guards struck him in the courtroom, Jesus challenged the judges to restrain such actions (John 18:23). There may well have been regulations against mistreatment of a prisoner, and Jesus was appealing to those rules. Paul affirms Jesus' emphasis on non-violence in Romans 12:14: "Bless those who persecute you; bless and do not curse" (NIV). This notion seems to have been the standard for Christians through at least the first three centuries of the Church. In fact, it is said that when Constantine was converted and became the first Roman Emperor to be a Christian, he had his entire army baptized, and each man, upon going into the water, was careful to hold his fighting arm up so as to not have it baptized, for it would mean he could no longer fight in war.

Violence and Vengeance in The New Testament

As we have already seen, there are strong New Testament teachings against violence, commanding loving service instead, even of enemies. But how did Jesus and the apostles deal with Old Testament violence?

But I tell you, love your enemies and pray for those who persecute you,

that you may be children of your Father in heaven.

Matthew 5:44-45

Jesus And His Mission

In Luke 4:18-19, Jesus sets out His mission by quoting from Isaiah 61:1-2: "The Spirit of the Lord is on me, because he has anointed me to proclaim good news to the poor. He has sent me to proclaim freedom for the prisoners and recovery of sight for the blind, to set the oppressed free, to proclaim the year of the Lord's favor" (NIV).

He went on to say that this scripture was fulfilled in Him. But notably, He chose not to complete verse 2 of Isaiah 61 (which He was quoting), which goes on to say, "and the day of vengeance of our God." There are several views on why Jesus omitted this section, but they all lead to the conclusion that Jesus was distancing Himself from violence as a means for fulfilling His mission. And arguably, He was correcting an Old Testament misunderstanding about God.

Paul And Violence

In the book of Romans, Paul often quoted Old Testament passages that included God's vengeance or condemnation of Gentiles – and each time he omitted those sections. In Romans 15:9-10, he quoted Psalm 18:49 and Deuteronomy 32:43. Both passages are surrounded by statements of revenge on the enemies of God's people, but Paul omitted these and only quoted the shorter sections on praise to God for His mercy. In Romans 12:19-21, Paul urged Christians not to take vengeance and again quoted Deuteronomy 32, but whereas the original passage was a celebration of God's vengeance, Paul turned it into an admonition to love enemies.

Then, in Romans 3:10-18, Paul quoted from a series of Psalms to illustrate human sinfulness. But the original context of most of these Psalms was the supposedly righteous writer calling on God to judge evil-doers, while Paul used the passages to teach that all of us, without exception, need the mercy and forgiveness of God, not His justice and vengeance.

How can we put it all together?

There are three ways we can make sense of these large differences.

1. Defend all statements in the Bible

Some Christians argue that the Bible stands in its entirety and all the apparently violent depictions of God and His commands can be justified. The people He commanded be killed were really evil and depraved and liable to lead the Israelites away from God or even destroy God's chosen people. And the children had to go because they couldn't survive without their parents. I cannot follow this course. I cannot see how ordering people to murder can be squared with God's character revealed in Jesus. Can I imagine Jesus carrying out that command? No, I cannot! I would rather give up believing in these Old Testament teachings than try to defend such a view of God.

2. The whole Bible is barbaric

Some non-believers, sometimes those who left the faith over issues like this, agree that the Bible stands in its entirety, and therefore must be rejected because the barbaric depiction of God in the early books of the Old Testament belongs to a long gone age. I cannot follow this course either. I believe in Jesus, and He taught and embodied a loving God. I cannot let go of that understanding because I believe it is the truth.

3. Believe what the New Testament shows us about the Old

There is a third way. I believe we can see that Jesus and the apostles rejected this violent portrayal of God and replaced it with something nobler and truer.

Comparing Emphases

The Old Testament contains several commands to seek vengeance (e.g. Numbers 31:1-3, Joshua 10:12-13, Judges 16:28-30, Jeremiah 50:14-15) along with others to be more loving, but the New Testament strongly teaches mercy, non-violence and not taking revenge. It is clear then that the New Testament has a different overall emphasis compared to the Old Testament. However, we might explain this, it seems likely that both Jesus and Paul were correcting faulty understandings of God's character that appeared in some passages in the Old Testament and explaining some passages in a new way. They seem to have felt free to reinterpret the Old Testament, something that isn't uncommon in the New Testament or in first century Judaism.

Interpreting the Old Testament's Portrayal of God

It seems then that both Jesus and Paul were not happy with the portrayal of God as taking vengeance and gave us a new emphasis on forgiveness and mercy. How can we understand this? It seems to me that there are two possible ways to resolve this apparent dilemma.

We All Make Mistakes

However much or little we may think it inspired by God, the Old Testament was written down by people, and these people used the language and thought forms of their day. It may be that they simply recorded their understanding of God at the time, and they were mistaken on this aspect. This easily resolves the difficulties but makes the Old Testament less useful as an authoritative revelation of God's true character.

God adapts himself to our human limitations, and His self-revelation has always been progressive, starting with what is most easily understood and gradually moving to a more complete revelation in Jesus. The early Old Testament belongs to an early stage when God's revelation was incomplete, and the commands to violence were part of the culture that God hadn't corrected yet.

I can't help feeling the truth is a combination of these. C.S. Lewis wrote: "If you take the Bible as a whole, you see a process in which something which, in its earliest levels .... was hardly moral at all and was in some ways not unlike the Pagan religions, is gradually purged and enlightened till it becomes the religion of the great prophets and Our Lord Himself. .... At first hardly anything comes through but mere power. Then (v. important) the truth that He is One and there is no other God. Then justice, then mercy, love, wisdom."

Is this selling the Bible short?

Our initial reaction may be to feel alarmed at this "answer" – it is compromising the truth of the Bible. But we have Jesus and Paul's example to show us that they were comfortable with that approach, so perhaps we don't need to be fearful after all. And anyway, which is most important: a true understanding of God's love or a doctrine about the Bible? On this understanding of the Old Testament, it is still inspired. It still points to Jesus, and it is still the scriptures Jesus used and which allow us to understand His mission. But we are in a new covenant now, and God is revealed in new ways through Jesus that make the Old Testament view of Him complete.

CHAPTER 10
GOD DOES NOT HAVE MOOD SWINGS.

Perhaps the most difficult biblical dilemma for those of us who affirm the classic view of an utterly sovereign and immutable God is how to make sense of the various divine affections spoken of in Scripture. If God is eternally unchanging—if His will and His mind are as fixed and constant as His character—how could He ever experience the rising and falling passions we associate with love, joy, exasperation, or anger?

Classic theism teaches that God is impassible—not subject to suffering, pain, or the ebb and flow of involuntary passions. In the words of the Westminster Confession of Faith, God is "without body, parts, or passions, immutable." God without passions? Can such a view be reconciled with the biblical data? Consider Genesis 6:5-6: "God saw that the wickedness of man was great in the earth, and that every imagination of the thoughts of his heart was only evil continually. And it repented the Lord that he had made man on the earth, and it grieved him at his heart." In fact, Scripture frequently ascribes changing emotions to God.

At various times He is said to be grieved (Psalm 78:40), angry (Deuteronomy 1:37), pleased (1 Kings 3:10), joyful (Zephaniah 3:17), and moved by pity (Judges 2:18). Classic theism treats such biblical statements as anthropopathisms—figurative expressions ascribing human passions to God. They are the emotional equivalent of those familiar physical metaphors known as anthropomorphisms—in which hands (Exodus 15:17), feet (1 Kings 5:3), eyes (2 Chronicles 16:9), or other human body parts are ascribed to God.

We know very well that God is a Spirit (John 4:24), and "a spirit hath not flesh and bones" (Luke 24:39)—so when Scripture speaks of God as having body parts, we naturally read such expressions as figures of speech. Almost no one would claim that the biblical tropes ascribing physical features to God are meant to be interpreted literally. But the texts that assign emotions to God are another matter. Many Christians are loathe to conclude that these are meant to be taken figuratively in any degree. After all, one of the greatest comforts to any believer is the reassurance that God loves us. But if love is stripped of passion, we think it's a lesser kind of love. Doesn't the doctrine of divine impassibility therefore diminish God's love?

To complicate matters further, when we try to contemplate how any of the divine affections can be fixed and constant, we begin to imagine that God is inert and unfeeling. Fearing such inferences, some veer to the opposite extreme and insist instead that God is even more passionate than we are. In one of the ubiquitous internet Bible discussions, I participated in, a minister who hated the doctrine of divine impassibility wrote, "The God of the Bible is much more emotional than we are, not less so! "Someone else sarcastically replied, "Really? Does your god have even bigger mood swings than my mother-in-law?" The point was clear, even if made indelicately. It is a serious mistake to impute any kind of thoughts to God that are cast in the same mold as human passions—as if God possessed a temper subject to involuntary oscillation.

In fact, a moment's reflection will reveal that if God is subject to like passions as we are, His immutability is seriously undermined at every point. If His creatures can literally make Him change His mood by the things they do, then God isn't even truly in control of His own state of mind. If outside influences can force an involuntary change in God's disposition, then what real assurance do we have that His love for us will remain constant? That is precisely why Jeremiah cited God's immutability and impassibility as the main guarantee of His steadfast love for His own: *"It is of the Lord's mercies that we are not consumed, because his compassions fail not"* (Lamentations 3:22).

God Himself made a similar point in Malachi 3:6: "For I am the LORD, I change not; therefore, ye sons of Jacob are not consumed." Still, many find the doctrine of divine impassibility deeply unsatisfying. After all, when we acknowledge that an expression like "the ears of the Lord" (James 5:4) is anthropomorphic, we are recognizing that God has no physical ears, so if we grant that the biblical expressions about divine affections are anthropopathic, are we also suggesting that God has no real affections? Is He utterly unfeeling?

The Misrepresented God

If we allow that God's grief, joy, compassion, and delight are anthropopathic, must we therefore conclude that He is really just cold, apathetic, and indifferent?

Scripture tells us that the eternally unchanged and unchanging God became so angry against Israel at Sinai that He threatened to annihilate the entire nation and essentially void the Abrahamic covenant. Exodus 32:9-11reads:*"And the LORD said unto Moses, I have seen this people, and, behold, it is a stiffnecked people: Now therefore let me alone, that my wrath may wax hot against them, and that I may consume them: and I will make of thee a great nation. And Moses besought the LORD his God, and said, LORD, why doth thy wrath wax hot against thy people, which thou hast brought forth out of the land of Egypt with great power, and with a mighty hand?"*.

A casual and logical reading of the above passage seems to suggest that God is the unkind and bad father, and Moses is the kindhearted and understanding one advising God. Look at Moses' reply to God in Exodus 32:11. *"And Moses besought the Lord his God, and said, Lord, why doth thy wrath wax hot against thy people, which thou hast brought forth out of the land of Egypt with great power, and with a mighty hand?"* Two things are perfectly clear from such an account: First, we are not to read this passage and imagine that God is literally subject to fits and temper tantrums. His wrath against sin is surely something more than just a bad mood. We know this passage is not to be interpreted with a wooden literalness. How can we be so sure? Well, Scripture clearly states that there is no actual variableness in God (cf. James 1:17). He could not have truly and literally been wavering over whether to keep His covenant with Abraham (Deuteronomy 4:31).

Moses' intercession in this incident (Exodus 32:11-13) could not literally have provoked a change of mind in God (Numbers 23:19). In other words, a strictly literal interpretation of the anthropopathism in this passage is an impossibility, for it would impugn either the character of God or the trustworthiness of His Word.

Nonetheless, a second truth emerges just as clearly from this vivid account of God's righteousness anger. The passage destroys the notion that God is aloof and uninvolved in relationship with His people. In other words, we can begin to make sense of the doctrine of impassibility only after we concede the utter impossibility of comprehending the mind of God. The next step is to recognize the biblical use of anthropopathism. The anthropopathisms must then be mined for their meaning. While it is true that these are figures of speech, we must nonetheless acknowledge that such expressions mean something. Specifically, they are reassurances to us that God is not uninvolved with or indifferent toward His creation.

However, because we recognize these anthropopathisms as metaphorical, we must also confess that there is something they do not mean. They do not mean that God is literally subject to mood swings or melancholy or spasms of passion or temper tantrums. And in order to make this very clear, Scripture often stresses the constancy of God's love, the infiniteness of His mercies, the certainty of His promises, the unchangeableness of His mind, and the lack of any fluctuation in His perfections. "With [God there] is no variableness, neither shadow of turning" (James 1:17).

This absolute immutability is one of God's transcendent characteristics, and we must resist the tendency to bring it in line with our finite human understanding.

Sorting Out Some of the Difficulties

To be perfectly frank, impassibility is a difficult doctrine, both hard to understand and fraught with hazards for anyone who handles it carelessly. And dangers lurk on both sides of the straight and narrow path. While the radical-Arminian open theists are busily lampooning the doctrine of divine impassibility by claiming it makes God an iceberg, a few hyper-Calvinists at the other end of the spectrum actually seem prepared to agree that God is unfeeling and cold as ice. Obviously, people on both sides of the open theism debate are confused about this doctrine, and that is to be expected. After all, we are dealing with something we cannot possibly comprehend completely. "For who hath known the mind of the Lord?" (Romans 11:34a).

We must begin by acknowledging that we are all prone to think of God in human terms. "You thought that I was just like you," God says in Psalm 50:21. "I will reprove you and state the case in order before your eyes" (NASB). "My thoughts are not your thoughts, neither are your ways my ways, saith the LORD. For as the heavens are higher than the earth, so are my ways higher than your ways, and my thoughts than your thoughts" (Isaiah 55:8-9). Again and again, Scripture reminds us that the affections of God are ultimately inscrutable (cf. Ephesians 3:19; Romans 11:33).

To cite just one example, consider that God's love never wavers and never wanes. That alone makes it utterly unlike any human love we have ever experienced. If we consider how the Bible defines love rather than how we experience the passions associated with it, we can see that human love and divine love have the same characteristics, which are spelled out in detail in 1 Corinthians 13. But notice that not one characteristic in the biblical definition of love has anything whatsoever to do with passion. Real love, we discover, is nothing at all like the emotion most people refer to when they mention "love."

That's why we must allow Jesus' life and teachings and the Epistles, not human experience, to shape our understanding of God's affections. Those who study the matter biblically will quickly discover that God's Word, not merely classic theism, sets the divine affections on an infinitely higher plane than human passions. We can learn much from the anthropopathic expressions, but to a large degree the divine affections remain hidden in impenetrable, incomprehensible mystery, far above our understanding.

Making Peace Is The Gospel

Peacemaking is at the very core of the Good News. "Even when we were God's enemies, he made peace with us, because His Son died for us" (Romans 5:10a). That is why peacemaking must also be a central component of what it means to follow Jesus. As Dom Jose Maria Pires, a Brazilian archbishop, put it, "What North Americans call nonviolence is simply living out the teachings of the Gospel." Tom Yoder Neufeld goes so far as to say, "For the sons and daughters of God, peacemaking is at the end of the day not a matter of tradition, denomination, or political ideology. It is a matter of gospel, period."

Put bluntly, those people who seek to follow Jesus' example of forsaking violence in order to extend love towards enemies should not be called pacifists; they are simply Christians. We are called to be peacemakers because God is a peacemaker. This is why the only people Jesus referred to as "sons of God" were those engaged in peacemaking. John and Paul used the phrase "sons of God" or "children of God" to refer to anyone who believed in Jesus. However, based on the recorded sayings of Jesus in the Gospels, Jesus exclusively reserved this title for those who made peace by loving their enemies. Here are some of these teachings from Jesus:

"Blessed are the peacemakers: for they shall be called the children of God". Matthew 5:9

"But I say to you, love your enemies, bless those who curse you, do good to those who hate you, and pray for those who spitefully use you and persecute you, that you may be sons of your Father in heaven." Matthew 5:44-45a.

"But love your enemies, do good, and lend, hoping for nothing in return; and your reward will be great, and you will be sons of the Most High. For He is kind to the unthankful and evil." Luke 6:35

The reason Jesus solely used the title "sons of God" for those who love their enemies is because they are the ones who most fully resemble the forgiving Father. If you go about making peace by loving your enemies, then everyone will know you're a child of God because you'll be the "spittin' image" of your Father! People will look at you and say, "Wow, you remind me of your Father. You look and act just like Him."

Jesus is our model and our motivator for cultivating peace. Jesus and His cross give our peacemaking efforts a distinct flavor. Jesus' life and teaching are our model for cultivating peace. Ours is a cross-centered approach to peacemaking. Ours is an approach rooted in being a people that extend mercy instead of judgment. One final point must be made. Jesus' voluntary crucifixion is not only the ultimate example of nonviolently loving one's enemies and making peace, but also the source from which we find the inspiration to do the same. We are to love our enemies as an act of gratitude to the One who loved us when we were still His enemies. As Philip Yancey stated so well in his book *What's So Amazing About Grace?*, "If I had to summarize the primary New Testament motivation for 'being good' in one word, I would choose gratitude."

We will never last long in our efforts to be a people of mercy that love their enemies if our motivation for doing so is solely a desire to obey Jesus' commands. This is a good desire, but it is not strong enough to sustain us long-term. Rather, our motivation for being Christian peacemakers ought to be the cross, or more specifically, the gratitude that will overflow from a life centered on the cross. Through the cross, God has been graciously unfair to us. The joy that comes from receiving such a gift empowers us to be graciously unfair to others as well.

Interpreting the Old Testament

A long time ago I noticed that when Jesus and the New Testament writers quoted the Old Testament, they did not always do it literally or accurately, but often used translations and interpretations that did not seem to be present in the original. I felt this was an important fact, so I researched the matter (the way to learn new truths is to examine difficult facts). What I found was interesting. I analyzed all the Old Testament references in the four gospels, plus Acts and Romans (using only English translations). And I found that while about half quoted the Old Testament passages accurately and in context, about half did not. Some just changed a few words, but some changed a lot or changed the meaning or quoted out of context.

But while this pattern was clear, I didn't really understand what was going on. Then I discovered a book that examines this very question: *Biblical Exegesis in the Apostolic Period* by Richard Longenecker, a Canadian professor of New Testament. Longenecker uses these concepts:

- iteral – the plain meaning of the text, more or less as a western scientific person would understand it;

-Midrash – based on Jewish rabbinical rules of interpretation, and some subsequent Christian emphases, that can lead to meanings that extrapolate way beyond the literal – for example, by linking passages on apparently quite different themes, because they contain the same word;

-Pesher – understanding and interpreting the Old Testament passage in the light of later events, particularly finding messianic meanings where none were previously obvious, or even intended by the writer (though doubtless intended by God).

-Allegorical – the passage is interpreted via symbolism.

Significantly, literal interpretation is not the most common approach in the New Testament. Jesus most commonly used Pesher analysis as He interpreted the Old Testament in non-literal ways based on his understanding of Himself as the Jewish Messiah. Paul most commonly used Midrashic interpretation (perhaps because of his background as a Pharisee). This shouldn't trouble us. We can well believe that Jesus had authority to re-interpret the Old Testament and choose between alternate translations, versions and understandings of the text as suited His purpose, and it appears the early Christians who wrote the New Testament believed the Holy Spirit working through them could do the same.

But it does mean we have to be careful when we insist on literal interpretations in every situation. God's truths can be conveyed through non-literal understandings – perhaps sometimes they can best or only be conveyed that way. We need to pray for the wisdom of the Holy Spirit to be given to the whole body of Christ, to enable us to understand the way he wants us to interpret the Bible and apply it in our lives or else we will keep describing a God that aligns with our political parties, ideological views, and religious views instead of the God who revealed and manifested Himself in Christ Jesus.

CHAPTER 11
THE GOD OF THE OLD TESTAMENT VS. THE FATHER OF THE NEW TESTAMENT

The angry, violent, vindictive God of the Old Testament often seems completely at odds with the loving Father of the New Testament. It is difficult to reconcile the two, and sometimes believers – along with non-believers and ex-believers – question the actions of God recorded in the Old Testament because they seem atrocious and outside the character of a good God.

Religious defenders of God often respond in one of two ways. Some try to explain how the seemingly cruel actions of God in the Old Testament are proper given the circumstances: God killed people because they were evil, as He did in the flood; and He killed Israelites in order to enforce obedience; and so forth. Others simply point out that God is not accountable to anyone and has the right and power to do as He pleases—He is above reproach. Neither answer seems satisfactory. The acts still seem incompatible with a good God. I believe both answers are misguided. One early bishop took this objection very seriously and concluded that the God of the Old Testament was not the same person as the Father of the New Testament. Bishop Marcion was the son of the Bishop of Sinope, a seaport city in northern Asia Minor. Recognizing the conflict between the concepts of God in the Old and New Testaments, Marcion taught that the Father whom Jesus describes is the universal God of love and compassion, while the God of the Old Testament was a lesser being and the jealous tribal god of the Israelites.

Marcion addressed a real issue, but I believe his answer was mistaken. I believe the answer lies elsewhere: God did not do what the Old Testament claims He did. Simple. The problem with the Christian defenders of God's violent behavior in the Old Testament, and with Marcion's conclusion that this God was a completely different being than the Father, is that they both believe that the things written about the God of the Old Testament were accurate.

But who wrote about God in the Old Testament? Was God writing His own story or were people writing about God as they understood Him? I think it was the latter. The Old Testament is a collection of material written by many people, in many situations, over a long period of time. What they had in common was that they felt a connection to God or with the nation Israel. Perhaps God provided special insight to some writers in some way, but we don't know to what extent. And it seems that they had a very incomplete understanding of God. The Old Testament idea of God certainly reflects many of the same assumptions about gods held by the surrounding cultures of that day—assumptions we should no longer maintain.

The writers of the Old Testament were bound by the times and cultures in which they lived, and their ideas of an angry, violent, vindictive God were products of their limitations. It is an incredible burden on them to expect that they were perfect in everything they wrote.

It is important to realize in this regard that violent images of God are not the only ones found in the Old Testament. There are many references to a gentle God. When Jesus announced His mission, He did so by reading from Isaiah 61. Luke 4 reports His words: *"The Spirit of the Lord is on me, because he has anointed me to proclaim good news to the poor. He has sent me to proclaim freedom for the prisoners and recovery of sight for the blind, to set the oppressed free, to proclaim the year of the Lord's favor"* (NIV). However, the angry, violent images are still in the Old Testament. They grab our attention, and we must account for them.

Inerrancy of the Bible

Inerrancy is the belief that every word of the Bible is inspired by God and is accurate and authoritative. Accepting and defending the Old Testament descriptions of God's behavior as fact is necessary for those who hold to inerrancy. A reader commented recently, "I am continually challenged when confronted with the thought that it isn't ALL INSPIRED by God. If it isn't, then what is the point of the Bible? Why bother believing any of it." This concern is sometimes called 'cherry-picking' the Bible. But were we to read a compilation of works on medicine from writers over a period of 2000 years, we would certainly use the best of the works and ignore the rest. We would not throw out the entire collection because of the varying quality. Neither must we accept the Bible's description of God in the Old Testament as inerrant in all things in order to accept the good news of Jesus.

Jesus and the Father

What does Jesus say about the Father? How did He get His information? How does it relate to Old Testament descriptions of God? Jesus talks a lot about the Father in the Gospels, but how does he know so much? Where does He get His information? On one occasion, Jesus told the Pharisees about His special relationship with the Father, and they were furious! What Father? Most of John chapter 8 is devoted to this conversation. Jesus said to the people in the temple courts, "I am the light of the world. Whoever follows me will never walk in darkness but will have the light of life."

The Pharisees challenged Him saying He had no witness to those claims but Himself. Jesus answered that He also had the witness of the Father who sent Him. So, the Pharisees pressed Him by asking, "Where is your father?" Jesus responded, "You do not know me or my Father...If you knew me, you would know my Father also." Later, the subject came up again when Jesus claimed He was not of this world. "Who are you?" they asked. "Just what I have been telling you from the beginning," Jesus replied. "I have much to say in judgment of you. But he who sent me is trustworthy, and what I have heard from him I tell the world."

They did not understand that He was telling them about His Father. Jesus told them the Father had sent Him. The discussion really heated up when the Jews insisted that Abraham was their father and Jesus replied, "I know that you are Abraham's descendants. Yet you are looking for a way to kill me, because you have no room for my word. I am telling you what I have seen in the Father's presence, and you are doing what you have heard from your father." "Abraham is our father," they answered. "If you were Abraham's children," said Jesus, "then you would do what Abraham did. As it is, you are looking for a way to kill me, a man who has told you the truth that I heard from God.

Abraham did not do such things. You are doing the works of your own father."

"We are not illegitimate children," they protested. "The only Father we have is God himself." Jesus said to them, "If God were your Father, you would love me, for I have come here from God. I have not come on my own; God sent me." So, the Jews now claim that God is their father. Jesus winds up suggesting their real father is the devil, and they retort that Jesus is a demon-possessed Samaritan. LOL.

But what does Jesus mean when he referred to what he has seen 'in the Father's presence'? Did He experience the Father's presence or was he actually with the Father? He also said that He heard the truth from God, that He came from God, and that God sent Him. This is a lot of information! Finally, the Jews asked, "Are you greater than our father Abraham? He died, and so did the prophets. Who do you think you are?" And Jesus gives even more key information about his relationship with the Father: "My Father, whom you claim as your God, is the one who glorifies me. Though you do not know him, I know him. If I said I did not, I would be a liar like you, but I do know him and obey his word. Your father Abraham rejoiced at the thought of seeing my day; he saw it and was glad."

"You are not yet fifty years old," they said to him, "and you have seen Abraham!" "Very truly I tell you," Jesus answered, "before Abraham was born, I am!" We learn so much from this short exchange. Jesus began by identifying His Father with the God of the Jews, which is the God of the Old Testament. So, it seems that Marcion was mistaken. Then we hear that Jesus existed before Abraham was ever born! This is a game changer. Whatever Jesus meant by His statement, it certainly sounds like a claim of pre-existence and a relationship with the Father before His birth among the Jews. Hearing this, the religious folks did the most natural thing and picked up stones to stone Him.

Throughout history men and women have wondered about the nature of God. That God exists is pretty much taken for granted by most. The question is not whether there is a God, but rather what kind of a God is He? Is He tough or tender? Is He laid back and easy going or demanding and strict? Does He notice the small fry or is He mostly concerned with world leaders and the rich, the famous, and the influential? Each religion has its own version of God. And many people who hold to no particular organized religion have created their unique view of the Creator, made after the image of the Creator they suppose He ought to be.

For evangelical Christians, the matter is settled by the pages of the Bible, that large collection of books written by prophets, kings, poets, and apostles that we believe has been inspired directly by God, the Holy Spirit. Gaining an accurate perception of God is the most important education one could ever hope to receive. It is far more valuable than computer skills, mathematical abilities, or a knowledge of world history. Jesus tells us, "God is spirit, and those who worship Him must worship Him in Spirit and in truth." Without a true knowledge of God, we become idolaters and religious pretenders. The Muslim who kills women and children while shouting, "Allah is great," the Hindu who beats Christians to death in defense of his idolatrous religion, and the cult leaders who persuade their followers to commit mass suicide are all acting out the consequences of a false and utterly deceptive view of the divine Creator.

Not only does Jesus tell us that we must worship God according to truth, He declares that He Himself is the purest and most complete expression of God the world will ever see. When asked by Philip to show them the Father, Jesus replied, "Have I been with you so long and you have not known Me. He who has seen Me has seen the Father" (John 14:9).

It is in Jesus Christ that we finally discover the exact and precise nature of our Creator. When we read the gospels, when we observe the healings, teachings, actions, reactions, and lifestyle of Jesus of Nazareth, we gain an understanding of God that is without distortion. We discover God as He manifests Himself in humanity. The Bible says, "No one has seen God at any time. The only begotten Son, who is in the bosom of the Father, He has declared Him" (John 1:18, NKJV). Through His words and through His life Jesus has placed the invisible God before us; none of us has any excuse on that day of judgment, nor will we ever be able to say, "Well, I never thought You were like that!"

The Teachings of Jesus

We learn much of God through the teachings of Jesus. Our Lord had much to say about God. He was called "Teacher," and His subject was God. He had not come to give us lessons in advanced mathematics or history or geography. His words and His life were all about God: His nature, His demands, His love, and His willingness to provide for His children. One of the most comforting insights He gives us is found in the title He gives the great Creator. He tells us that when we pray we are to call Him "Our Father which art in heaven." Not our heavenly General, not our Big Boss, not our King, not our divine Commander, not the Man upstairs, but "our Father."

The idea of God being a heavenly Father was not a popular or common concept among the Jews. There are a couple of Old Testament references to God as Father, but this idea had never really caught on with the Jews. God was too holy, too strict, too remote, and too distant to think of Him as Father. And yet Jesus insisted this was how we were to begin our prayers, reminding ourselves at the outset that we were in a loving relationship with our divine Maker. The theme of God being our Father and we His children runs throughout the New Testament. John writes, "Behold what manner of love the Father has bestowed on us, that we should be called children of God!" (1 John 3:1). The early Christians called each other "brother" and "sister," emphasizing the family nature of the church. Yes, it might be argued that we are the army of God, and Paul referred to the church as the vineyard of God and the building of God. But the idea of the family of God is given far greater weight.

Jesus taught that this Heavenly Father is a very generous Father, saying: "Do not worry about your life, what you will eat or what you will drink; nor about your body, what you will put on. Is not life more than food and the body more than clothing? Look at the birds of the air, for they neither sow nor reap nor gather into barns; yet your heavenly Father feeds them. Are you not of more value than they?" (Matthew 6:25-26)

Not only are we taught that the Father will gladly and freely provide for His children, but we are encouraged to recognize that we flawed, mistake-prone, thick-headed children possess great value in the eyes of our divine Father. We are not to worry. Our Heavenly Father thinks so much of us, His children, that food, clothes, and physical needs will be provided as a matter of course. Our Father will see to it that we have all we need.

The Father's Eyes

Jesus also insisted that our Father in heaven is keenly aware of us and our circumstances. He declares: "Are not two sparrows sold for a copper coin? And not one of them falls to the ground apart from your Father's will. But the very hairs of your head are all numbered. Do not fear; therefore, you are of more value than many sparrows" (Matthew 10:29 NKJV).

The idea of God having all our hairs numbered has made for a lot of preacher jokes; they love to tell us that He has an easier time of it with some of us than others. But we need to go beyond the jokes and see what Jesus is saying: Our Father is keenly, intimately, acutely, and absolutely aware of every minute circumstance of our lives. No tear we cry, no crisis we face, no attack that threatens our health, our relationships, or our lives has escaped the eyes of the One that Hagar called, "The God who sees." Our Father's intimate and perfect awareness of everything that pertains to His children should be a source of incredible comfort to us.

We don't have to shout and fast for days and weeks or jump up and down to get His attention. His eyes are on us constantly as He tenderly observes and directs our lives and circumstances. Jesus taught that our Heavenly Father is highly responsive to our prayers and petitions. As a generous, kind, and caring Father, He will not withhold good things from those who ask Him. Jesus tells us: "What man is there among you who, if his son asks for bread, will give him a stone? Or if he asks for a fish, will he give him a serpent? If you then, being evil, know how to give good gifts to your children, how much more will your Father who is in heaven give good things to those who ask Him!" (Matthew 7:9-11, NKJV).

Just as it is natural for earthly fathers to provide for their children, it is far more natural for our Heavenly Father to supply and sustain His children in all their needs and wants during their allotted time on this earth. We do not have to coerce the Father through forceful, bombastic prayers. It is not necessary to feverishly attempt to summon a huge measure of faith and spiritual power in order to squeeze a drop or two of heavenly blessings from Him. A simple "Give us this day our daily bread" will do the job. And when God opens wide His hand and pours out blessings and sustaining grace on our lives, He is not doing something that is alien and contrary to His nature. He is doing that which is precisely in line with His personality. He is being who He is and doing what He does. He is the God who "gives to all liberally and without reproach" (James 1:5).

The sum and substance of Jesus' teachings about the Father in Heaven are found in the word love. In what is unarguably the most famous verse in the Bible, Jesus tells us that "God so loved the world that He gave His only begotten Son" (John 3:16). Jesus spoke of a Creator who cares deeply about His creation and eagerly seeks their well-being. His classic parable about the prodigal son demonstrates the forgiving, loving, tender nature of the One who "in the beginning made the heavens and the earth." John, who was, of all the disciples, closest to Jesus, summed up Jesus' teachings about the Father with these simple words: "God is love" (1 John 4:8).

But Jesus did not merely teach the world about God as a lecturer, giving dry addresses about the qualities of the divine Creator. He actively went about demonstrating God's nature and manifold attributes. He revealed the generosity of the Father when He fed the multitudes by multiplying the fish and loaves to such an extent that not only were 5,000 people well fed, but there was food left over. David describes the Lord as a Good Shepherd who anointed his head with oil and made his cup to overflow. Jesus proved to be that Good Shepherd who supplied even more than was necessary.

He demonstrated God's intimate awareness of us when He stopped below a tree and called the tax collector, Zacchaeus, by name, and when He astonished the Samaritan woman at the well by mentioning her five previous husbands. Just as He taught that the Father would respond to our prayers and petitions, Jesus demonstrated that quality again and again as He went where He was asked and healed all who came to Him. There is no record of any person requesting healing who did not get it. Zero, zilch, nada.

Jesus Christ is called the "the brightness of God's glory and the express image of His person" (Hebrews 1:3, NKJV). And just as God is love, so Jesus revealed to the human race what this love looks like with human skin wrapped around it. His love was so intense He could never turn it off, not even on the Sabbath. Lepers were healed; the hungry were fed; sinners were forgiven; children were blessed; the despairing found hope; and the outcasts were made to feel special as Jesus of Nazareth "went about doing good." The nature of the Deity was revealed, and to our surprise and joy we learned that God really, really does care about us. He is truly "our Father which art in heaven."

God's Ultimate Provision

As encouraging as all of this is, there is another attribute of God that Jesus both taught and demonstrated which we must consider. Jesus taught that God is holy, in fact so holy that He finds sin utterly abhorrent. This has serious ramifications for sinful, flawed human beings (such as we all are) who hope to go to heaven and live with Him forever. Jesus preached the concept of repentance and told us that apart from repentance and a transformation of heart, we will never be accepted in that place where God dwells. He declared emphatically, "Unless you repent, you will all... perish" (Luke 13:3, NKJV). This process of repenting and trusting Jesus for forgiveness and salvation He calls being born again, and states, "Unless one is born again, he cannot see the kingdom of God" (John 3:3, NKJV).

Because it is in the heart of the Father to provide for His creation, He has made a way, but only one way, for us to go to heaven. It involves faith in Jesus, trusting that His substitutionary death and His resurrection the third day made up the atoning sacrifice by which we may be saved. To fully trust Christ, His sacrifice on the cross, and His resurrection is to receive Him. The Bible tells us, "As many as received Him, to them He gave the right to become children of God, to those who believe in His name" (John 1:12, NKJV). The cross of Jesus is God's ultimate provision; it represents our loving, generous, kind, merciful God providing for the deepest, greatest, most desperate need that men and women will ever have – the need to be reconciled to the One Jesus called "our Father which art in heaven."

Believers Should Never Have A Fear Of God

Many believers today are driven by fear—especially in very theologically conservative groups and churches. Leaders in those groups teach that God is often angry, harsh, and vindictive. And this is easy to believe when we read certain Old Testament stories; for these reasons, many believers do have a strong fear of God. And from this misunderstanding of God flow other great fears: the fear of hell, the fear of making a mistake, the fear of being wrong, and the fear of being rejected by God and the church.

When I was part of those churches, I had considerable fear, too. But I have since learned there is no reason a believer should ever fear at all, and overcoming fear begins by better understanding God's character and nature in Christ. There is No Need to Fear God at All. Some parts of the Old Testament can really strike the fear of God into you! We read that God destroyed the entire world population in a flood (except Noah's family) because He was upset with them. We read about strict laws from God that required death for those who did not observe them. Then there are the stories of God ordering the Israelites to exterminate entire nations including women, infants, and livestock.

God did not spare His own people, either. He swallowed Korah's followers into the depths of the earth, struck Uzzah dead for steadying the ark of the covenant, and heavily punished Israelite kings who displeased Him. All this should put the fear of God in us for sure! Except...Except that God did not do any of these things. Yes, those who wrote the books of the Old Testament said He did, but often they were just trying to explain calamities that occurred or even create stories about God. They assumed that their God did all these things based on His displeasure. However, their ideas arose from the limitations of their eras and cultures and from their limited understanding of God.

Jesus gives us a much better understanding of God. He taught that God is not angry and vindictive but is instead like a loving Father/Mother. One of Jesus' followers captures this teaching very well. In 1 John 4:15-18 he writes: "If anyone acknowledges that Jesus is the Son of God, God lives in them and they in God. And so we know and rely on the love God has for us. God is love. ... There is no fear in love. But perfect love drives out fear, because fear has to do with punishment. The one who fears is not made perfect in love" (NIV). His point is that God really loves us and there is no fear in love; this is our true relationship with the Father. Believers should never have a fear of God who loves us. But Didn't Jesus Warn Us Specifically to 'Fear God'? This common assertion is based on something Jesus said that is found in both Luke 12 and Matthew 10. Luke 12:4-5 reports Jesus as saying: "I tell you, my friends, do not be afraid of those who kill the body and after that can do no more. But I will show you whom you should fear: Fear him who, after your body has been killed, has authority to throw you into hell. Yes, I tell you, fear him" (NIV).

Jesus is talking to his friends (disciples) and warns them about the Pharisees. A moment later He tells them not to fear those who can kill them—probably still having the Pharisees in mind; and, as we know, many of Jesus' earliest followers were indeed killed by authorities. Jesus says don't be afraid of them; don't be intimidated by them; don't regard them to the extent that you stop sharing the good news. He goes on to say who they should really 'fear' instead of those who threaten them—and that is God. But I don't think He meant for them to be 'afraid' of God but to regard God's work above the concerns of human threats and intimidation. While the authorities are indeed capable of killing Jesus' followers, God is able to totally destroy people in Gehenna (hell). Jesus does not envision an eternal burning hell but an image of total physical destruction found in the Old Testament that He often uses in hyperbole.

Actually, the charge to 'fear God' doesn't seem to apply so much to the disciples as to the Pharisees themselves. In fact, Jesus immediately tells the disciples of the Father's tremendous care for them and uses the words 'Don't be afraid.' "Are not five sparrows sold for two pennies? Yet not one of them is forgotten by God. Indeed, the very hairs of your head are all numbered. Don't be afraid; you are worth more than many sparrows."

So, I don't think this passage should be stripped of its context to teach believers that they should 'fear God.' This is my message to believers today: There is no need at all for us to fear the Father who loves us. You might recall that, in addition to fear of God, there are four other great and common fears believers should never have: the fear of hell, the fear of making a mistake, the fear of being wrong, and the fear of being rejected by God and the church. You might well ask, 'What about those fears?'.

5 Unnecessary Fears Believers Should Never Have

Many believers think God is harsh and vindictive—always ready to catch us and punish us when we mess up. But Jesus tells us a different story–that God loves us deeply. And Jesus demonstrates God's love for us in His own teaching and example. So there is no need to be in fear of God.

Fear of Hell

There is no need to fear Hell. Those who think God is easily angered, harsh, and vindictive also think God punishes us in eternal burning hell if we don't make the grade. Who wants to risk that? I certainly don't. But the Bible does not teach such a thing; rather, some believers have collected a number of unrelated passages and forced them together to create a place of eternal conscious torture, featuring fire, darkness, and gnashing teeth.

The passages themselves do not support this understanding. Some Bibles translate three different words as 'hell.' The first two are 'Sheol' in the Old Testament, which simply means death or the grave, and 'Hades' in the New Testament, which means the same thing; no punishment is implied in either case. The third term sometimes translated 'hell' (as in the KJV) is 'Gehenna,' an Old Testament image Jesus sometimes uses; but it does NOT indicate eternal torment in burning fire. Another problem with the idea of eternal punishment in 'hell' is that it is contrary to the character of the Father who loves us so deeply.

Fear of Making a Mistake

Because many people think God is easily upset with us when we mess up. Many believers are insecure in their relationship with God and think that if they violate any of God's 'rules' God might send them to burning 'hell' forever. Their response to this fear is legalism: trying to discover all God's rules and making sure not to cross them. In practice, most of these groups have general lists of 'sins' they teach that God will punish us for.

These believers see God as very picky and thin-skinned. Anything can set Him off so that we are always in danger. These two beliefs re-enforce each other and are both sadly misguided. Jesus was killed because he confronted Jewish and Roman society. Significant things did happen at Jesus' death, but by far the most important is that he rose from the dead and established eternal life for us. As we follow Jesus, we should follow His teaching and example, but we all make mistakes. However, they are not fatal to our relationship with God. In fact, we will continue to grow as followers of Jesus until our last breath. There is no need to fear making a mistake.

The Fear of Being Wrong

There is no need to fear being wrong. Because they think God is picky and thin-skinned, many believers fear they might be wrong about some religious doctrine and be punished forever for it. Detailed doctrinal beliefs are considered essential, and woe to the person who strays from them! Believers are warned to never doubt the beliefs they have been taught or they will be led astray from the true faith and burn in hell.

But Jesus did not load us down with detailed doctrines we must believe and defend. His emphasis was on loving God and people and living in the kingdom of God. Of course, we want to be as accurate as we can about such matters, but there is no need to fear being wrong on doctrine. We are all mistaken about something.

The Fear of being Ostracized by God or the Church

Finally, because they think God is easily angered and focuses on religious rules and 'correct' beliefs, many believers fear that they will mess up in some way and that God and the church will ostracize them; and they don't want to be alienated from God and the church. But let me say this strongly: the Father loves each us and wishes to heal us of our brokenness and bring us peace, love, and reconciliation. The Father is not interested in abandoning us when we mess up. There is no need to fear being ostracized by God. Now, being ostracized by the church is another matter; if we change the way we follow Jesus, the local church might very well disfellowship us. That is on them, not on us, and there is little we can do about it. However, other churches are ready to embrace us as we follow Jesus together.

Let me leave you with a saying of Jesus from John 14: *"My peace I give you...Do not let your hearts be troubled and do not be afraid."* So, follow Jesus and do not be afraid about anything.

The Fear of Doubt and of Questioning Religious Beliefs We have been Taught

Growing up, I witnessed a lot of fear and experienced significant fear myself. The religious environment I grew up in was fear-centered. The fear of God, fear of hell, fear of making a mistake, fear of being wrong, and fear of being rejected by God (and the church) and fear of Satan himself. One must constantly tow the line on God's many requirements, believe all the right doctrines, and never waver.

One of the greatest dangers is doubt. Doubt is portrayed as being from the devil, and we are warned of the dire consequences of being led astray—punishment in eternal hellfire. Security is found only in accepting tradition passed down as God's own certain truth from one generation to another to another. In these circles, having doubt is considered a loss of faith, so it is no surprise that when a believer begins to question their beliefs it often induces a lot of fear. Taking action on those doubts can be even more fearful. But there is NO REASON to fear!

Doubt, Faith, and Authority

Doubt is not the opposite of faith; doubt is the opposite of gullibility. Doubt is not the opposite of faith; doubt is an element of faith. Until we question beliefs we have received, those beliefs are not our own but someone else's. Until we examine what we have been taught, we are actually putting our faith in some human authority or system. And, often, 'Do not doubt!' is a strong part of their message.

Appeals are made to the authority of the Bible, but in reality much of what people believe is based on an interpretation of the Bible and not a 'clear teaching' of the Bible itself; so our authority is not really the Bible but some particular understanding of the Bible, which is not at all the same thing. For our beliefs to be our own, we must question whether our underlying assumptions are correct and whether our beliefs make sense generally. As followers of Jesus, we must also consider whether they align with His teaching and example. We must investigate aspects of our belief that just don't seem right; we must pursue them diligently even if that means we can no longer accept them. This is called critical thinking—where we think for ourselves instead of depending on an outside authority. This is key for an effective and smooth relationship based on knowledge.

The term 'Do not doubt' means 'Do not think.' It means accepting what someone else thinks (or what the group thinks) without questioning whether what they think is valid. Of course, we are warned against such questioning. We are warned not to heed false prophets or to be tricked by the devil. But doubt means only that we examine our beliefs to see whether they are indeed valid. Do they reflect the most reasonable understanding of reality? When I was young, a verse in Proverbs 14 guarded me against the danger of questioning my beliefs. It reads: "There is a way that appears to be right, but in the end it leads to death."

I didn't want to be tricked into following the wrong path—one that led to death. This verse was very effective against my harboring doubt until one day I realized that it could apply to any 'way'– even my current belief system. I was shaken. It was only then that I even considered there might be flaws in my beliefs. But as I began to embrace logical thinking, I was afraid, sometimes intensely afraid, because I had been warned not to fall into the dangerous error of questioning my beliefs. I was afraid God would punish me for my doubts even to the point of sending me to eternal burning hell. This is a tremendous deterrent to doubt—and independent thinking!

I feared I might be making a huge mistake, that the conclusions of my quest might be wrong, and that I would be rejected by God. But these fears were unfounded. No one should fear honest doubts and questions about beliefs they have been taught.

Discovering Errors in the Religious Baggage I Inherited from Others

As I began to question my inherited beliefs, it is interesting that I asked some of the same questions many other people from such religious circles ask: Is God angry, harsh, and vindictive or a loving Father as Jesus tells us? Does God want us to follow long lists of religious rules (commandments) or to follow Jesus and His principles of the kingdom and of loving others? Does a loving God really send people to eternal burning hell, and does the Bible even teach such a thing? Should we assume the Bible is God's very word throughout or should we read it as a record of how people understood God within their own eras, cultures, and limited grasp of God's character? These are not all the possible questions, of course, but are some of the most common ones. And I think there is a reason for this—these beliefs, passed down in some traditions, are seriously mistaken and lead to baggage, bondage, and erroneous understandings of God, Jesus, and the Bible; and at some point they just don't feel right.

I bet you have wondered some of these questions—perhaps fearfully. Faith in these and other mistaken beliefs, based on someone else's word and understanding, is not true faith but a dependence on human authority. And once we realize this, fear vanishes.

God is Not Angry at You or the World

Belief in an angry God is perhaps the most damaging, misguided Christian belief of all. What is more central to our religious experience than our relationship with God? But some believers understand their relationships with God much differently than others do. Most of us believe God loves us and cares about us. We even talk about God's unconditional love. And I think we do this because this is the way Jesus presents God to us; and it is also the way Jesus Himself acted toward people in the Gospels.

Jesus loves us, and God loves us. I know that almost all believers would say the same thing and even believe it in some way, but in reality, many believe in an angry, violent God who is very demanding and vindictive toward us. We don't want to get on the bad side of this God! What kind of God is this angry God we are talking about?

- A God who will punish people in eternal hell fire who do not measure up to His expectations.
- A God who is consumed with wrath toward our sins, though He poured out that wrath on Jesus.
- A God who has specified a host of specific rules for us to follow in order to please Him; and
- A God who will afflict us with tribulation horrors if we mess up and miss the rapture.

From this perspective, God is in control of the Universe, in control of our lives, and in control of our eternal destinies. There is no place for us to hide and nothing we can do to escape God's power and wrath, and we are helpless and hopeless before God unless we are able to meet His expectations. But the truth, as revealed by Jesus, is that this notion is false. Attempting to relate to this angry man-opinion-made God often involves a great deal of fear and apprehension. If I believed these things, I would have to cry out with the writer of Hebrews 10: "It is a dreadful thing to fall into the hands of the living God". But I don't believe these things about God—because of Jesus. In fact, I think the idea of Angry God is the number one foundational harmful belief because so many other harmful beliefs are rooted in the fear of Angry God.

Why would we even think that God is so angry, violent, and vindictive? I believe it begins simply by reading the Old Testament. Beginning with Genesis, we don't read very far before we learn that God decides to kill practically everybody on earth in a huge flood because of His great disappointment with them. Is this not a frightening God? It would be frightening if this story were historically true, but it isn't. Instead, it is a story written by the Israelites reflecting their limited understanding of who God is; and I think they got it wrong.

To the Israelites, God was not only powerful but promised to punish them severely if they disobeyed Him. Deuteronomy 28:22-27 (NIV) describes their punishment this way: *The Lord will strike you with wasting disease, with fever and inflammation, with scorching heat and drought, with blight and mildew, which will plague you until you perish. The sky over your head will be bronze, the ground beneath you iron. The Lord will turn the rain of your country into dust and powder; it will come down from the skies until you are destroyed. The Lord will cause you to be defeated before your enemies. You will come at them from one direction but flee from them in seven, and you will become a thing of horror to all the kingdoms on earth. Your carcasses will be food for all the birds and the wild animals, and there will be no one to frighten them away.*

This is an angry, violent, vindictive God. It's easy to believe that indeed God is capable of causing those bad things in Deuteronomy 28 to befall the Israelites, but friends, that's not God. Why? Because Jesus revealed the Father to us. The mistake we have made as Christians is this idea that because God is sovereign and can do anything, the terrible events like sickness, flood, genocide, mass killings, diseases, and wars are the works of God. "Why would we not think that God is angry, violent, and vindictive? We can also ask why we should NOT accept this depiction of Angry God in the Old Testament as true and accurate. After all, God is whatever God is and not obligated to be what we want God to be. And, again, I think we find that answer in Jesus who is God revealing Himself to us. What we find when Jesus talks about God is that He describes Him as 'Father.' Now, there can be angry, violent, vindictive fathers, but this is not what Jesus had in mind about God.

In Matthew, Jesus introduces the 'Father' relationship in the Sermon on the Mount. His first clue into what the Father is like comes when He tells us: *"Love your enemies and pray for those who persecute you, that you may be children of your Father in heaven. He causes his sun to rise on the evil and the good and sends rain on the righteous and the unrighteous. If you love those who love you, what reward will you get? ...Be perfect, therefore, as your heavenly Father is perfect"* (Mathew 5:44-46,48 NIV).

Is this statement from Jesus who is the express revelation of God not different from what the Israelites thought of God in Deuteronomy 28:22? You can see from Jesus' own mouth the Father's attitude toward all people, and Jesus called upon us to be like our Father. This is no angry, violent, vindictive God. This is not a God who destroys people in floods. This is not a God who brings wasting disease, scorching heat and drought, and blight and mildew to plague people until they perish. So, someone in the Bible is mistaken about the character of God. Were the Old Testament writers right who thought God was angry, violent, and vindictive? Or was Jesus, who tells us of a Father who loves both the righteous and unrighteous? (And remember that Jesus also patterned His entire life on loving others as God did.)

I don't think Jesus is mistaken, friend, and I strongly advise that we believe what Jesus said about God's nature and character instead of what the Old Testament writers said about God. This is not in any way discrediting the Old Testament writers. Rather we are accepting the fact that just as we are growing in our knowledge of God, the Old Testament writers were growing in their knowledge of God. The fact that their writings were inspired by the Holy Spirit does not mean that their depiction of God's nature and character was absolute or flawless. So, let us embrace, without fear, the God who truly loves us—Loving, Caring, Healing God.

CHAPTER 12
GOD IS NOT SCHIZOPHRENNIC?

One reason God can be so easily discredited is because people don't really know Him by His word. The only way we can truly know anything about God is through Jesus. Everybody on earth has an opinion about what God is like and what He will do. But the only thing He gave us to know Him – and the only source that is eternally reliable – is Jesus Christ and His written Word. Most Christians don't read God's Word on a regular basis. They just get a little here and a little there, maybe some from a preacher on television and then a little on Sunday morning from their churches. But that is not going to be enough to make a real difference in their lives and, especially, in their understanding of God and His nature.

Some people read and study God's Word on a fairly regular basis. But even then, a lot of passages in the Bible appear to give a "schizophrenic" revelation of God. I'm just being honest with you! Of course, God is not schizophrenic, but that is the way it appears to some people from a casual reading of the Scriptures. In one Scripture, God commands death by stoning for picking up sticks on the Sabbath day (Numbers 15:32-35), and then in another, He forgives and does not condemn a woman caught in the very act of adultery (John 8:3-11). Examples like that have given people a rather strange impression of who God is. The Word of God does not contradict itself. There is a perfect harmony to it all. The purpose of much of what is in this book is to harmonize the Old and the New Testaments to reach a better more complete understanding of the nature of God. In the Old Testament, we see a picture of God that is incomplete. It is not incorrect; it is just incomplete. People who create their understanding of the nature of God based only on the Old Testament usually do not end up with a fully accurate picture.

The Old Testament is only a partial picture. It is not a perfect representation of God. Unless we understand the New Testament and are able to harmonize it with the Old Testament, we are going to end up misunderstanding the love and the whole nature of God. C.S. Lewis said, "It is Christ Himself, not the Bible, who is the true Word of God. The Bible if read in the right spirit and with the guidance of good teachers will bring us to Him. When it becomes really to know whether a particular passage is rightly translated or is Myth or history, we shall no doubt be guided to the right answer. But we must not use the Bible (our ancestors too often did) as a sort of Encyclopedia out of which texts (isolated from their context and read without attention to the whole nature and purport of the books in which they occur) can be taken for use as weapons."

What an amazing statement from one of the most influential Bible teachers of the past century. His view of the Bible comes from his expert knowledge of ancient literature, history, language, and culture. I think he points us to a better and more faithful understanding of the Bible, especially the Old Testament, that can help us all understand difficult aspects and explain them to others. God is not schizophrenic. It sounds simple enough, but on closer inspection, you might want to seriously consider its implications. When I looked for a biblical reference point, there were actually too many to quote. I mean, the Bible is full of confirmation regarding God's consistency and His unwavering faithfulness to us. God does indeed keep His promises, and in His unpredictability, He is predictable.

God loves us no matter how hard we try to deny this. We can never remove ourselves from this truth. It/He never changes. Warts and flaws and faults, God loves us. That means you and all your hidden secrets too. Deal with it. The problem with God's consistency is our inconsistency. When put into that perspective alongside God's steadfastness, our fickleness screams out almost as some kind of bizarre trick.

What I'm saying is our behavior can become unsteady and sinfully shaky. But our faith should not. In the context of our faith, the consistency of God's promise and His covenant with us should flourish. It should provide us with that proverbial 'rock' that we need to lean on. After all, we're not dealing with trick questions, sleight of hand or spiritual illusions when it comes to God's promise of eternal life and everlasting salvation. With faith comes the understanding that "God is not schizophrenic." Someone once told me that there should be some things and people in life that you can always count on, folk who will be there for you no matter what! The reason we can relate to this is we know so many things and people in our lives that we cannot count on, or certainly shouldn't. So-called friends will let you down. Family will fail you. Circumstances will change. Results are inconclusive, and fame is fleeting. Being a Christian does not exempt us from every day and every people challenges. They can be severe and debilitating.

Tests and testimonies are real. Yet God is steadfast. He does require however — or should I say, demand — the discipline of faith. Unfaithfulness, schizophrenia, relapses, and backsliding all combine to get us into spiritual trouble. Faith, fortunately, always gets us out. That's because God is good all the time. And God is God all the time, always was, always will be. He is not lost. He has not moved without leaving a forwarding address. He's at the same place where you originally found Him, and blessedly for you, He's patiently waiting for you to acknowledge His presence there again and again and, if needed, again.

My Bible says faith proves itself by its obedience to the Lord. The more we accept His steadfastness, the clearer our paths become. When all is said and done, once you know where home is, you're never lost. Because when we acknowledge the Almighty and who we are in relation to Him, we too will never be lost or forsaken. May God bless and keep you always. In wanting to be "great men or women of God," many Christians go back and begin to emulate some of the Old Testament examples. Anytime it is said to certain folks that they are prophets or have the gift of a prophet, some begin getting hard or cruel. They think that they are acting like Elijah, an old, bony-fingered prophet who would get right in your face and let you have it. People think of Elijah as someone who would rebuke you, lambaste you, starve you out with famine, or burn you out with fire to teach you something.

Now, there are some examples of true prophets who were not hard and cruel, but when people think of the typical prophet, they usually have an impression of someone like Elijah. Young believers who think they are prophets believe they are God's lighting rod in the earth – they are going to attract all the judgment and wrath of God and smite people if they get out of line. But that's not a total understanding of the ministry of the prophet, and certainly not of God's nature. Under the Old Testament, some things were done in that manner, but that is not the whole nature of God. It is vital to know who it is we are really dealing with. If we don't know God's nature or really understand Him, then we'll never effectively walk in the blessings and the power of God. I don't care what scripture we learnt or whose teaching we sit under. As I have said before and will say many times throughout this book, we have to come to a place where we really know God and have intimate relationship with Him.

Religious ideas arising from a misunderstanding of Scripture block people from entering into close relationship with God. Many are really afraid to come before God because they have been taught or have gotten the impression that He is going to "hit" them with something. So many believers feel they have to bow and scrape and duck every time they come before God. That's not the relationship God desires or that His word teaches.

Old Testament Judgment

Ahab and Jezebel are probably two of the most wicked people in history and certainly the most corrupt king and queen of Israel. In 1 Kings 21:1-24, they conspired together to kill an innocent man named Naboth in order to acquire his vineyard. They had Naboth stoned to death and had his body thrown into the field, where the dogs came and licked up his blood. While Ahab was walking through his new vineyard, he saw Elijah the prophet and said, "Hast thou found me, O mine enemy?" (1 Kings 21:20).

Elijah replied, "I have found thee: because thou hast sold thyself to work evil in the sight of the LORD" (1 Kings 21:20). Then, Elijah began to rebuke Ahab. "Thus saith the LORD, in the place where dogs licked the blood of Naboth shall dogs lick thy blood, even thine… the dogs shall eat Jezebel by the wall of Jezreel" (1 Kings 21:19, 23). It took a while for those prophecies to come to pass. Ahab was killed in a battle, and when he was brought home, the people washed out his chariot. As they did, the dogs came and licked up Ahab's blood (1 Kings 22:38). As for Jezebel, when a man named Jehu became king, she was thrown out of a tower and landed on the ground by the wall. Jehu rode his chariot over her, mutilating her body. Then he went into the palace, sat down, and began to eat. Right in the middle of the meal, he said something like, "Well, she's a king's daughter, and even though she was a wicked woman, she ought to be buried." Jehu sent some people out to bury her, but all that was left were her head, hands, and feet. The rest of her had been eaten by dogs (2 Kings 9:30-36)! Elijah's awesome prophecies came to pass exactly the way he had said, so you wouldn't want to mess with Elijah, right?

In 2 Kings 1, we move on to the story of Ahaziah, the son of Ahab. Ahab and Jezebel had sinned against God to such a degree that Elijah had declared the terrible ways their lives would end. Ahaziah had seen those prophecies fulfilled, but he didn't like Elijah any more than his parents had. Ahaziah followed right in the footsteps of his parents. He wasn't seeking the one true God; he was seeking pagan gods. When he got sick, instead of seeking God and inquiring of Him for his healing, Ahaziah sent a messenger to Beelzebub, the god of Ekron.

When Ahaziah's messengers were on their way to inquire of his pagan god, Elijah met them and said, "Is it not because there is not a God in Israel, that ye go to enquire of Beelzebub the god of Ekron? Now therefore thus saith the LORD, thou shalt not come down from that bed on which thou art gone up, but shalt surely die. And Elijah departed. And when the messengers turned back unto him, he said unto them, Why are ye now turned back? And they said unto him, There came a man up to meet us, and said unto us, Go turn again unto the king that sent you, and say unto him, thus saith the LORD, is it not because there is not a God in Israel, that thou sendest to enquire of Beelzebub the god of Ekron?

"Therefore, thou shalt not come down from that bed on which thou art gone up, but shalt surely die. And he said unto them, What manner of man was he which came up to you, and told you these words? And they answered to him, He was a hairy man, and girt with a girdle of leather about his loins. And he said, It is Elijah the Tishbite" (2 Kings 1:1-8).

The king knew it was Elijah and was seized with fear, so he sent his armies out to capture him: "Then the king sent unto him a captain of fifty with his fifty. And he went up to him: and, behold, he sat on the top of a hill. And he spake unto him, Thou man of God, the king hath said, Come down. And Elijah answered and said to the captain of fifty,

If I be a man of God, then let fire come down from heaven, and consume thee and they fifty. And there came down fire from heaven and consumed him and his fifty" (1 Kings 1:9-10). That's pretty strong, isn't it? You just didn't mess with Elijah. Ahaziah sent out an army – fifty men and a captain over them—to take Elijah, but Elijah called fire down out of heaven and destroyed the king's men.

"Again, also he sent unto him another captain of fifty with his fifty. And he answered and said unto him, O man of God, thus hath the king said, come down quickly. And Elijah answered and said unto them, If I be a man of God, let fire come down from heaven and consume thee and thy fifty. And the fire of God came down from heaven and consumed him and his fifty" (2 Kings 1:11-12). That's 102 men! Somebody might think, "Well, Satan must have done that." But it says in verse 12 that it was the fire from God that came down from heaven. Elijah had access to the power of God to such a degree that he could consume people. He could kill people with the power and the anointing of God. This is similar to Revelations 11:5 where the two witness will have the power of fire coming out of their mouths, destroying anybody who stands against God.

God, in defense of Elijah, released fire from heaven and killed 102 men. Finally, a third captain and his fifty men came, but this captain was a God-fearing man. A paraphrase of what he said is, "Have mercy on me. All I'm doing is what he the king told me to do." So, God told Elijah to go down with him to Ahaziah.God protected Elijah, and he wasn't touched by any of the king's men. He didn't have to call fire down out of heaven to strike anybody else. Did you know that's the only way Elijah could have handled the problem? But this is an Old Testament example of the power, the anointing, and the wrath of God in defense of one of His prophets.

New Testament Grace

Now let's compare this story of Elijah with one in Luke. "And it came to pass, when the time was come that he should be received up, he steadfastly set his face to go to Jerusalem, And sent messengers before his face: and they went, and entered into village of the Samaritans, to make ready for him. And they did not receive him, because his face was as though he would go to Jerusalem" (Luke 9:51-53). It had been commanded by God that Jerusalem be the center of worship for the Jews (2 Chronicles 6:6). That's where He put His temple and where the Ark of Covenant was located. God had commanded His people to worship Him only in Jerusalem. There was a time when the children of Israel rebelled against God and He allowed the northern ten tribes to be taken into captivity by the Assyrians. The two southern tribes, Benjamin and Judah, remained undisturbed in the land because they had maintained worship in Jerusalem.

After the northern tribes were taken captive, the king of Assyria sent colonists from Assyria to inhabit the land of the northern ten tribes, so the field wouldn't go to waste. These colonists intermarried with the remnant of the ten tribes who had remained behind. This remnant forsook their identity as Jews and intermarried with the Assyrian pagans, in direct disobedience to God's commandment not to marry people who did not worship Him. Because the Assyrians didn't know the ways of God, the beasts of the field began to multiply. The Bible says in 2 Kings 17 that God sent lions among them. The people were being killed and devoured. The Promised Land that was a blessing of abundance to the Jews had begun to produce beasts that were devouring the Assyrians. When the king of Assyria got word of this situation, he released some of the Israelite priests to return to the Promised Land and teach the Assyrians the ways of the God of Israel, assuming that if they pleased God, they would not be consumed by the wild animals.

The Assyrian colonists began to learn the outward practices to please God, but they didn't change their hearts. They were still pagan worshipers, and they incorporated their pagan practices into Israelite rituals. They did the necessary things to appease God and get rid of the wild animals, but it was not true worship of God. As a result, the northern tribes became a mixed race of people, called Samaritans, which led to racial problems in Israel. The devout Jews who were living in Jerusalem hated the Samaritans who had a corrupted worship. This is verified in John 4 where Jesus talked to the Samaritan woman at Jacob's well. There was tremendous hatred involving religious and racial prejudices between the Jews and the Samaritans. The Jews had no dealings with the Samaritans at all.

By Luke 9, Jesus had already ministered to the Samaritans. He had seen the entire city of Samaria respond to Him. They had accepted Him as Messiah. But now, when He came through their town, they would not receive Him because it looked like he was going to Jerusalem to worship with "those hypocrites down there." The Samarians rejected Jesus because of His association with the Jews, a rejection based upon religious and racial prejudices. To reject Jesus under those conditions was pretty serious, and His disciples, James and John, had a knee-jerk, Old Testament reaction: *"And when his disciples James and John saw this, they said, Lord, wilt thou that we command fire to come down from heaven, and consume them, even as [Elijah] did?"* (Luke 9:54).

Certainly, James and John were as justified in wanting to kill the Samarians for their rejection of Jesus as Elijah was in calling fire down to kill the soldiers who had rejected the God of Israel. This was a serious rejection of the Lord Jesus, and they were simply imitating Elijah, a great man of God. The two disciples were taking a Scriptural example, acting on the Word of God, and doing what Elijah did. Yet how did Jesus respond to His loyal, zealous disciples? Luke 9:55-56 reads: *"But he turned, and rebuked them, and said, Ye know not what manner of spirit ye are of. For the Son of man is not come to destroy men's lives, but to save them"*.

Jesus rebuked James and John for trying to do what was done under the Old Testament. He rebuked them for trying to be like Elijah, one of the most powerful men of God who had ever lived. Does that mean Elijah was sinning in 2 Kings 1? No, because at that time God was dealing with men differently. Jesus is the walking, living word, and when we see Him, we see the Father. However, many Christians are seeing God through the Old Testament instead of through Jesus. They misunderstand and are confused about who God really is and the relationship He wants with them because they see Him according to the Old Testament. In the Old Testament, God had to deal with mankind and sin in a different manner. We will study the Scriptures that tell us that in the following chapters. But when Jesus came, He brought the true revelation of the Father to mankind, and He operated very differently.

I personally believe if Jesus had come to earth in His human form in Old Testament times, He would have rebuked Elijah; Joshua never would have killed every man, woman, and child in those cities in the land of Canaan; and Moses would have been rebuked for a lot of things he did. You may be thinking, "Brother, how can you say such things?" I believe it's clear from the teachings of Jesus that God's nature is mercy and forgiveness. That is His real nature and character. But because we haven't known this, we have a mixed impression of God. We haven't seen Him in His fullness.

God did not change; mercy and forgiveness have been His nature and character from creation. It's our understanding of Him that has seen changes through history as we grow in our relationship and knowledge of His nature and character. This growth process in our knowledge of God is a beautiful thing, but the problem is that many Christians are so dogmatic and firm in their religious mindset that they have refused to give room for the Word of God to reveal God to their hearts and minds. Most of us don't really recognize or understand the depth of love, mercy, and compassion God has towards us. This mistaken impression of God keeps us at arm's length from Him. That's why it is so important to harmonize all of the words of God. Only then can you get a firm understanding of His true nature.

Hebrews 1:1-4 reads: *"God, who at sundry times and in divers manners spake in time past unto the fathers by the prophets, Hath in these last days spoken unto us by his Son, whom he hath appointed heir of all things by whom also he made the worlds; Who being the brightness of his glory, and the express image of his person, and upholding all things by the word of his power, when he had by himself purged our sins, sat down on the right hand of the Majesty on high; Being made much so much better than the angels, as he hath by inheritance obtained a more excellent name than they."*

Jesus is the brightness of God's glory and the express image of His person. In other words, Jesus is an exact representation of God, His true nature revealed. The love, mercy, and forgiveness God offers to us in the New Testament through Jesus Christ were always available to mankind, even in the Old Testament. But man's response to God's goodness in the Old Testament forced Him to deal with mankind more harshly than He desired. As we harmonize the Testaments, we are going to see clearly that God is not schizophrenic!

How Some Misguided Christian Beliefs are Very Harmful

Christianity is an overly broad group of more than 2.3 billion people throughout the world, according to 2015 figures. Christians form the biggest religious group by some margin, making up nearly a third (31%) of Earth's 7.3 billion people, according to a new Pew Research Center demographic analysis. There is tremendous variation in doctrinal beliefs among us. What we have in common is that we all, in some way, recognize Jesus as God's anointed One. It might be nice if we agreed on everything we believe, but we don't. And I have no problem with that.

People come to different conclusions on just about everything because we are different. We have different experiences, different ways of thinking, different understandings and insights, and different perspectives. Therefore, we often arrive at different conclusions, and religious beliefs are no exception. It doesn't bother me (and I don't think it matters to God) that we don't agree on everything. But what does concern me is when religious beliefs become harmful—when they begin to hurt either those who embrace them or those who do not embrace them. Harmful Christian Beliefs

I sometimes refer to harmful beliefs in my writing and even have lists of those I consider most harmful. The first is a list of what I consider foundational beliefs that harm people:

Five Foundational Beliefs that Do Great Harm:

1. Angry God. God is angry, demanding, and vindictive toward us
2. Inerrancy. The Bible is essentially written by God and every word is inerrant propositional truth
3. Punishment in Hell. God will punish those in eternal fire who do not measure up to His expectations
4. Legalism. God has specified a host of specific rules for us to follow in order to please Him

5. Penal Substitutionary Atonement. God poured out his wrath for our sins on Jesus at the cross.

From these foundational beliefs derive other beliefs that also do great harm. Now, you might embrace every one of these beliefs and not feel you are being harmed at all. That's okay; I am only concerned for those who ARE harmed. I was taught all these beliefs as a young Christian, and I am witness to the pain and damage they caused me and others. My objective is to assist and support those who were taught these beliefs and now question some of them. Those who are happy with these beliefs are not my primary audience.

In What Ways are these Beliefs Harmful?

I understand these misguided beliefs do hurt people in several ways, and some beliefs tend to lead to one harmful result more than another while others promote more than one harmful result. Three very significant damaging results are:

1. Fear
2. Unnecessary religious burdens and restrictions
3. Judgment, condemnation, and rejection

Do you ever experience fear in relation to your spiritual life? I hope not, but millions of believers do; and it is all unnecessary, as I explained in chapter 11 of this book. I think fear is perhaps the most harmful result of some of these beliefs—fear of Angry God, fear of eternal hell, fear of failure to follow all of God's commands, fear of missing the rapture. And I am not talking about that fear which is the awe, respect, and reverence we feel for God. I'm talking about being afraid—very afraid! The message of Jesus, as God's representative, is GOOD NEWS! It should not generate fear. Are we afraid of Jesus? Of course not. Jesus' teaching and example are based on large measures of love—not fear. And as God's representative to us I think Jesus demonstrates God's own attitude toward us, which is love—not fear. I agree with author of 1 John 4: "There is no fear in love. But perfect love drives out fear, because fear has to do with punishment. The one who fears is not made perfect in love" (NIV).

The Severely Garbled Message of John 3:16

I suppose most believers think John 3:16 is one of the most wonderful passages in the Bible—and I agree! This passage tells of God's love for us in a very proactive way. "John 3:16" is found everywhere: on T-shirts, bumper stickers, posters, mugs, at ball games, and in an endless number of other places. It is as though the mere reference to John 3:16, without comment or elaboration, is a strong message of God's love.

However, I am concerned that many believers who heavily promote John 3:16 have a fundamental misunderstanding of what it means, so their use of the passage is really a misuse, and the message of God's love is corrupted and severely garbled. When reading John 3:16, many believers infuse it with harmful doctrinal beliefs that really aren't there, and the message of God's love is lost and twisted from good news into what is essentially bad news. The meaning is transformed into something very different than what the passage says.

The message of God's love has been seriously garbled! Instead of good news it has become bad news. The bracketed sections are not part of John 3:16 and do not represent its message. This understanding assumes God is angry and upset with us; God must satisfy his sense of strict justice by killing his own Son (penal substitution); God requires us to perform a salvation ritual in order to accept us; God will punish us forever if we do not comply; and eternal life is only in heaven. This is not at all like the loving Father Jesus tells us about; this is an angry, harsh, and vindictive God. And this is BAD NEWS. This terrible misunderstanding of God originates in harmful doctrinal baggage that developed and accumulated over centuries to produce an idea of God completely at odds with the God Jesus knew.

The truth is God loves us unconditionally, God accepts us as we are: broken, hurt, and alienated, God desires our healing and reconciliation and requires no ritual transaction of us, God does not punish any of us in some imagined hell, and to crown it all, eternal life begins now. God is like a loving Father/Mother who wants the best for each of us and sent Jesus to tell us of his/her wonderful, unconditional love for every person. This is the good news, friend!!

John 3:16 Is Only Part of the Context

We need not stop with John 3:16 because the thought continues. Let us see what it says and note that some believers insert misguided understandings into this passage too [in brackets]. John 3:17-18: *"For God did not send his Son into the world to condemn the world [to hell], but to save the world [from hell] through him. Whoever believes in him is not condemned [to hell], but whoever does not believe stands condemned [to hell] already because they have not believed in the name of God's one and only Son."*

Certain believers (and there are a lot of them) understand that the goal in accepting Jesus is to go to heaven and avoid eternal hell, which is where angry God will send us if we don't do the right things. This assumes God to be angry, harsh, and vindictive, but this is NOT the case. There is no reason to be afraid of God, and God is not going to punish anyone. Verses 17 and 18 do not refer to being condemned to, or being saved from, 'hell.' If hell is not in view, then what does it mean to not condemn the world but save it? Save it from what? Or that those who do not believe in him (Jesus) are condemned already? Condemned to what? These are good questions. If people are not being condemned to hell or saved from hell, then what is it they are condemned to or saved from?

I submit that we are being saved from a life of brokenness, pain, alienation, and death. Jesus came to bring good news such as:

- God is not angry, as many of us supposed, but loves us deeply;
- God's love for us takes away our fear, guilt, and condemnation;
- We are not asked to follow burdensome religious rules but to love people;
- As followers of Jesus, we are agents for expanding God's kingdom on Earth; and
- Death is not the end because Jesus offers eternal life and happiness.

But what of those who are condemned already because they do not believe in Jesus? I think this means they are still in a state of brokenness, pain, loneliness, alienation, and despair. But it does not mean this is a permanent condition. When one does hear the good news of Jesus and begins following Him, this condition begins to change. Reading John 3:16 should give us great joy, but misreading it (as many do) garbles the good news message entirely. So, let us read the passage for what it says instead of what some people mistakenly think it says. For it is GOOD NEWS indeed!

Harmonizing Old and New Testaments

When people don't look at the whole Word of God, examining the Old Testament in light of the New Testament, they generally get an Old Testament picture of God as a God of wrath, judgment, and punishment. They believe this is truth about God, and those who don't accept the love and forgiveness of the Lord Jesus Christ will one day experience a terrible day of God's judgment. But wrath and judgment are not the essential nature of God. God's nature is not judgment. You can't find that in the Word of God. He does judge, and He is just and holy; but scripture reveals to us in 1 John 4:8 that "God is love." Love is God's real nature. He doesn't just have love or operate in love. God is love. Love is the true character of God.

Elijah's actions in obedience to God were not the complete representation of the nature of God, and the Old Testament cannot give the nature of God, and the Old Testament cannot give us a total revelation of God by itself. We need the New Testament to understand the fullness of God.

GOD'S GRACE IN THE OLD TESTAMENT

You are probably asking, "Well, if Jesus represents the true nature of God, what exactly was God doing in the Old Testament?" The Word of God tells us clearly what God was doing. *"For until the law sin was in the world: but sin is not imputed when there is no law."* (Romans 5:13). When we use the term "law," we can be referring to all of the Old Testament, but the law used in the context of this scripture is more specific. When Paul said "law" here, he was referring to the Mosaic

Law, which includes the Ten Commandments, judgments, punishments, and all of the ordinances and ceremonial observances. Romans 5:13 shows us that before the law, or before the Law of Moses was introduced, sin was in the world, but sin is not imputed where there is no law. The word "impute" means to take what has been done and apply it to one's account, or to hold transgression against someone. In other words, sin was not being held against people until God gave the laws to Moses.

Grace Extended After the Fall

Most people's concept of God comes from that moment sin entered the Garden of Eden, and the wrath of God was released upon mankind. People believe that God was holy, and that man was unholy. Therefore, God separated man from Himself and drove Adam and Eve from His presence because His holiness could not stand to look upon sinful flesh. But there was a period of time from Adam until Moses when God dealt with people out of love, mercy, and forgiveness instead of wrath and judgment.

Now, of course, I believe God is holy and I know that man is sinful, but God's love is so great that He did not just expel man from His presence. As a whole, God dealt in mercy toward man, and He did not impute their sins (hold those sin against them) until the days of Moses, when the law was given. Sin entered the world when Adam and Eve fell to the temptation of the serpent in the Garden of Eden. Let's take a good look at how God dealt with them. Genesis 3:22-23 *reads: "And the* LORD *God said, Behold, the man is become as one of us, to know good and evil: and now, lest he put forth his hand, and take also of the tree of life, and eat, and live forever: Therefore the* LORD *God sent him forth from the garden of Eden, to till the ground from whence he was taken"*. When you see the "therefore," you're always supposed to look and see what it's *there for*. So "**therefore**" means this verse is tying in with what was said previously.

Therefore, link the expulsion of Adam and Eve from the garden with what was just said. What would happen if God didn't send them out? He didn't want them to eat of the tree of life, which would mean all of mankind would live forever in their sinfulness. God didn't send them out because He couldn't tolerate mankind. Adam and Eve transgressed against God, but God did not expel them from His presence. The presence of God went with Adam and Eve and their descendants outside the Garden of Eden. I'm going to show you that even after Adam and Eve sinned and left the Garden of Eden, God was still walking and talking with them in the cool of the evening. He was still fellowshipping with them. Contrary to what most people have thought, a holy God was still fellowshipping and present with sinful mankind.

The reason God sent Adam and Eve out of the garden was because He loved them so much, He didn't want them to partake of the tree of life and live forever in bodies that were corrupted by sin. Sin gave Satan the opportunity to put sickness, diseases, and all kinds of curses on man. Can you imagine what it would be like for cancer to destroy your body, and yet because you have eaten of the tree of life, you couldn't die? Can you imagine what it would look like to live for eternity with diseases destroying your body, yet you couldn't die from them? It was God's mercy that sent mankind out of the Garden and away from the tree of life. For a person who knows God and accepts His provision, a glorious, glorified body is coming that won't be subject to the things this earthly body is subject to in this life. God sent Adam and Eve from the Garden of Eden because He didn't want them, and us, to live forever in corrupted bodies, subject to all of the things we are subject to because of sin.

In Genesis 4, we see that God was still fellowshipping with mankind after the fall, outside the garden. We know that because God was talking to Cain and Abel. How did Cain and Abel know to bring sacrifice? How did they know to bring a blood sacrifice and give the first fruits of their labor to God? Adam and Eve didn't have blood sacrifices explained to them in the garden, because they had no transgressions to atone for yet. The Bible doesn't say this outright, but it's evident to me that God was still talking with Adam and Eve and with Cain and Abel. He was talking and communicating with them because they understood about sacrifices and how to approach Him.

After Cain and Abel offered their sacrifices, Genesis 4:5 says, "but unto Cain and his offering he [God] had not respect." God did not respect Cain's offering. How did they know God did not respect Cain's offering? If you and your brother came and offered a sacrifice today, how would you know which one God respected and which one God didn't? As born-again Christians, we have a witness of God in our spirits. But Cain and Abel weren't born-again Christians, so they didn't have God inside them. It's evident God was talking to them. They were aware God was walking, talking, and fellowshipping with them, because in Genesis 4:6 it says, "The LORD said unto Cain."Here, we have God speaking in an audible voice to Cain just the same as He did with Adam and Eve in the Garden of Eden. "And the LORD said unto Cain, why art thou wroth? and why is thy countenance fallen? If thou doest well, shalt thou not be accepted? And if thou doest not well, sin lieth at the door. And unto thee shall be his desire, and thou shalt rule over him" (Genesis 4:6-7).

God was walking face to face with Cain and Abel. As I stated earlier, most people thought God had to separate man from His presence because man was unholy, and God was so holy there could be no fellowship. That's the concept most people have developed, but it's not proven by scripture. When Cain saw God respected Abel's sacrifice more than his, he was overcome with jealousy and killed Abel in anger. The Bible shows us that God spoke to Cain about it in Genesis 4:9: *"And the LORD said unto Cain, Where is Abel thy brother? And he said, I know not: Am I my brother's keeper?"* Now, stop and think about this. Here's the very first murderer on the face of the earth, and while he still had the blood of Abel on his hands, an audible voice from God said, "Where is Abel, your brother?"

What would you do if you just murdered somebody, still had the murder weapon in your hands, and God spoke to you in an audible voice? You would probably die of heart attack! You might do a lot of things, but you wouldn't just turn around and say, "I don't know where he is, God. Am I my brother's keeper?" Do you know why Cain did that? He was used to talking to God. He talked to God every day. It wasn't unusual. There had to be familiarity with the audible voice of God. God was still walking and talking with man, even after sin entered the world and mankind was expelled from the Garden of Eden. He was not imputing sin or holding their trespasses against them. God was not treating them the way the Old Testament law has revealed sin should be treated. He was operating in love, mercy, and forgiveness. Still, God showed His disapproval of Cain killing Abel and let Cain know what the consequences would be in Genesis 4:11-12.

Cain became fearful and said, "God, I'm going to be a vagabond, wandering throughout the earth, and everybody who finds me is going to try to kill me" (Genesis 4:14). Do you know what God did? Instead of bringing judgment on the very first murderer on the face of the earth, God put a mark upon Cain and protected him. (Genesis 4:15). Now, isn't that contrary to popular religious ideal? God did not approve of the sin, but He protected the first murderer! In contrast, under the Old Testament Law, if a man went out and picked up sticks on the Sabbath day, God commanded the man to be stoned to death (Numbers 15:35). God protected Cain, who murdered a man, but he commanded Moses to stone to death someone who just picked up sticks on the Sabbath day!

Doesn't that look inconsistent? It looks like the man who picked up sticks on the Sabbath day got the raw end of the deal! The reason it looks that way is because until the law came, God was not holding mankind's sins against them, He was overlooking (not imputing) sin as pertained to man's fellowship with Him.

CHAPTER 13
GOD IS NOT JEALOUS LIKE MAN

Medical science has proven that if it is done slowly and with the right antibiotics, the human body can actually accept animal organs. Scientists believe that one day it will be feasible to use the hearts of monkeys, sheep, and even pigs to save lives. All it takes is the right drugs to persuade the body to accept the alien heart. The trick is fooling the body into believing that this beastly organ is actually human.

This same concept is true when it comes to our corrosive perceptions of love. It is astounding to see what people will accept over time. We are routinely fooled by the counterfeit until many people's spirits and souls are functioning with a version of love that bears a resemblance to the heart of a baboon. It doesn't happen in a day but gradually over time. And in the spiritual case, instead of saving a life, before we know it, the counterfeit makes our hearts think and believe things that are absolutely hideous and unacceptable.

When envy or jealousy is presented in its most raw form it reeks with an obvious odor. Surely no one would mistake its ugly presence for being love. It stands in such opposition to what love is about. I have found, however, that over the years we have all experienced a gradual transition in our thinking. When it comes to love, not only have we learned to accept the opposite, but we actually expect it. Envy is ugly and self-serving. At its core, it's jealousy. Envy and jealousy are *anti-relationship*. This attribute of envy leaves a person in constant "receive mode." The "give mode" required by love gets shut off and even becomes nonexistent, making relationship impossible. Selfishness leads to relational death, and jealousy is a frantic *self-protection* that paralyzes relationships. Born out of self-love, it leaves nothing for the other person. Nothing can survive it.

We say we don't believe that love envies, but when you think about it, many of us believe that envy is the true inception of love. We believe that without it, love can't even begin. Selfish envy can be equated with lust. Envy and lust share the same heart; they are fueled by a flesh desire to gratify one's self. Our generation doesn't even believe that love is possible between a man and a woman without the initial presence of lust. If a friend wants to introduce you to a friend of the opposite sex, your first question is bound to be "What does he (or she) look like?" The treasure within is not nearly as important as the outside.

We've learned to present ourselves in a certain way to incite lust. Having someone lust after us is how many of us find our personal value. Our world has taught us that if we are sexually unattractive, we are worthless, and I believe that, sadly, most people in this generation have bought into that idea. Women especially have been taught to actually desire the look of lust from men when they enter a room. This look is envy in its most raw form. Many people have become addicted to the look of seduction, and they can't find their personal worth without it. Envy and lust share a common heart; they both *take* from others for personal gratification.

I've watched women in clothing stores purposefully buy things that will entice such looks from men. They don't even realize how obvious their intentions are to those around them. They put the jeans on and immediately turn around to see what their backside looks like. They put the blouse on and check their cleavage in the mirror. Many times they'll ask their girlfriend how their backside looks in the pants they're trying on. It's all an attempt to acquire that seductive and selfish response from others. How ironic.

The problem with inner treasures is that they can't be possessed by another person for personal gratification. They can only be admired. Selfish people have nothing personal to gain by discovering someone's inner beauty. The outer beauty is quite a different thing. That can be seen, touched, taken, and used. It requires no intimacy or emotional closeness. This is why so many people put the flesh at the top of their list of desires in a mate. Because people believe that love *does* envy, they attribute it to God's character as well. When I fell in love with the people in my congregation for the first time, my eyes were opened to how widespread this upside-down view of God's heart has become in modern-day Christian thinking.

I have heard preachers thunder from the pulpit that "God is a jealous God." Because we see God's jealousy and envy from this upside-down human perspective, we have created a black cloud over Christianity that ultimately strangles to death our relationship with God. Envy, lust, and jealousy are synonymous. All three leave a person in constant receive mode, and their heart core is "anti-relationship." Jealousy is a frantic, self-protection frenzy that completely paralyzes a person relationally. It is born out of self-love and absolute apathy for the other person. Nothing can survive this!

We are being conformed into God's image. If He does it, we can do it. If He doesn't do it, we are not supposed to do it. This is why it's imperative that we know the truth about His image. Whatever we believe to be true about Him is what we will ultimately be changed into. If we believe that God envies and is a jealous God, we will ultimately become envious and jealous people.

Unfortunately, our human perspective of a *jealous* God has attached itself to every slice of our religion. The results are catastrophic. We have become like the terrified woman who is enslaved to her husband's jealousy problem. She can't have friends or a life of her own because her world centers on her jealous husband. She rationalizes to herself that he acts this way because he loves her, but deep in her heart she is confronted with the truth that he doesn't even know her and his motives are based on love for himself. The most she can do is follow his rules and make him think he is the only one in the world that matters. Hopefully, if she proves herself to be faithful, he might release his death grip on her and give her the few remaining crumbs of her life back.

As awful as this sounds, it is astonishing how frequently I hear Christians talk about their God in this same repulsive manner. Because of our misconceptions about God, we have become just like this woman in our relationship with Him. Worse, we don't even know we are doing it. We've grown up with it all our lives, so it's not that upsetting. We begin to see through the same demented mind-set as the woman who believes jealousy is the result of love. Think of this. We say things like "God wants you to give Him your life," and it doesn't even sound bad to us anymore. Over time it actually begins to sound beautiful. We even encourage others to give their lives to Christ because we are certain that this is what God wants.

Christ came that *you* may have life and have it more abundantly. He never asks you to give Him your life. *It's your heart He is after.* Only an envious God would give you life and then require you to give it back to Him. He gave it to you, and He wants you to enjoy it to the fullest.

This upside-down thinking is seen when Christian musicians are plagued with the notion that their songs must all be about Jesus. If they dare to write a song about anything other than God, the Christian community scoffs at them. Their faith is called into question, and they are ultimately viewed as backslidden. It is heartbreaking to God that this wonderful gift of expression is never allowed to express itself freely because the receiver of the gift believes that God would be jealous.

Many Christians are skeptical about listening to any secular music because they believe that God would rather have them listen to Christian music or nothing at all. This mentality is born out of a belief that God envies. They think He might get jealous if they gave any part of their day to something other than Him. They see Him as a jealous husband who doesn't want them to have lives of their own. They're encouraged by their Christian friends to go through their houses and throw everything away that doesn't glorify God or pertain to Him. How sad.

I've watched in amazement while people check themselves to make sure they don't love their mates too much, for fear that God will get envious and either remove their mates or remove His presence. I've seen dating couples even break up because the partners fear that the person they are in love with has become an idol before God. They constantly measure whether or not their thoughts are more focused on God than on the ones they love.

Several years ago, a young couple came to me for advice concerning their six-month-old baby. This child evidently had suffered from a string of recurring medical problems that seemed to be getting worse. I almost began to cry as I listened to them explain their theory as to why this was happening to their baby. This poor couple blamed themselves, because they felt they might have made their child "an idol" in their lives. Because they loved this baby so much and had given everything over to him, they believed that God was allowing illness to attack their baby out of jealousy. Poisoned by modern Christianity's interpretation of a jealous God, they even quoted a Scripture from the Bible that said God would destroy any idols that His people set up in their hearts before Him.

There is a look I give my wife that can be described in only one way. I cherish her. It's a deep, soul-piercing gaze that travels way beyond the surface and lands deep within her spirit. It's a look that sees every hidden thing within her heart and adores it all unconditionally. My eyes literally scream "valued" to her when she looks into them. When my wife sees that look in my eyes, she knows that I've discovered another beautiful thing about her. She finds her inner value because she sees me finding it every time, I give her that cherishing look. Inside every one of us is a treasure chest that waits to be opened by our Father. Until a person is cherished, his or her treasure chest remains closed. The cherishing look happens when the one giving the look has discovered inner value in the one they see. I've seen many people wait an entire lifetime for just one person to discover value in them. When that look comes from our Father, we know for certain who we are. Because we are a fatherless generation, most of us were never cherished by the one person we really needed it from. And we've become lost as a result.

God is a jealous God, but He is jealous on behalf of you. He is not selfishly jealous as human beings are. His righteous jealousy is actually the opposite of what we understand jealousy to be. Until we understand this principle of God's heart, we will always see Him upside down from what He truly is. We have taken the Scriptures that describe Him as a jealous God and have given them a selfish and Satan-like interpretation. It has become so common that we don't even recognize it anymore. When the Bible says that the Holy Spirit envies, it's speaking in the context of love. A father gets jealous when his daughter is dating a man who doesn't love her as much as he does. He's not jealous on his behalf. His jealousy is on behalf of his daughter. He wants her to have the best, and when he sees her giving herself to someone who doesn't see or understand her heart the way he does, he immediately becomes jealous for her.

God is not in competition for your love. I am always mystified when I hear people boastfully say, "I love God more than my wife." The only way to love God more than your spouse is to love God *through* your spouse. Your husband or wife would be the direct recipient of that love. Don't ever think that He would even raise such a question as to whom you love more. He is quite all right with you giving all of yourself over to your mate. The God who is love loves it when we love. He doesn't concern Himself with whether or not someone else is receiving more than Him

I once approached a little boy in our Church and told him what a good boy I thought he was. I was mortified when this five-years-old child began to inform me that he was a "bad little boy" and a "stupid little boy," and there was no good in him. As I walked away with a heavy heart I thought, *What kind of parents does this little boy have?* This is what the world thinks when we talk this way about ourselves in an effort to bring our Father glory. It's morbid and twisted. It paints a picture of our heavenly Father that is cold and ugly. <u>God is never in competition with your love for people!</u> *<u>Anytime you love a person, you are not far from God.</u>* <u>Your love for people is the evidence that you love God. All people are the direct recipients of our love for God. It is impossible to have a relationship with God aside from relationships with people. He doesn't get jealous or envious of our love for His people; He delights in it because that is how He created life to work.</u>

It shocks me to see so many people who honestly believe that God desires a separate and secret relationship with them aside from their family members. Many men will lock themselves in their prayer closets while their wives are in another room watching the kids alone. I call this adultery. It comes from a mentality that God wants His personal time with them separate from their wives. I am not putting down a personal prayer time, but I am confronting a mind-set that is directly against God's heart. If I stayed two hours in my office praying while my wife needed me downstairs with our children, that would not be called prayer; that would be called sin.

Only selfish people ask the question "Whom do you love more?" Don't ever think God behaves this way. The moment we buy into this way of thinking, we will have permanently shut ourselves out from knowing His heart. A true relationship with God is impossible unless we love people. He is never envious of our love for others; He created it! God is love. Why would He ever contradict who He is?

God is not insecure. His heart is that you love people more and more. Release yourself to love wholeheartedly because your Father in heaven made you for this purpose. Jesus told us that the way to love God is to love His people. It was at the very moment I fell in love with the people in the market square that I came to know the deepest parts of God's heart. I immediately began to find specific attributes of His character woven into the love I had for others. When I analyzed that love, it would speak to me and reveal what it would and would not do. It told me many things and answered many questions about my faith that had kept me bound and miserable for so long. This love did not speak audibly. I just suddenly came alive in my spirit. As if it had been there matter-of-factly my entire life. Suddenly I knew why love does not envy: because the very scent of selfish envy is repulsive when we love. And just as love does not envy, it does not boast.

The doctrine that God is a jealous God comes from the Old Testament law of Moses. The "jealousy" is always in the context of idol worship, beginning in the Ten Commandments of Exodus 20. "You shall not worship them or serve them; for I, the LORD your God, am a jealous God, visiting the iniquity of the fathers on the children, on the third and the fourth generations of those who hate Me" (Exodus 20:5, NASB). "For you shall not worship any other god, for the LORD, whose name is Jealous, is a jealous God" (Exodus 34:14, NASB). "For the LORD your God is a consuming fire, a jealous God" (Deuteronomy 4:24, NASB). "You shall not worship them or serve them; for I, the LORD your God, am a jealous God, visiting the iniquity of the fathers on the children, and on the third and the fourth generations of those who hate Me" (Deuteronomy 5:9, NASB). "For the LORD your God in the midst of you is a jealous God; otherwise, the anger of the LORD your God will be kindled against you, and He will wipe you off the face of the earth" (Deuteronomy 6:15, NASB).

What these five verses have in common is that they all share the same Hebrew adjective, *qannâ' translated* as the English word "jealous." The interesting thing about this word is that it is only used in reference to God. In no instance is the word *qannâ'* used to describe human jealousy. The reason that God is "jealous" is because He wants people to choose to love Him. Jesus said that the most important commandment was to love God. The way we view God today reminds me of how we view rock stars. He has thousands of groupies who claim to know and love Him, but in the end it's not Him they adore; it's His words, His power, and His amazing, good looks. His groupies aren't interested in knowing His heart. They are dazzled by all that surrounds Him. This is precisely why God became a man. He wanted us to know Him for Him. Though God loves the angels in heaven, they are basically groupies. All they can see is His glory and majesty. They can't help but cry, "Holy, holy, holy." God's incredible splendor and beauty are so overpowering that anyone or anything that comes into contact with Him immediately falls to the ground in worship and awe.

There is an inner part of God that remains hidden and veiled behind the radiance of His shimmering glory. It's a part of Him that is tucked so deep within the blinding brilliance of His presence that unless all that is great and magnificent is stripped away, no one can ever know this inner part of God. In Christ, God became nothing so He could have real intimacy with you. Jesus is the center core of who God is in His heart. He desires true intimacy with you so much that He shed all His outward glory and splendor so that you could make a clear-minded choice of whether or not to have a relationship with Him. This is the only way God can know for sure that you truly love Him.

God became something a little lower than you in order to lift you up! He not only became a man; He became a servant of men, and then died a criminal's death on the cross. One of the last things we see Jesus doing just before His crucifixion was perhaps the most astonishing example of a non-boasting God in all of Scripture. He was on His hands and knees washing dirty feet. God does not boast about who or what He is. He isn't interested in bragging about His highest truths.

I have found only one undisputed way of lifting people up. It may not be popular or spiritually attractive, but it always works. The best way to lift hurting people up is to get beneath them. In my travels, people often thank me for "being real." I think they mean they can identify with me. I didn't leave them feeling like I had arrived at a perfect spiritual plane they could never reach. They felt they were on my level, and if I could do it, so could they. I do this for one reason and one reason only; I love them, and love does not boast. When I fell in love with people, I found that with everything in my heart, I wanted to meet them on their level for their benefit. This is the opposite of boasting. Boasting is bragging about our strengths, but if we truly love, we will boast about our weaknesses for the purpose of elevating the ones we love.

Boasting is bragging about the truth. It's exalting the highest truth about a person, place, or thing. The problem with boasting is that it ultimately pushes others down around us. It leaves people feeling like failures, or at the very least, inadequate. It cultivates spiritual inferiority. Boasting is based on comparison thinking. When we boast, we are letting others know that they don't add up. When they don't add up, relationship is impossible. Love does not boast because love is only about relationship. An unreachable person is not someone we human beings can relate to. We must be able to *relate* before we can have a *relationship*. People who claim to have reached a spiritual level that is far beyond the average person's ability to comprehend are usually pretty lonely people. They're lonely because there is no such spiritual level. I've found that people create this super spiritual facade as a subconscious way of retreating from intimacy with others.

This is the greatest obstacle I have to overcome when I go to a church to preach. Most people immediately believe several things about a guest speaker who comes to their church. They think that he is better than they are, or he has some special powers that they don't have. People will never give me their hearts until they know that I'm the same as them. The moment I get those stars out of their eyes is the moment I can connect with them on a truly intimate level. I'll be honest with you. At first, I enjoyed the attention. It made me feel good. After all, there is a certain gratification that goes along with being famous. It feels good to have people think you're a spiritual guru of sorts. My flesh loved the entire exalted experience. But I had to give it all up because I truly wanted to help people, and I knew they would never connect with someone they couldn't relate to.

Peter understood fully who Jesus Christ was, and he tried to put a stop to all the demeaning foot-washing. He refused to accept God in this way. He was much like modern-day Christians who are insistent on seeing the highest truths of His nature and nothing else. The response that Jesus gave Peter is His response to many of us today:

"You must be washed by the Carpenter! You must know Me in this way if you ever want to have a part of Me." Unless you can receive the simplest side of God, you will never have intimacy with Him. It's impossible.

Imagine if a man broke into my home and was planning on killing my wife and children, but I convinced him to take my life instead of theirs. If he let them escape and then proceeded to take me into a back room and film himself torturing me for hours until finally taking my life, do you think I would ever want my family to see that videotape? Absolutely not! I would want them to remember my life and my love for them. There is nothing inside me that would ever want them to view the pain I underwent to save their lives. That would break their hearts. This is how God feels when we reenact the Stations of the Cross in an effort to riddle people with guilt and condemnation. It doesn't motivate; it exasperates. This is not what love desires.

Why are so many people more excited about the Crucifixion than they are about the Resurrection? God never boasts about what He went through to reconcile you to Him. The account of the Crucifixion lasts only a few sentences in the Bible, but the result of the Resurrection is seen throughout the entire New Testament. God does not boast about the Cross. He downplays it, and He rejoices in the possibilities of relationship with you today because of the Resurrection.

Don't ever feel that you have to repay God for the suffering He went through for you. This was a gift to you! Anytime we attempt to repay someone for a gift they gave us, we are diminishing that gift. An attempt to repay someone for a gift is really a rejection of that gift. You'll never know how much it cost to see your sin upon the cross because God removed the price tag from the gift before He gave it to you. Just receive it and go on. It's free. Boasters always expect repayment, and they make sure everyone knows what their gifts cost them. God is not this way. He never boasts!

God also never wants you to compare your relationship with Him to someone else's relationship. There is no comparison. What He has with you is entirely unique. No other person in this world will ever have what He and you have together. Don't ever wish your relationship could be like someone else's. He doesn't wish that. The more I began to look intently into the heart of love, the more I began to know the truth about God's heart. I began to find that what I had been taught in church all my life was untrue. As my journey continued I began to discover a God who was more like me than I had ever imagined.

Our next step in this journey might be the scariest prospect of all. One of the main concerns I have after observing Christians over the last 8 years is that boasting has become a way of life. It has found its way into many churches and has become even more accepted in the larger world.

One of the biggest ways boasting is manifested is through what I call "God-told-me-ism." I'm talking about people who feel that they have to boldly and bluntly announce to the world that "God told them" to do this or that. It wouldn't be so bad if these people reserved their claims of divine revelation for things such as "God told me to go to college" or "God told me to write a book," but it seems with some people God dictates every jot and tittle of their lives. He tells them what clothes to wear in the morning, what roads to take to work, what to order for lunch, and what pen to use when writing a check.

The reason these people feel so inclined to inform the rest of us that they are hearing from God is not because they are, but because they want to ensure that we *believe* they are. They're trying to validate their spirituality in the eyes of the person they're talking to. The problem is that in doing so, they step on the hearts of everyone in the room. They leave people wondering why God doesn't love them or speak to them as much as He does that person. People walk away feeling there is something wrong with their Christian walk, and they ask themselves why they can't hear the voice of God with as much clarity as this person does. It causes people to give up because they feel a million miles behind. Ultimately, "God-told-me" people do more harm than good.

Sometimes, the spirit of boasting is played out in people's testimonies. Many times, testimonies become a way to titillate the crowd. I have found that almost every time you investigate further into someone's rags-to-riches testimony, you find that it didn't happen nearly the way he or she told it. It is often exaggerated for effect. Christians have been taught to outdo one another when telling their stories, and in the process they exaggerate the truth to make their stories appear even more exciting. As a result, we create a God that doesn't exist. People are left wondering why God isn't moving in their lives the way He did in the lives of the people in all those amazing stories they grew up hearing.

Many people accentuate their testimony because they actually think they're doing God a favor. They're making Him "look good." I think most Christians are afraid that if people knew how things really happened in their lives, they might not be attracted to God. Boasting and embellishing the story in an effort to make God a superman is usually done in an honest effort to sell God to a lost world. We do this because we honestly believe God is a boaster and He likes it.

It also grieves my heart when I see people who have become "expert prayer warriors" (how's that for an oxymoron?). They know everything to say and just how to say it. It's amazing to listen to them confront the enemy, bind the demons, call down the blessing, and release the anointing. Their prayers sound like an ER doctor calling out orders in the spiritual realm in a language that only the truly educated can understand. The most disturbing thing about all this is the look of spiritual insecurity on the faces of the poor people who are being "prayed for." When it's all over, they feel worse than they did before they requested prayer. They feel like loser Christians whose prayers are bland and boring. They feel a million miles behind the rest of the world in their spirituality. This boastful way of praying puts many precious people in such spiritual bondage that I sometimes wonder if they wouldn't be better off without prayer at all.

Boasting generally has the effect of making people smaller. It shrinks their self-esteem and diminishes their spiritual confidence. Boasting has an anti-relationship quality that paralyzes people's hearts and forces them into emotional and spiritual seclusion.

What would cause us to pray or speak in a way that is boastful? It seems so clear that love wouldn't boast, right? Could it be, perhaps, that we are doing what we believe our Father in heaven does? I want you to go through what you've been taught about God and think about that for a moment. Does God boast? I truly think it would be impossible for any Christian in today's church world to think otherwise. Most of us think it's okay because, after all, He's God. He has a right to boast.

We think He boasts about His accomplishments, and we think He boasts about how great He is. This is why we amplify these two things in our church services.

We have scientifically based teachings that walk us through the pain and suffering Jesus must have gone through during the Crucifixion. We make movies that dramatize the flogging and beating He underwent on our behalf. At Easter we put together pageants and invite outsiders to come and watch Jesus get the tar beat out of Him for their sins. We have come to believe that it is in God's heart to hold this moment over the heads of His children in an effort to get them to obey the rules. If we are graphically reminded of the pain and suffering He underwent on our behalf, perhaps we will do our best to repay Him by living a right life.

The God I grew up with was like the mother who constantly reminds her kids of the pain she went through during childbirth in an effort to guilt them into doing what she wants. By the time I was sixteen years old I had witnessed more than a thousand reenactments of the Crucifixion. Over a hundred preachers had reminded me that Jesus "took the nails for me" and "hung on a cross for me." Even our Communion services, rather than being a time of remembering Him, had been reduced to going through a list of the awful things He went through on our behalf. Sadly, the gospel message has been affected by this way of thinking. "God loves you; come to Him," has been turned into, "Jesus got a major beating that was meant for you, so come to Him."

CHAPTER 14
GOD IS NOT ANGRY WITH YOU OR THE WORLD

One of the reasons Jesus came was to reveal God to us. Among all the truths that Jesus revealed to us about God, one of the most critical in connection to the violence of God in the Old Testament is that God is not angry. The violence attributed to God in the Bible makes it appear that God is angry with us, and one way He deals with His anger is by slaughtering people through floods, earthquakes, pestilences, diseases, and enemy armies.

When people believe that God is angry with the world and is actively punishing us for the sins, we have committed by sending us diseases, famines, earthquakes, storms, terror, and death, we malign the character of God. God does not torture, rape, kill, and murder in order to teach us to love and obey Him. While there is indeed blood on God's hands, this blood is His own. God does not force us to bleed for Him so that we might learn some sort of lesson about obedience. This way of thinking takes the cruel arbitrariness of life and deifies it by projecting it onto God. When this is done, the beautiful clarity of God's loving will be revealed in Christ and centered on the cross is obscured by a nonbiblical picture of a God of power. And Jesus' simple words "If you see me, you see the Father" are qualified by every terror-stricken scream of torture throughout history.

God does not punish, kill, torture, or maim so that by some inscrutable aspect of His mysterious will, He might teach us a lesson. Quite to the contrary, as I have shown you in the previous chapters of this book, God's nature and character are revealed in Jesus Christ. God does not bring about suffering in order to discipline a person. This presumption morphs to cruel absurdity when we are speaking of horrors like a man mourning his murdered wife or a mother grieving over her stillborn child. God is not out for bloody revenge folks.

How Jesus Reveals God is Not Angry

When Jesus began to minister in Galilee, one of the common threads of His miracles and message was that God is not angry at us. Instead, God loves us and wants to redeem, deliver, and rescue us from the clutches of Satan, the bondage of sin, and the sting of death. Jesus reveals the love and forgiveness of God through everything He says and does. Such a study would reveal that the consistent message of Jesus is not that God is angry with us and has departed from us, but that we have misunderstood God and have departed from Him, and now, finally, God is bridging that divide by drawing near to us and reconciling us to Himself once and for all in the person and work of Jesus Christ.

The parable of the prodigal son reveals that God is not angry. We all know the story. A man had two sons. The younger asked for his portion of the inheritance, and when he received it, travelled to a far country where he squandered his inheritance on parties. He eventually found himself living and eating with the swine and so decided to return home to his father in the hopes that he might be taken on as a servant. But when he was a long way off, the father saw him coming and ran to him. Then the father threw a party for his long-lost son, which lead to a teachable moment for the older son. I understand that there are multiple levels of interpretation to this parable, but one is sufficient for our purposes here.

The prodigal son is not just a story about a wayward Christian but is a story of cosmic proportions. It is about a father who loved his son so much, he let the son think the worst of him, insult him, slap him in the face, treat him as if he were dead, and then on top of it all, depart to a foreign land. Note that the father goes nowhere. The son has done all the leaving while the father stays right where he was. When the son returns, the father has clearly been watching for his return; for when the son is still a long way off, the father sees him coming, and runs to meet him on the road. For a wealthy middle eastern man, any sort of running was considered shameful, and to run to meet a son who had betrayed you was extremely shameful. Nevertheless, due to the father's great love for his son, he runs to meet him, and not only that, gives him a warm welcome and throws a party for him.

The Misrepresented God

The only thing that is different about this parable and how God behaves toward prodigal humanity is that God came Himself into the far country to seek and save the lost. Then, when God found His lost child, the child killed Him. But other parables represent this aspect of what God has done for humanity in Jesus Christ. The point of this parable, as well as many of the other parables by Jesus, is to show humanity how badly we have misunderstood God, what God is doing in this world, and that God is not out to destroy us, slaughter us, or punish us, but is seeking to bring us back into His family, to rescue us from the pigsty we find ourselves living in, and to throw us a party when we are reconciled to Him.

This sort of message is found not just in the parables of Jesus, but in all the other teachings and miracles of Jesus. By the love of God, those who were once far off have been brought near and have been accepted once again into God's family. The violent portrayals of God in the Bible are actually part of this rescue operation of God. He is not the one commanding or performing these violent actions, but is instead, taking the blame for them. Just like the father of the prodigal son, out of His great love for us, God is shaming Himself for our sake. How can a God who says "Love your enemies" (Matthew 5:44) be the same God who instructs His people in the Old Testament to kill their enemies?

Folks, this might be shocking to some people, but it's the truth as revealed by Jesus Christ who is the only express image of the Father. God has never killed, and God will never kill. This doesn't mean that God cannot kill, no!! He can. He is sovereign, but He has not and will never kill. Do you know why? Because it's not His nature and character to kill. Before you start quoting Scriptures, I'd like you to hold on and study it holistically in context and then weigh it through the life of Jesus Christ. It's this misguided view of God that makes a Christian pray for God to kill his or her enemies who hurt them. Folks, this issue is very dear to my heart, and I'm constantly broken in my spirit when I see Christians with a distorted view of God.

Why is it important that we understand God's nature through Jesus? Because Jesus is God revealed to mankind. The Bible is not a revealer of God, but rather Jesus is. We see a lot of killing in the Bible, especially in the old Testament, that were all attributed to "God," ranging from the story of Noah and the flood to the drowning of the

Egyptian soldiers to the massacre of the Canaanites to the wars Israel as a nation fought with other nations, and others too numerous to mention. At first glance, we Christians feel that these actions were God's ways of protecting us, "His obedient and chosen people." But the more I have studied and asked the Holy Spirit for answers and explanations, the clearer it has become. We are constantly misrepresenting the Father to the world and our children, and our children in turn will pass this same false perception of God to the next generation. And who wins in all this? The Devil. Ignorance of our Father is a gift to the devil and he so loves it.

We read that God killed Ananias and Saphira for lying, but no. It was not God. Peter lied, but he was not killed. Many Christians today lie, but God has not killed them. We read that God killed the first-born sons of the Egyptians, drowned their soldiers, and sent plagues to their land because they enslaved the Israelites. But no, God did not. If you say He did, then God should have also destroyed America and Britain for the Euro-American slave trade (Transatlantic Slave Trade) which lasted from the 16th to the 19th century and transported approximately 10-12 million Africans to America and Europe. Yet today the United States is the richest, strongest, and most powerful nation in the world, and Britain remains a strong nation. Whatever killings and evil you see in the Old Testament attributed to God are a product of a people who were still growing in their knowledge of God.

Romans 5:8 reads, "But God demonstrates his own love for us in this: While we were still sinners Christ died for us" (NIV). I believe that there's something seriously wrong with our knowledge of our Father, and that's affecting our relationship with Him and how we treat people. I think it hurts the heart of God to see His children with such a skewed knowledge of Him. Ten years ago, if someone had told me the same thing I'm writing now, I certainly would have rebuked such a person and gradually stopped talking to him/her. But you see, I feel the Holy Spirit is available to reveal this truth to as many as are willing to open their hearts and minds to Him like I did.

John 10:10 reads, "The thief comes only to steal and kill and destroy; I have come that they may have life and have it to the full" (NIV). God has never killed and will never kill anyone. God did not even kill the first murderer on earth, Cain. One reason why so many of us has a misguided view or perception of God is poor contextual reading of biblical events. I'd like you to know that the English language today is only one thousand five hundred years old. The Bible was not originally written in English. A good steward of the Word must look for the origin of words and how they are being used.

We need to be cognizant of pretext (text before), context (middle text), and postext (text after context). Doing this helps you get a better picture and understanding of what you are reading in the Bible. Folks, this issue is very dear to my heart and I'm constantly broken in my spirit when I see Christians with a distorted view of God. I leave you with this prayer of Paul to the Ephesian church: "[I ask] that the God of our Lord Jesus Christ, the glorious Father, may give you the Spirit of wisdom and revelation, so that you may know him better" (Ephesians 1:17, NIV). It would be too easy to reduce the subject of this chapter to "anger" alone. Though it is true that love is not easily provoked to anger, the fact is, love is not easily provoked to anything. Love cannot be moved from one emotion to another. It cannot be content and happy in one moment and be hurled into anger, depression, unhappiness, or offense the next. Love is stable and real, and it cannot be controlled.

The issue here is really control. There is a term in our society that baffles me. It's a label we put on people who constantly seek to control others. We call them "control freaks." While there are many people who are controlling and overbearing, I am amazed that they are the ones being called such a name. If you ask me, the people allowing themselves to be controlled are the real freaks. Why would anyone want to do this? There is something about losing control that becomes strangely addictive. If fact, giving up self-control is the essence of addiction. This is why it is so hard to recover from things like alcoholism and pornography and drug addiction. Having no control becomes a convenient pattern of life, and the prospect of regaining self-control feels almost un-natural. It takes too much personal responsibility. It requires us to stand on our own two feet and be accountable. It is much easier to lie back and allow others to control us. It doesn't take any work.

Our view of love in this generation has been so distorted that we actually expect a loss of control to come over us when we are in love. In fact, love has been turned, tied, and twisted around so much that we now call it 'falling' in love. We actually relieve ourselves of all personal responsibility. It's looked upon as an accident that was unavoidable, and those to whom it happens are not to blame. It's not surprising to see that people who subscribe to this mentality often "fall" out of love as quickly as they "fell" in love. After all, accidents happen, and who can you blame when love is involved?

I have watched families in which a three-year-old child has complete control over his mother and father. It's almost comical to observe. Psychologists tell us that it's just the child starving for attention, but I don't think is stops there. I honestly believe that the child is starving for control. Many children play their parents like a fiddle. The child literally decides the mood of the home moment by moment. The parents become like puppets in the child's hands. Whatever the child wants to happen can be manipulated into existence simply because the mother and father are easily moved. At the end of the day, both parents blame their love for their child as the reason they were controlled by him so easily.

The downside of this game is that while little Billy may be able to control his parents. Billy also has an unavoidable inner sense that parents who are controlled are parents who don't love. Children need stability in their parents. Just like the rest of us, they have the truth of love written on their hearts, and that truth is that love is not easily provoked. Ironically, they test it and try it, but that child needs his parents to stand strong and not be controlled.

The moment the parents cave into manipulation, intimacy is put off to another day. Children will not give their hearts to mothers or fathers they can control. There is no security in that. They need something bigger than a screaming, angry daddy or a sobbing, worried mother. Children are looking for something bigger than they are, and until they find it, they will never share their true selves. This is why kids who can provoke their parents are almost always blatantly disrespectful to them as well. Parents also try to provoke their children in a number of ways. They'll use fear or shame to get their children to obey. Threats of pain and punishment are always waved in the child's face. Many times, guilt is the great provoker; and with some parents, the threat of withholding love and affection does the trick. Whatever the technique, the mentality behind it is the same. It all comes from a heart that doesn't understand the truth about love.

We have become a society of broken people who have mastered the art of pushing the right buttons in others to get what we want. Unfortunately, we never feel a sense of security in any one relationship, and without that, we are empty and alone. Some people become experts at provoking others. They are known as being "provocative." We all are familiar with this term. When we hear it, we immediately associate it with someone we know personally. You might even have a list of people who fall into this category. If you don't, just pick up any one of the thousands of women's magazines that promote provocation. Even department store catalogs are laced with it. Turn on the television and you will see it in every commercial, sitcom, and movie. We not only believe that love is easily provoked, but we want it no other way. We feed on it.

I feel bad for those women who believe love is easily provoked. This false understanding causes many to become trapped in degrading experiences and abusive relationships where they feel "loved" by men who act crazy and lose control. The morbid satisfaction many women derive from this kind of relationship becomes addictive, and many begin to feel they aren't loved if their men aren't easily provoked to fly off the handle at them. Some abused women admit they purposefully push their men's buttons to get that response because it's the only form of "love" they understand.

And I submit to you that this is the cracked lens through which we view God today. Sadly, we've been taught that being provocative is how to get answers to prayers. In fact, most Christians seem to believe that God simply will not move unless provoked. We've created a remote-control God who jumps into action the moment the right buttons are pushed, and many people spend their entire lives trying to figure out the correct code to punch into the God keypad so they can get what they want.

We act out what we think God wants to see and hear, hoping He will be fooled into reacting on our behalf. Some people even speak in Bible verses when talking to Him because they think it makes them sound super spiritual, spurring God to respond. Others might try to appear to be weeping before Him or in great pain so He will feel bad and answer their prayers. It seems the majority of today's teachings on prayer are "how-to" teachings regarding provoking God.

There are many beautiful and authentic times when people sincerely wail and mourn during their prayers. When strong emotions come from a broken heart that is calling on God to bring healing and comfort, He is truly moved. Many of us were raised with a God of anger, and not only that, but we were also taught He's easily angered. It doesn't take much to set Him off. We quote Old Testament passages that seem to depict Him as a volcano waiting to erupt. We study passages where people were put to death and use them out of context as evidence against Him. Then we hold the threat of God's anger over the head of anyone who might be thinking of leaving the church or doing something sinful. It becomes the dark cloud that follows us wherever we go.

Not only do we believe in an angry God, but we also depend on His anger. He has to be short-tempered or we might just go out and sin. Many Christians in America believe that we need an angry God in order to keep other people and ourselves in line. Why do those who need to believe in an angry God to motivate them to holiness sometimes react with anger toward anyone challenging their beliefs? I have watched people panic at the mere mention of this message of grace. The power they've drawn from to quit destructive habits and abstain from sin was rooted in their fear of punishment from an angry God. And when grace threatens to strip that power away, they are left with only themselves and an overwhelming fear of what they might do.

Fear has become the glue that holds the institutional church together. If ministries were to eliminate fear as a motivator, their businesses would cave. The infrastructure that holds them together would be gone. Our beliefs about God are laced with this same poison. Offering, sermons, altar calls. Communion, and even sermons about salvation rely on fear to motivate people and "seal the deal." Amazingly, we now hear that it's holy to be terrified of God.

The claim that God will turn on you if you sin is dead wrong. Yet this very fear is the reason many people call themselves believers. Most of Christianity is built on the fear of hell. It's as if God has given us an offer we can't refuse: "Turn or burn!" If Christians found out hell was officially closed, how many would really choose a relationship with God? Interestingly, people either see God as hostile and angry, or as depressed. The teachings I grew up with depicted the Holy Spirit as being easily hurt and offended. It didn't matter what we did; the Holy Spirit was bound to get His feelings hurt. Like many people, I learned to live in fear of hurting His feelings. God reminded me of an earthly stepfather who got a hurt, disappointed look on his face every time I did something wrong. He was the teary Native American looking down from his horse on the trash left on the side of the road. I always felt like I owed Him a lifetime of apologies.

I remember a time I became nervous when a preacher said those infamous words: "The Spirit of God is in this room." I felt like the audience was being encouraged to be sensitive to the fact that the Spirit was there because the Spirit was so sensitive. It seemed the preacher was saying that if anyone stepped out of line or said something wrong, the Holy Spirit would get His feelings hurt and lock Himself in the bathroom and cry His eyes out in disappointment. I got to the point where I didn't even want Him to come around anymore. It was exhausting trying to spare His feelings and protect His sensitive heart.

God Is Not Easily Provoked

Make no mistake about it: God will never turn His face from you! His eyes are constantly on you in loving affirmation. To even say that God would turn from you is an anti-Christ mentality. It denies the work of Christ on the cross. It will simply never happen. Don't ever worry that God is not watching over you. You are everything to Him. Nothing you ever do will cause Him to be provoked and turn away from you. Many times, we confuse natural consequences with withholding blessings. If you give nothing, God will not love you any less than if you give everything you have. In the spiritual realm there are laws, and the laws that govern giving in the spiritual realm are not about blessing or lack of blessing. They're governed by natural consequences, and they apply to every human being on earth, believer and nonbeliever alike.

God is as grieved by those who try to provoke Him through counting to make absolutely sure they give the required 10 percent as

He is by those who don't have "cheerful hearts." He is also grieved by those who beat themselves up because they fell short. We have been taught to expect nothing from God, that He can't bless us unless we first "pay" our tithe. This is preposterous and straight from the Old Testament. God is not provoked when people purposefully put themselves in financially dangerous positions in the name of faith. Of course, there are accounts in Scripture where someone was down to their last penny and when they gave it, God created a miracle. Sometimes life brings you to a place of devastation, and the promise of your Father is that when you get there, He will hold you up and deliver you. Manufacturing that situation on purpose is mocking the gospel of the Lord. Why take something beautiful and force it into something mechanical? He doesn't need Scripture brought up to Him, and He doesn't need to be reminded of what He said. Your Father doesn't need to be provoked into helping you; He finds personal pleasure continually blessing the ones He loves.

Since I fell in love with people, I've noticed there are two perspectives about what it means to be sensitive. Ironically, they stand at opposite poles from each other. We call a person "sensitive" when he gets offended so easily that people have to walk on eggshells around him. Another person is "sensitive" to the needs of others. Yet both people are sensitive even though they're reflecting opposite definitions. I'm astonished at the number of Christian teachings that depict the Holy Spirit as being like the first definition. As a result, we've become terrified of "grieving the Holy Spirit." In fact, many people will admit that they secretly feel as if they've hurt the Holy Spirit more times than they can count.

God's Spirit is the second definition of sensitive. He is sensitive to our needs. He knows everything about us. He waits for the perfect time before speaking, and when He does, He speaks in the perfect tone and says the perfect thing. The Holy Spirit is focused on your heart. He is sensitive because He is sensitive to you. Don't ever worry that you've hurt His feelings. Believe it or not, the Holy Spirit is extremely difficult to hurt because He's an amazingly secure person. You can't easily "provoke" the Holy Spirit to anger or to grief. His emotions are stable because He loves you, and love is not easily provoked.

God is not provoked with our "spiritual tools" either. When I speak my Ashley's name, it erupts with power the moment it leaves my lips. The essence of Ashley fills the air around me. I can hear her voice the moment her name is spoken. I can feel her hair in my hands and smell her breath as if she were standing right before me. That name has power within it because of the relationship I have with that woman. She has become all that I am. The power is in the relationship. Before I knew Ashley, her name meant nothing to me. It was just another name among millions. But once I knew her personally, it exploded with meaning and power. The name of Jesus is much the same way. It was never meant to be used as a bobby pin to pick a lock in the spiritual realm, or as a clove of garlic to ward off vampires. Its power is contingent upon relationship. Only in relationship can the essence of Jesus hit the air when the name is spoken from your lips.

The same is true with faith. These things that we use as tools to be the aroma of relationship, not keys to get what you want. Believe it or not, when your name is spoken by God, it explodes with power in the same way. God does not use things like your job, your children, and your marriage as tools to manipulate you to greater performance. The power comes from relationship. Faith viewed through the lens of love and relationship will come to be more than you ever dreamed, something beautiful and life-changing. Never again will you think the same. And never again will you worry about God being easily provoked.

God is not a "wrong-doing" List keeper

In the opening chapter of this book, I talked about the love chapter in Paul's letter to the Corinthian church. Have you heard someone say to you that there is a judgement book in heaven for everyone? I grew up hearing things like this. I was told that the angels are recording all our actions on earth, good or bad. I believed this lie for a long time in my early Christian life, and there are Christians who have such a belief about God. But friend, this is false. God is not the great list keeper who keeps or documents all our actions on earth. that keeping a record of wrongs and reminding us of our past is a tool of the enemy. He is the accuser and to do that, he needs a list of what he will accuse us of This is kind of scary if it were actually true but thank goodness it's not.

Psalm 130:3 reads, *"If you, LORD, kept a record of sins, LORD, who could stand?"* (NIV).

Several years ago, I was with my senior pastor when a troubled married couple came to talk with him. They came prepared. Both had brought a yellow pad on which they had carefully kept a record of what the other person had done wrong. They took turns reading their grievances out loud. Whether written on paper or etched in our memories, our lists of wrongdoings show how well we can keep score of other people's faults and sins! Let us thank God that He does not keep a record. God could fill one yellow pad after another with our sins, toss them in our faces, and refuse to have anything more to do with us. If He did, according to Psalm 130:3, we would not stand a chance.

But instead, there is forgiveness, or, in the words of Romans 8:1, *"There is now no condemnation for those who are in Christ Jesus"* (NIV). In fact, according to Jeremiah 31:34, God says, *"I ... will remember [your] sins no more"* (NIV). He won't hold our sins against us. He won't act toward us on the basis of our sin. God has pushed the delete button on our guilt. God does not cast us off. He continues to give His grace in spite of our failures. That's the reason God can continue to use us to share with others the grace we have received through all generations.

Love Keeps No Wrong Doings

1 Corinthians 13:5 tells us that love *"keeps no record of wrongs"* (NIV). What do you think of when you read that Bible verse? Do you feel a little defensive, wondering if I'm about to point my finger at you and "force" you to forgive somebody who hurt you? Does it feel like relief because blame and shame has been nipping at your heels for years? Is it just plain confusing? Or are you not exactly sure how this scripture applies to you? Join the club. The verse is used all over the place. It's thrown in for good measure in sermons that champion forgiveness and getting along with each other.

It's spoken liberally in support groups, where members stumble beneath the burden of self-loathing and pain. In some religious spaces, it's written on bathroom mirrors and bulletin board note cards as reminders for us all. It's an amazing verse! But what does it actually mean as we attempt to put it into practice? In 1 Corinthians 13, the "love chapter," we have a list of love's attributes. Included in the description of love are some things that love is not. Verse 5 says that love "keeps no record of wrongs." Or, as the Amplified Bible translates it, "It takes no account of the evil done to it [it pays no attention to a suffered wrong]."

This idea of keeping no list of wrongs directly connects with Paul's words to the Corinthian believers earlier in the epistle. Some in the church were bringing lawsuits against other Christians. Instead of settling church matters among themselves in a spirit of humility and love, they were dragging each other to court. Paul takes a firm stand on the matter: "The very fact that you have lawsuits among you means you have been completely defeated already. Why not rather be wronged? Why not rather be cheated?" (1 Corinthians 6:7, NIV). To combat the attitude of demanding one's "pound of flesh," Paul wrote that love "keeps no record of wrongs." In fact, it is better to be cheated than to be unloving.

Jesus Christ provided the ultimate example of this type of love. He paid the price for the sins of the entire world on the cross. While we were still sinners, Christ died for us (Romans 5:8). Jesus kept no record of wrongs; rather, He prayed, "Father, forgive them," from the cross as He died (Luke 23:34). Colossians 3:13-14 also ties forgiveness to love: "Forgive whatever grievances you may have against one another. Forgive as the Lord forgave you. And over all these virtues put on love, which binds them all together in perfect unity." Refusing to keep a record of wrongs is a clear expression of God's love and forgiveness. Often, people say they love each other, but as soon as one gets angry, out comes the list of past sins! Accusations fly, painful memories are dredged up, and bygones are no longer bygones. This is not love. True, godly love forgives and refuses to keep track of personal slights received. The focus of love is not one's own pain, but the needs of the loved one.

Obviously, we should not allow people to continue to hurt or abuse us or others. That's not what 1 Corinthians 13 is teaching. The goal is to have a spirit of reconciliation, to forgive those who seek forgiveness, letting the past stay in the past. Some people have an axe to grind, but Christian love seeks to bury the hatchet. Love keeps no record of wrongs, for we forgive as Christ has forgiven us. When Peter asked Jesus, "Lord, how often will my brother sin against me, and I forgive him? As many as seven times?" Jesus said to him, "I do not say to you seven times, but seventy-seven times" (Matthew 18:21-22, ESV). That is love. Any time we keep a record of a wrong that someone did to us, we are imprisoning that person in a world where they will be caught in a continuous cycle of doing that same thing over and over again. This is the biggest reason most people persist in their grinding routine of sin. They have never been set free from the things of their past. The only way to set someone free is to throw away the records and give them a clean slate.

Condemnation is devastating to human hearts because it paralyzes. When someone feels condemnation, it's because they feel there's a record somewhere of what they've done wrong. Sin's power over us is in this feeling of condemnation. This line of thinking has tortured so many Christians it's difficult to know the far-reaching effects it's had on our larger faith. But condemnation is certainly why faith has become more about making it to heaven than intimacy with our Father. Possibly the greatest evidence that people believe God keeps records of their wrongs is the fact that they keep such accurate records of their own wrongs. If we really believed in our hearts that our Creator doesn't keep such records, would we? Still, I've found that most people do.

It becomes a habit that won't allow any undeserved comfort to creep in and give a dose of freedom. Forgetting personal wrongs seems irresponsible or even fraudulent. Before they know it, they begin calling themselves names that correlate with the sins they've committed. People do this because they believe that in God's eyes, they deserve it. They start to believe that when they are on a personal bashing binge, it is actually the voice of God talking to their hearts like that. They'll imagine they are practicing humility by being so inwardly honest, and yet nothing could be further from the truth.

The result of this upside-down thinking is that people become "sin-focused." Their relationship with God becomes about the list of all the wrongs they've committed. Even their prayer lives are saturated with apologies and promises of purity. They end up spending so much time trying not to do certain things or attempting to break free of other things that they miss the heart of what it means to be a believer. As I've stated, most Christians believe that God keeps a record of their wrongs because they keep records as well, not only of their own wrongs but of other people's wrongs. They've become conformed to the image of who they believe God to be. And in many cases, it's His exact opposite, the accuser.

I am not sure that the average person has ever stopped to think about how much of their faith is based on a belief that God is a record keeper. Most of us believe our calling in life has everything to do with the mistakes we've made in our past. If a person was a drug addict in the past, he immediately thinks God will call him to minister to the drug world. If a person was a prostitute, God will surely call her to reach out to prostitutes. This is a recordkeeping mentality. This perception comes from a belief that God associates our past with our future, which simply isn't true. God is not limited to or by the mistakes or problems we've had in the past.

God doesn't define your future by your past. He has no record of your past, so your future is free and clear. Though many people may have a special heart for others who have come from their previous lifestyle, this does not mean everyone is called to have a ministry that pertains to their past. Your purpose may have nothing to do with the life you used to lead, because your Father has no record of it in heaven.

God is in the business of restoring people, not labeling them. Look at how divorce has become the unpardonable sin in many churches. The moment someone gets a divorce, he or she is labeled for life. This is truly heartbreaking and is a result of a generation of people who believe God keeps records. Our belief in a record-keeping God is so pervasive many Christians believe that if you commit "the unpardonable sin," God will never forgive you. It's perhaps the most frequent fear brought to me. This has been held over the heads of millions of people as a tool of manipulation. I remember worrying about this for the first ten years of my Christian journey. It wasn't until I understood love that I was set free from this ridiculous notion

Our testimonies show this focus on record keeping as well. We commonly hear about the sinful things in someone's past, and yet a testimony is not about what sins you used to commit before you met God. The purpose of a testimony is to share who God is now. And this alone is powerful enough to win millions of hearts. God is not excited about what you came from; He is excited about having a relationship with you today. Out of that relationship, you will become a testimony.

Our Heavenly Father doesn't keep a record of your sins because He doesn't want anything. You would be caged in a cycle of repetition. This is the ugly being held over your head. He is the expert record shredder. Everything He touches becomes like new. There is no such thing as an "unpardonable sin" when you're in the family. This particular Scripture applied strictly to the Pharisees who were trying to discredit Jesus by knowingly attributing His works to the devil. They were nonbelievers, not Christians. While we are at it, I would also like to state that I don't believe suicide earns a person a guaranteed one-way ticket to hell. Many Christian denominations preach this, and not one of them has scriptural proof of their opinion. Yes, suicide is a terribly selfish act that destroys many lives, but that does not mean it guarantees hell.

You are precious to Him, and when He looks at you, He sees only the picture of His perfect creation. He doesn't want anything unholy or unattractive to appear in that picture. Imagine writing down the sin that one of your children committed against you on a piece of paper and then holding it over his or her head. This would be labeling your own child. When you love, this is the last thing you would ever want to do. God is no different. He is the loving Parent who is constantly wiping your face clean and fixing your hair before a family picture. He wants you to always look your best, regardless of where you have been or what you have done.

It is God's desire that you let go of your past He doesn't need you to make sure everyone knows how bad it used to be. He has truly let every wrong thing in your past go. In fact, He has cast it into the sea of forgetfulness. Believe it or not, God doesn't even refer to you as a "sinner, saved by grace," like so many Christians proudly proclaim. This, once again, is a mentality born out of the belief that God keeps records of past wrongs. He sees you as perfect forever! If you, Jesus, and Billy Graham were to stand before God to see who was the cleanest and most perfect, God would declare to you that you're all the same. Further, God does not label people "divorced" because it's not the action He has a problem with. He hates emotional walls and the willful decision to be emotionally hidden and unknown. The sin of divorce is the divorce from intimacy and oneness that couples allow to take place in their marriages long before the legal papers are filed. Sadly, there are millions of self-righteous married people in the church who don't realize they are as guilty as the people at whom they point their fingers.

God is not impressed or more predisposed to bless you because you've come so far in your spirituality. He's proud of you because you are His child. He loves you because you are His child. His heart for you is because of your position in His family, not because you follow the rules well and don't sin as much as you used to. God does not bless us for being good little boys and girls. God blesses us because God blesses. When you receive a blessing from Him, just accept it and know that it's because you are His child. Believe it or not, God doesn't even keep records of what you do right. He doesn't need to. He doesn't need a reason to love you and bless you. Because you are in His family, you can know for sure that His grace is extended to you forever, irrespective of what you do. This is the truth of God's heart He is not a keeper of records, and the more we know the source of love, the better and freer we will become.

CHAPTER 15
GOD ISN'T DISAPOINTED IN YOU

God does not delight in fear tactics. Love simply never thinks this way. When we use fear either to convert people or to get them to follow the rules, we are partnering with evil. All fear is evil. God does not delight in the use of evil to manipulate His children into salvation or repentance. Instead, the kindness of God leads people to repentance. He will never bully anyone into doing what He wants them to do. He doesn't use evil to fight evil, and He certainly doesn't delight in prayers that suggest He will perform evil. There is a power in love that can soften the hardest heart and bring the dead to life. The reason we resort to using fear and evil is because we don't believe love is enough. We've never encountered authentic love. We're ignorant of its power. We see love as one of several things of use in religion. And yet in relationship, love is everything.

Threats of hell were never meant to be the argument that drew people to God. The Bible says that the Holy Spirit draws us to God. Threats of hell bring fear and condemnation. Only a loveless person could think of such a thing. If someone told our children that we might abandon them if they didn't mind us, wouldn't we be enraged? It's unthinkable. We adore our children. Yet this is common practice in many Christian circles.

God finds no delight when people believe He might take one of their children or destroy their business if they don't give their lives to Him. While it may cause people to respond, they will also shrink back from God's heart. God didn't create men to save their souls from hell. He created men and women to have relationships with one another and with Him. Fear tactics make that impossible. The end does not justify the means. Yes, God does work through life's tragedies but contrary to modern-day teachings, He's never the one who causes them. His promise is that in the midst of life's hardships He will be there to comfort and heal. Even when those hardships are caused by our own actions! God never delights in people getting what they deserve. He is about saving us from what we deserve.

If a drug addict breaks into your home and steals your television for drug money and gets away, God exacts "vengeance" by taking that man out of addiction and freeing him to live his life in the knowledge of love. God's vengeance is never on people; it's on the devil. God does not delight in getting revenge on people, and He never participates in it. God delights in forgiveness. And when you forgive someone, you're freeing that person to receive a touch from God that will release him from hell's grip. Our battle isn't against flesh and blood – and neither is God's. Nothing about the evil of our past glorifies God. God desires what is true, holy, pure, lovely, and of good repute. He would much rather you talk truthfully about what you have with Him now than who you were before. It isn't that He's secretly hoping we'll skip over the details of our lives before Him. Leaving out details for the sake of making Him look good is false advertising. Unfortunately, thousands of people won't have anything to do with God now because they're either terrified of Him or they believe false things about Him. We shouldn't try to sell God; He can stand on His own.

What if before I married my wife, I sent a friend to tell her that if she didn't marry me, I'd be "very disappointed" and set about messing up her life? She may agree to marry me out of fear, but she'd never give me her heart. What kind of marriage would that be? God wants people to love Him for Him, not so they can escape hell. He will never threaten our families or our health in an effort to coerce us into a relationship. When we win people with the power of fear, we make them "sons of hell," not sons of God. Using fear only proves that we haven't personally experienced a goodness that exceeds our faith in hell's evilness.

The only way to understand God's heart is to love people. When I give my daughters a gift, I'm not going to ask God to bless me because I gave. When I present my wife with a new dress, I don't tell her I'm "giving it to her in faith" that she'll be good and do what I ask. That would break her heart. She wants to know that I gave it to her because I love her. In the Old Testament, spiritual realities were shown in the physical realm. In the New Testament era, spiritual things are played out in the heart. In the Old Testament, people received a physical blessing after they gave. Now, giving creates a blessing in the heart. If we don't love, we will always be drawn back to the "What's in it for me?" mentality. The new covenant with God must be understood through the eyes of love. God never gives for the purpose of receiving. He gives because He is love, and love gives.

Contrary to many popular teachings, God doesn't plunder people or rob the wicked. He blesses them. When we tell stories that seem to show God doing such things, we misrepresent the truth of His heart. He will never do this. He loves the atheist as much as He loves you. He sent His Son to die for the entire world. Christ died for sinners. He didn't plunder them. This is His heart. He will never abandon His own children.

All New Testament references to the Rapture were to encourage Christians to look forward. Never were they used to terrify people into repentance. Only now do we do this. Imagine being with the people you love most in this world on the happiest day of your life. And just before you go to meet your loved ones, someone comes and informs you that they're hiding in a broom closet because they're afraid of your coming. Would you want to come for that? Until we understand who God is, this is what we're doing to Him.

Imagine having no friends at school. All the kids make fun of you, and even teachers humiliate you in front of the class. Then, in the midst of that, you remember, "My daddy is picking me up today, and he will make it all better." That's what God hopes for us to feel about Him. You need to know right now that if you have ever opened your heart to God, you are safe. Nothing you do will make you any more ready. You are going with Him when He comes because you are His child. Nothing you do will ever cause Him to leave you behind. Don't let anyone tell you anything different. The Rapture was never meant to be used against you; its purpose is to encourage you.

Can you imagine someone going to your child's elementary school and standing before the kids to tell them that their parents might abandon them if they step out of line? How would that make you feel as a parent? How do you think God feels when someone does this to His children? The only way anyone could do such a thing would be if they didn't have love in their hearts. When you love, something so awful is inconceivable. Yet this is what's threatened every day in many Christian circles, and it breeds insecurity in people's hearts.

The nature of love is that it expands. All things of God expand. Living together without a promise of absolute security requires an intentional constraint on the heart. Because love comes from the heart, non-secure relationships ultimately restrict the heart from growth until it dies. Much as a fish grows only to the size of the tank, he's in, if you don't believe your relationship with God is secure, your relationship with God can't grow. Without an unbreakable covenant, you're merely "living together" with God, and your spiritual fulfillment will be stunted.

Security is free, open space. All relationships need to grow. You have that in God. Don't allow anyone to tell you different. Your relationship with God and your security with Him can never be taken from you. The moment you lose sight of your security, you will cease to grow spiritually. God calls it a promise, and you can believe that. The starting point of all true relationships is the knowledge that we will never be abandoned. Our experience of love will never be taken away for any reason. This is the foundation of relationship with God and, therefore, the very foundation of faith. Yet sadly, millions of Christians haven't crossed the starting line of faith because they've been convinced, they can lose God's love and acceptance.

My friend, you must believe in unconditional love if you want a true relationship with God. What other kind of security is there if it's not total and absolute? Anything less than that is no security at all. We give it to our children without a thought. Why wouldn't God, who created us, give the same and even better than our earthly Parent.

Love is the author of forever covenants, and when you truly love someone unconditionally and with all your heart, you see things in them they themselves can't even see. The next chapter discusses another thing only love can show us.

TOWARDS A RENEWED KNOLEDGE OF HIM

Because we haven't really understood the nature and the character of God, we haven't understood how God deals with us and why He answers prayer. Therefore, we haven't been allowing God to truly manifest Himself in our lives by meeting our needs.

"His divine power hath given unto us all things that pertain unto life and godliness, through the knowledge of him that hath called us to glory and virtue" (2 Peter 1:3). God said all things that pertain unto life and godliness. Did you know that includes healing, joy, deliverance, prosperity, and anything you can think of that results from our redemption? "All things that pertain unto life and godliness" come through "the knowledge of Him." If you have *wrong* knowledge about God, you are not going to receive "all things"! Proverb 23:7a reads, "For as he thinketh in his heart, so is he." As a man thinks in his heart, so is he. If you have a wrong impression of God, you will expect the wrong things from God – judgment, punishment, and withholding of what you are asking for in prayer. You'll get what you expect or believe. Jesus affirmed this in many places, including Mathew 9:29 which reads: "According to your faith be it unto you."

Many believers have the wrong attitude and concept of God – who He is and how He operates in their lives. I'm not saying people have it all wrong, but I am saying many people have things mixed up in their theology. Satan is using that misunderstanding to keep them from receiving the fullness of what God has provided for them through Jesus. If we can receive this and let God reveal Himself to us in the way Jesus revealed His nature and character, then I promise we'll come to truly know the way God is. And then we'll find out faith isn't something hard. In fact, it's really hard to disbelieve God once we really know God.

For people who really know God intimately and have true revelation of His character, it would hardly be possible for them to believe it when Satan says God won't bless them or their faith won't work for them. The devil could not deceive people who really know God and have intimate relationship with Him. We know what God is like when we look at Jesus. Once we understand the true nature of God and how much He loves us, "the love of God [will be] shed abroad in our hearts" (Romans 5:5). That will help us to have new relationship with God, something we've never had before. I don't excuse myself either. I'm not saying God doesn't care whether we sin. But Jesus is the payment for that sin and has borne all that sin, so it no longer separates us from God.

GETTING OUR NEEDS MET

I really believe that one of the biggest problems in the body of Christ is that we learn the *mechanics* of how Christianity works. We learn about faith; we learn about confessing God's words; we learn all of the things to do; and many times we try to put them into practice without really knowing God.

The mechanics of Christianity do not produce the "all things" that we need from God for our lives. The fruit of the Christian life comes out of really knowing God. Faith comes from knowing Him and knowing Him is the basis of everything else in Christianity. Remember, 2 Peter 1:3 said that through the knowledge of God, He has given to us all things that pertain unto life and goodness. If we really knew God, all of His fullness would already be ours. I believe in and am not against prosperity, but sometimes things nearly have to be overstated to keep people from misunderstanding. People tend to put preachers in just one category. Either they are faith preachers, or they're doubt and unbelief preachers. The first think driving luxury cars proves they have faith, the second that God wants them to walk around with holes in their shoes. Well, I'm not either one of those!

I believe in prosperity, but I also believe that if people really knew God, all the teaching on prosperity could be put into its proper place. People wouldn't have to know all of the ins and outs of prosperity techniques because if they are really seeking *first* the kingdom of God and His righteousness, everything will be added to them (Mathew 6:33)! Many of us have taken our faith teaching and used it to get houses and cars and more things, but I believe God gave us faith to overcome the devil, tear down his kingdom, and see people born again, healed, and delivered. There is nothing wrong with houses and cars, but that's not what faith is for.

We should not have to spend so much time believing for material things. God didn't give us faith so we could have things. God gave us faith so we could know Him. Then, because His divine life is flowing through us, cars, houses, boat, and things like that would find us. They would come as byproducts of faith in Him. They are the extras that comes after seeking first the kingdom of God and knowing Him. If we really knew God in an intimate way, believe God would shower more upon us than we could ever use. Do parents have to teach their children how to manipulate them – how to confess, ask them just the right way, and do all of the right things – in order to supply the children's food, clothes, bikes, and all of the things they need? We don't do that! We just love our children and provide for them because of our love. We take delight in giving them surprise gifts.

How much does our Heavenly Father want to bless us? We need to renew our mind and eliminate teaching that has told us God wants us to be poor, sick, and stupid, but we also must be careful not to focus our attention on the *mechanics* of how things work. I'm not saying that faith and prosperity are false teachings, but they can actually be used to destroy people if they don't have their lives focused on the central figure of *all* of life – the Lord Jesus Christ. We are more concerned about the mechanics of how to work Christianity and all of the things we have to do than we are in knowing Jesus. On the order hand, if we know Jesus, and we really know Him, it is amazing what we can get done and how blessed we become without a lot of formulas.

After a few years of counseling others, I have found that every relationship that ends in a breakup, including mine in the past, had one thing in common: the reason for the breakup came about because of something that was evident in the beginning but consciously overlooked. We're never surprised when our world of lies blows up. Though we lived the lies, we knew the truth all along. As long as we're feeling that dreamy feeling again, we'll let just about anything slide. The romance of the fantasy is the name of the game, and no more so than when it comes to love.

Romance is defined as "a strong, sometimes short-lived attachment, fascination, or enthusiasm for something; a dreamy, imaginative habit of mind; a disposition to ignore what is real; not based on fact; imaginary or fictitious; fanciful; marvelous; extravagant; unreal" (Dictionary.com).

It's not surprising to find that what we consider the heart of love today is actually an outright lie. We've been taught too long to put untruth at the conception of relationships. This is catastrophic. When women desire a romantic man to sweep them off their feet, many are figuratively saying, "I want a man who will lie to me." Romance has become a game of fantasy and manipulation to gratify the flesh. We all know romance isn't reality, but we desire it because it feeds our flesh. Many times, it's innocent fun that can easily become an addiction to fantasy.

A man who is charming can get many things from women. Women dream of being "charmed" by a cunning man. Love stories and romance novels are packed with charming men who seduce women. It seems innocent enough but look at the meaning behind it.

To charm means to cast or seem to cast a spell on; bewitch; to use magic spells; to subdue, control, or summon by incantation or supernatural influence; to affect by magic; to overcome by some secret power, or by that which gives pleasure; to allay; to soothe. Many women are completely addicted to this form of manipulation. It provides a high that's hard to beat, and as with most addictions, the end is a string of failed relationships and broken hearts. Should we be surprised such devastation follows trickery?

Because we have learned to romanticize love, we end up romanticizing God. Modern-day churches create hype and disperse it to sell people on God.

Some promises I've heard from the pulpit about Christian life are plain lies that appeal to the flesh. Instantaneous deliverance from sickness, a life without struggle, and financial prosperity are just a few of the charming things I've heard presented to desperate people. We think God wants us to tell the world what they want to hear in order to win them over, so we give Him an accent, a dozen roses, and a stack of winning lottery tickets to get up onstage and sell, sell, sell! Many churches have creative experts for selling what I call "spiritual pornography." It's a false, superficial spirituality geared toward tantalizing the carnal nature. It sells extremely well, but once you've signed on the dotted line, you find it's useless.

When we promise people all their problems will go away the moment, they ask Jesus into their hearts, we're setting them up for disappointment. It happens to people every day, but in my twenty years of ministry, I have yet to hear someone share this testimony in a church. I suspect it takes years (and possibly a lifetime) to recover from the guilt and condemnation of not being able to produce what was promised in the sales pitch. I've found that Christians will admit they felt charmed into a religion that never lived up to its promises, yet they still feel compelled to fake it so no one will know it's not working for them the way it is supposedly working for others.

When we invite our neighbors to dinner for the purpose of inviting them to church, we're not acting in love. Many Christians are encouraged to become deceitful and calculating in search of new converts. Such a mindset sidesteps love and often relies on cunning wit and manipulation. With our skewed perception of love, it's no wonder we are confused about God's heart. Do we believe that God rejoices in truth? How could we? Most of our lives are spent listening to lies about Him from super spiritual leaders who claim to be experiencing Him on levels we can only dream about.

But here is the truth. Are you ready? Super spiritual people will never find God on the path they're taking. You know the kind of person I'm talking about. They're a dime a dozen. They're not human; they're superhuman. Every facet of their humanity has been burned up by their mystical ideas of true spirituality. They float through life with a glassy eyed distant gaze in their eyes, and all normalcy and reality have been abandoned for something "deeper." These people truly believe that the truth of God is found in rejecting their humanity and embracing their idea of mystical spiritual enlightenment. I call them spiritual porn addicts; they can't see the truth of God because the foundation of their beliefs is based on lies.

Sadly, I've rarely seen anyone addicted to this form of accentuated spirituality recover to find contentment with truth. Almost always, when a spiritual porn addict is faced with the truth about who Christ is and how spirituality really works, he's disappointed and turned off. His experience with God is usually based on fantasy, and because of his commitment to embellished spirituality, he becomes blinded to God's true heart.

Here's another shot across the bow: the number one reason so many people miss God is because they're looking too deeply. They want something huge and spectacular, and they won't accept anything less. Their hearts crave revelation beyond a dirty, homeless carpenter. They find themselves studying the Greek and Hebrew words in the Bible and looking carefully between each line in an effort to find something deeper than what is plainly stated. They will read it over and over, waiting for a deep spiritual explosion to give them that much needed rush they've become addicted to. And when they are finally faced with the real Christ on a lowly donkey telling them to deny this superiority they're so attached to, it's a colossal letdown.

The Pharisees were this way in their time. They were the experts in deep revelation about God; however, when God came and stood right in front of them, they didn't recognize Him from Adam. Instead of rejoicing with the Truth (Jesus), they despised Him. They couldn't fathom accepting anything less than their lofty super spiritual fantasies about who God was. Surely, He was more profound than a simple carpenter! Jesus Christ was a complete letdown to the religious leaders of His time. And very little has changed since then.

Today, we describe the Messiah in the same high terminology the Pharisees used in their day. Do we not reject the humble Carpenter every bit as much as the people who first met Him? Religion doesn't rejoice in the truth about Christ; religion hides it. We embellish and exaggerate and accentuate the truth the best we can in order to sell Him to the world. But He isn't the high and lofty fantasy we've concocted. He's far more.

We want to believe that God rejoices in truth, but strangely enough, when I ask anyone if God rejoices in the truth about them, they almost always cringe. We are taught that the truth about us is BAD. We're even encouraged to abandon our hearts for His because there's nothing good in them. This is spiritual castration, and it's encouraged the moment someone joins the faith. We are bombarded with Scriptures about how evil our hearts are and how we should never trust them because "the heart is deceitful." Once we buy into this nonsense we begin to behave like a castrated dog.

We become docile and obedient and a thousand times less likely to think for ourselves and consider the truth beyond what we'll find in this kind of church. It's a fine teaching if obedience is what you're after.

But when spiritual procreation is needed, you end up with a bunch of impotent and sterile followers. And sadly, we accept this willingly because we're told that God doesn't rejoice in the truth about us. Think about that for a moment. If you are like most people, you probably believe that God knows the truth about you, and He's repulsed by it because you're certain He's kept track of where you've been and what you've done. Those things repulse you personally, so how can God think any differently?

God Rejoices in the Truth

God rejoices in the truth about you because it's truly something to rejoice about. Do you believe you know the truth about yourself? What most people think is the truth is not. Religion has taught us to confuse the facts of our lives with the truth about ourselves. You are not your sin. In God's eyes, the two are as far apart "as the east is from the west" (Psalms 103:12). The truth about you has nothing to do with what you have done or where you have been. God's eyes are fixed on the truth, and He rejoices in it because it's beautiful.

God has taken your heart of flesh and given you a new heart of love. He has made you a new creation. He delights in your heart because it's good! You can trust your heart. Life with God is lived out through the heart. What sense would it make for you to reject your heart when you ask Jesus to live in it? Your Father rejoices in your heart, and He's grieved when you talk as if it's deceitful and ugly. Your heart is the place He has chosen to live, and now your heart is connected to His forevermore. God is not bound by time and space. He knows our future as well as our present. When He looks at us. He calls us by what He sees in our future, not by what we see now. With God, the future is as solid and real as the present is to us. When He looks at us, it's important to know that He is not "hopeful" for what we could become, but of who we are in the "eternal future," what we will become and already are to Him outside of time. This is the truth that God rejoices in, and this is the name by which He calls us.

God saw the future of a man named Abram, and He gave him the name Abraham. God said He would make this childless man "the father of many nations." Then He went on to say, "It has been done." God didn't say it would happen in the future. To Him, it was the truth in the present and He called him by that name. God approached a cowardly man hiding in a cave and called him a "mighty warrior." Gideon's reaction was the same as ours would have been. He began to correct God with a long list of things by which he defined himself – anything but a warrior. But God interrupted him and told him the truth. He was a mighty warrior whether it had come to pass yet or not. It was the truth, a truth that God rejoiced in.

When God looks at you, He calls you by a name that has nothing to do with your present situation or mindset. Be excited about that! And stop calling yourself the lying names of your present. There is a truth about you that is so wonderful and enticing that God can't contain Himself when He looks at you. He sees that and only that. God is pleased to reveal Himself to the world in the most common and easily understood way. He rejoices in the fact that everyone can connect and relate to Him. God has made the truth so basic and simple that even little children can know Him personally. God rejoices in the bare facts about us and the simplicity of who Christ is. Love rejoices in truth, unvarnished and ever so uncomplicated.

God also rejoices in the truth about spirituality. Jesus once looked up to heaven and said, "Thank You, Father, for keeping this hidden from the wise and learned and revealing it to the little children." As I said in chapter 1, anytime someone gives you a new deep and profound spiritual truth about God's heart that you didn't already know in your own heart, you can pretty much count on it not being true. The truth is not some deep well of knowledge that only the educated professors can unlock. It doesn't take four years of Bible college and knowledge of Greek and Hebrew. The truth is already in you. It's in little children. When you hear it, it should be something that you already knew in your heart to be true. With Jesus Christ, what you see is what you get. You either accept it or reject it. Jesus is the mystery revealed. He is not a mystery that is still being revealed. He plainly said that if we love, we will know God; if we don't love, we won't know God. Don't look any deeper. People who truly love never to question the truth of this. Only those who don't love to reject this truth, probing the Scriptures for something more filling for their spiritual bellies.

Keep this in mind. All truth must pass the "child test." If a child intuitively understands it, it's probably truth. But if it's too complicated or doesn't match what a child inherently knows, it's probably a lie. If you want to know God's heart, you must learn to think simply and with your heart as a little child does. The harder you try to intellectualize faith, the further away you'd get from understanding. The love in our hearts is what wins people to God. We don't have to embellish the truth to get people interested in Him. Love is the truth. This, and only this, is what God delights in. He delights in love because it's the most powerful force in the world. If we don't know this love, we're left to nothing but our own deceitfully coercive efforts to convince people to come to our churches. When we understand that God rejoices in what He sees in us, we can be freed to believe our next subject as well.

God Is Not Distant

We all have something in our lives we wish we could have been protected from. But what we want isn't always what's best for us. In the name of protecting our kids, we sanitize our homes to keep harmful bacteria out, never thinking that children may need to develop the ability to fight off those bacteria to survive later in life. They need to get sick every now and then. Sometimes what we think of as protection could actually be a curse. We've come to define being protected as nothing bad ever happening to our flesh. As long as the flesh is protected, we think we're fine. But what about the spirit and the heart? What of the selfishness that breeds this upside-down view of protection? The problem with our modern-day definition of protection is that it's shallow and nearsighted. We've actually depersonalized it and made it into a mindless concept that should fit every person in every situation. And this cookie-cutter view of protection also depersonalizes our relationship with God. Eventually we begin to expect everything, including God, to work in a one-size-fits-all way, like a vending machine. This mindset is not conducive to relationship. In fact, it's anti-relationship. Let me explain.

We've all heard stories of someone in a severe car accident who escaped without a scratch. Someone will say, "God protected him." And maybe He did. But when we define God's protection this way, we make a grave mistake. What about the thousands of loving people who haven't escaped accidents without a scratch? Was God not protecting them? If we define protection this way, we're forced to assume God protects some and not others. This is how people in the church I was raised in believed, and it's how many people see God today.

These robotic expectations of protection have woven themselves into every area of our religious thinking. His ways eventually become a mystery to us because they don't coincide with our idea of this universal law. God becomes like an irritating soda machine that has a mind of its own. It's not supposed to work this way, but for some mysterious reason it does. This is why so many people behave as they do when the soda doesn't come down the chute. They get angry and start slamming the machine with their fists. This isn't supposed to happen. They followed all the rules. They put the exact amount in the slot they pushed all the right buttons. Yet they didn't get what they were "promised."

If you ask people if they believe that God always protects, they may say, "Yes. Of course." But most Christians agree that God doesn't always protect those who believe. They usually believe His protection is contingent on our towing the line and earning it. So, we say things like, "If that person doesn't turn from what they're doing. God will 'lift His hand of protection' from them." This is how we explain tragedy in other people's lives. We think He does this because our mechanical definition of protection tells us that's what it is.

I've heard God's protection described as an umbrella, and if we step out from underneath it, we'll get rained on. We have a one-dimensional understanding of God's protection that is contingent on our following an impossible list of laws and guidelines in an effort to earn it. At any point when something bad happens, we can always find a rule on that list we overlooked and blame ourselves for stepping outside His protection. I became an expert at finding these things in my life. I could find a reason to blame myself for every bad thing that happened to me. I know people who can't drive their cars to the grocery store without asking God to place angels around them for "protection." The heart of that kind of prayer is fear that we don't already have that protection. We fear it because we've been taught that nothing is free, and love does not always protect us unless we somehow pay for it.

Thousands of well-meaning Christians offer up daily prayers to "Father God" for His hand of protection over their families, businesses, and homes. They approach Him with fear. "Father God, I've paid my tithe this month, so please protect my business." "Father God, hold back the demons from attacking my family." "Father God, please put angels around my home to guard it and protect it." What they really mean is, "Godfather, remember me." Modern Christians teach that we're to pay tithes to God, like buying protection from a mafia kingpin who first requires our loyal payment. This is the picture we've painted of our Father in the twenty first century, and it's repulsive and heartbreaking. I don't know if there is another teaching that's so far removed from love. And yet amazingly, like marching droids, we accept it as fact and write the check in fear, hoping God will do what the preacher promised.

How difficult is it to believe that God will always protect you when you've grown up with the wrath of God hanging over your head at every turn? When I was a kid, I was more worried about finding someone to protect me from God than I was about getting God to protect me. It seemed every other sermon made mention of His wrath in some way. He was the last person I'd run to if I was in trouble. If anything, I'd run the other way. If I wasn't going to be destroyed by His wrath, one of His tough lessons where He sends unbelievable hardship in life would eventually do me in. Expecting protection from Him became a ridiculous notion, especially when everything I had been taught suggested He was the one causing the bad things to happen in the first place. Most of my Christian friends felt the same way. I believe that with this understanding of God's heart, it is next to impossible to believe that love always protects.

God Always Protects

God Always Protects you because He loves you. Not because you're being good and following the rules. Protection is a sacred thing with love. It's never used to manipulate or control. He would never threaten to take it away for the purpose of getting your attention. Just as we would never think of using this against our children. God won't do it with you. There are plenty of loving ways to get someone's attention without using fear.

Know that God will never, ever lift His hand of protection from you! Your security is sacred to Him. Without it, you are nothing, and He knows that. We live in a world where things go wrong. Bad things happen to all people eventually. It's just a fact of life. Don't ever suspect that God has removed His protection in an effort to correct, rebuke, or punish you when something bad happens in your life. He never once promised us that nothing bad would ever happen to us. As long as you are here on earth, you will experience adversity and pain. Everyone does. You must know in your heart that when you do, it's not a sign that God has ceased to protect you, and it certainly is not God bringing on the bad thing in order to teach you a lesson. At times, you might allow your children to experience hardship to teach them a lesson they'll need later in life. But intentionally hurting your child? Love never thinks this way.

God's protection is a Father's promise to always hold us up in the midst of all circumstances no matter how terrible. Love bears up under anything! It is the support beam that will never give way, even in the midst of unimaginable pressure. The pressures and pains of life are not evidence of a lack of protection; they are the things that prove God's protection. Understand that there is no escape from adversity and hardship as long as we live in this world. Bad things happen not only to bad people but to all people. The good news is that God will never cease to support and grow our hearts regardless of what is thrown at the flesh. God will never override the heart to save the flesh. Everything He does is for the heart because that's the part of you that lasts forever. Love always thinks this way. It's all about the heart.

God is a heart person, and we are created in His image. Though the flesh and the heart are interwoven, it's imperative that all things of God are seen and understood through the lens of the heart and not the flesh. The flesh is temporary, but the heart is eternal. This is why teachers who say we cannot trust our hearts are so paralyzing. When we think of the modern link between paying tithes and God's protection, it's interesting to note that none of the New Testament writers talked about paying tithes. Why would that be? Maybe it's because the New Testament is all about relationship. And if you love, giving only 10 percent is ridiculous and offensive because love gives everything.

I'm not suggesting God has changed from Old Testament times. God never changed, nor will He ever change; but circumstances have changed. Until we understand what has changed because of Christ, we will always be bound to the unmarried mentality of the Old Testament. In many ways the church resembles a couple who dated for fifty years and never entered into marriage. This is what our teachings do today. They reject the intimacy that Christ died for and embrace an anti-relationship mentality of solitude. In the Old Testament, people paid. Under the New Testament, we give. The difference between the two is the revelation of love. You don't have to pay God for His protection. God always protects you, and His protection is free because He's married to you.

The wrath of God should never scare you. All human beings have something in them that needs to know that their dad can beat up all other dads. It's a security issue. From the earliest ages on the playground, kids are disputing back and forth as to whose dad is invincible. The wrath of God is never pointed toward His children. It's used on behalf of His children. Sadly, however, we believe He would someday point His wrath toward His own children. Because of this, we suspect that every bad thing in our lives is God giving us what we deserve. When we get a vaccination, we are actually being injected with the very thing we are trying to avoid. With a smallpox vaccination, the doctor is purposefully shooting smallpox into our bodies. The same is true with the measles, the mumps, and even the flu vaccine. Ironically, this is what it takes to be inoculated from these deadly diseases.

Many people live bitter lives thinking the pain of their past is evidence that God wasn't there to protect them. They never stop to ask what it is they've been inoculated against because of those experiences. Rather than embrace who they are today as a result of those vaccinations of the past, they choose to focus on the pain of the shot. People who grow up in a stressful home where tension is always looming are inoculated against being unable to face tense situations later in life. They become uniquely qualified because of it. Emotional vaccinations often uniquely fit our futures. With God, our protection has to do with our purpose. When He created you, He knew your purpose and what kind of vaccinations you'd need to shape you. God did not delight in that torment you may have endured, nor did He cause it. He did not even plan for it to happen. In the midst of it happening, however, He used it to strengthen your ultimate purpose in life.

CHAPTER 16
THE PURPOSE OF THE LAW

The disobedience of man in the Garden of Eden gave birth to the ultimate loss of fellowship of Man with God. Man became sundered from God in his mind and lost the awareness of his immortal relationship with His Creator. He misplaced his identity, his rights, and his privileges and became a slave in a realm he was originally to dominate and control. This rebellion introduced the Sin "Nature" in Man and marked the beginning of his sufferings and ultimate spiritual death. As I ponder on this, I can't help but wonder if the "fall of man" in the Garden took God by surprise. Of course, that is a capital NO, as the Omnibenevolent, Omniscient, and Omnipotent Loving Father God planned that Jesus would die for Mankind's sins. The Scripture boldly declares that Jesus is the Lamb that was slain before the foundation of the earth.

Until Christ's death, God set in place a system where animal sacrifices had to be offered for the partial covering or reparation of Man's sin under the old covenant. It was complicated, expensive, and a great burden in the life of Man. People sinned every day, just as we do now, and so these sacrifices were offered yearly for atonement or based on the specific spiritual needs of the people. The old covenant is a sort of agreement between Man and God. It can be likened to a *quid pro quo* agreement, which simply means to get this, you must do that. Man needed to keep the commandments in order for God to bless him, forgive his sins, and, hopefully, gain eternal life after death. The old covenant was a covenant filled with dos and don'ts. Believe me, it was not funny at all.

Man, who originally had an intimate fellowship with God in the garden, could not even enter the Holy Place of the Temple. He needed a high priest to intercede on his behalf. All he knew about God was subject to what the priest and prophet could reveal to him, which were subject to personal interpretation or opinions of prophets who also had never seen God themselves. He was completely lost and could not redeem himself. All he could do was offer sacrifices of rams, goats, bulls, and turtle doves to atone for his sins, but all these animal sacrifices could do was cover Man's sins. Man was still alienated from his Maker.

Man was created in the image and likeness of God, with His full glory and authority. Satan made Man doubt who he was, and he fell for it in what I call the "Identity Deception" – the highest deception of all ages. With the fall, Man became lost, and all he began doing from that day forward was geared towards finding his true purpose and identity. The search for redemption, relationship, and identity by Man gave birth to all kinds of false doctrines, religious rituals, and practices that enslaved the old Man. Many religious lords and false prophets have used ignorance and crisis in Man to enslave and extort the ignorant man.

These religious masters have intelligently used Man's ignorance of the Scripture to put him on a never-ending quest to try to save himself through works. But the more Man tries to save himself by his works, the more frustrated he becomes. Why? Because he always ends up doing the things he vows to not do again. Since he cannot stop, he simply becomes a hypocrite. The birth, death, and resurrection of Jesus Christ are the greatest miracles for Man and God's ultimate Gift to mankind. With Christ's death and resurrection, God redeemed mankind back to Himself once and for all – not through the blood of animals that could only cover Man's sins temporarily but through the precious blood of His begotten Son Jesus Christ. With the death of Jesus, Man now has a new life, a new spirit, and above all, the precious gift of salvation.

With the death of Christ, the Veil that separated Man from God was torn. There is, therefore, no condemnation to Man if he believes in Christ. Man is now a mobile temple of the embodiment of the Godhead. He needs no mediator, no more animal sacrifice for the atonement of sins. Rather, with this new life, his past, present, and future sins are forgiven. With the removal of this Veil, Man gained direct relationship with his Maker. In fact, this new relationship is even better than what the first man experienced in the Garden of Eden. The first man had God visit him periodically, but this new, recreated man has God residing inside him forever. What an intimate relationship!!!

A careful study of the Old Testament reveals the hopelessness we were under due to lack of faith. As I studied the Old Testament, I noticed that most of the people that God had a closer relationship with were people who walked in faith: Abraham, David, Esther, Solomon, and lot more. Life before the Cross was a life built on lies and showmanship; it was a life filled with the blood of animals. Indeed, such a life was not the kind of life God destined for us. We brought it upon ourselves. People who really understand the goodness of God run straight to Him when they mess up, yet many of us, when we get into problems, and especially if we aren't living godly lives, run from God. What's the first thing that happens when we sin, and our conscience convicts us that we've done wrong? The first thing that happens to most believers is that they start feeling guilty and condemned and begin avoiding God. They know they have broken God's law.

Usually when believers know they have broken the law, they don't want to be confronted by God. They are afraid He is going to reject them or inflict some terrible punishment on them if they go near Him. So, they forget their Bible studies and skip their prayer times. They avoid church and the people of God because they are afraid, they will be exposed. Do you relate to what I'm sharing? Maybe you know somebody who got into sin and eventually stopped going to church, or maybe I am describing you. When you sin, you may not even think it through enough to verbalize what's happing, but in your heart, you are fearful of coming before God. You are afraid of having your sin exposed, that God will reject you as a person, that He will find no value in your life.

Then there's the punishment part. Most of us who are born again don't believe God is going to send us to hell for a few sins, but we believe He won't continue to fellowship with us, protect us, or provide for us. We think there has to be some groveling in the dirt and major humiliation to get God to go easy with us. The old covenant couldn't make anything perfect, so God had to bring in something better. This was the new covenant, sealed by the blood of Jesus Christ. The new covenant brought greater glory to God than the old covenant. If it hadn't been for the Old Testament law, brought into being through Moses, sin would not have had strength to destroy us. I know us. I know this may be challenging your theology. In fact, this may just make everything tilt on the inside of you. But we need to come to grips with some truths to harmonize the Old Testament law with the New Testament grace, love, and forgiveness.

We have discussed how the Old Testament is not an exact representation of God, but it goes much deeper than that. The old covenant was an inferior covenant to the new covenant. The whole book of Hebrews addresses this concept in detail, but here are a few scriptures to illustrate my point. Paul wrote in Romans 7:7-10 saying: *"What shall we say then? Is the law sin? God forbid. Nay, I had not known sin, but by the law: for I had not known lust, except the law had said, thou shalt not covet. But, sin taking occasion by the commandment, wrought in me all manner of concupiscence. For without the law sin was dead. For I was alive without the law once: but when the commandment came, sin revived, and I died. And the commandment, which was ordained to life, found to be unto death."*

Did you know there was a period of time in our lives when sin was "dead"? Then we gained the knowledge of right and wrong, and the law came into our understanding. Sin was present before, but it wasn't dominating or controlling us. Sin was "dead." Once we were confronted by the law and we saw God's perfect, holy standard, we realized how sinful we were. "Concupiscence" in the verse above is uncontrolled lust or desire. Did you know that the Old Testament law actually drew uncontrolled lust and desire out of us? We heard the commandment "thou shall not covet" (Exodus 20:17), and we saw ourselves as covetous maniacs!

The law points to our sin, brings it to life, and condemns us for it. Romans 3:19 reads: *"Now we know that what things soever the law saith, it saith to them who are under the law: that every mouth may be stopped, and all the world may become guilty before God."* Have you ever felt guilty? Do you know where that came from? You got that through the law, through the Old Testament administration. The law makes you feel guilty. It condemns you, according to 2 Corinthians 3:9 and Romans 3:19. Condemnation is not to be confused with the conviction of the Holy Spirit, however. Thank God for the convicting power of the Holy Spirit! He's inside of you and will get you immediately if what you are thinking of doing or have done is sin or not God's will for your life. Conviction draws you to God and leads you in His ways, but condemnation drives you away from intimacy with God and make you feel helpless to do anything but sin.

Most believers would agree that Satan is the author of condemnation, but one of the biggest things he uses to administer condemnation to us is the Old Testament law. We frequently rebuke the condemnation of the devil, but sometimes condemnation comes from thoughts established in us through religion. We need to cleanse ourselves from thoughts that have Old Testament scriptures attached to them. You might be thinking, who cares about the Old Testament covenant? I don't offer blood sacrifice. I don't sacrifice goats and sheep. I'm not under the old covenant. But I promise you, your theology, thinking, and attitude are probably influenced by the old covenant to some degree or another. You may not be offering sheep and goats, but you may be offering works of self-sacrifice and self-punishment to atone for your sin and guilt.

The religious attitude of the law will keep us from what we should do, from walking in intimacy with God. When we sin, the law causes us to focus on our sin. And focusing on sin will keep us from entering the Holy of Holies and calling on God, which is the only way we can get free of sin! The law keeps us from that kind of intimacy because we only see the wrath, the judgment, and the punishment of God upon our sin. When the law reveals our sin, our unworthiness, and our guilt, we generally run from God instead of to God. Now, not everything from Genesis to Malachi is the law. There is also a tremendous amount of faith in the Old Testament, but we've got to look for it. This is because the Old Testament was basically an administration of law, and the Bible says in Galatians 3:11, "But that no man is justified by the law in the sight of God, it is evident: for, the just shall live by faith."

I'm glad Paul said that instead of me! I would get in trouble with the religious crowd for saying "the law is not of faith." Put that together with Romans 14:23: "Whatsoever is not of faith is sin"—and it becomes plain that a New Testament believer trying to please God by living under Old Testament law is not in faith and is actually in sin. Did you know that trying to serve God the same way Elijah or King David did is sin for the New Testament believer? "Whatsoever is not of faith is sin," and the Old Testament law "is not faith."

Four books of the New Testament were written for the sole purpose of trying to renew our minds from serving God under the Old Testament law: the entire books of Romans, Hebrews, and Galatians and the majority of the book of Ephesians. In general, all of Paul's epistles are strong on this. The book of Romans was written to renew people's minds from the Old Testament law and work and justification by works and by effort. The book of Hebrews strongly emphasizes that we recognize Jesus has superseded everything in the Old Testament. Jesus is now our High Priest, and we aren't operating under the blood sacrifices of bulls and goats but are set free by the shedding of His sinless blood.

The church has accepted the truth that we no longer sacrifice animals, but the Scriptures also go on to say that we are no longer operating under that same system of the law where our consciences should condemn us. The Bible says believers should have their consciences purged to have no more consciousness of sin. That means no more awareness of sin. Quite a few people would probably like to stone me for saying this. They would say, "Brother, how dare you! We've got to keep the Ten Commandments; we've got to live the Old Testament law."

A lot of people believe we must keep the law, but most of them couldn't recite the Ten Commandments. Besides that, there are not just Ten Commandments in the Old Testament law. Most people don't know what they are, and yet they insist we've got to live under them! At best, that's just being inconsistent. People who really believe that should know what the commandments are. Many scriptures bear this out. Did you know that the death of Christ Jesus is of no effect if living under the Old Testament law is the way to please God and be justified to Him? It would frustrate the grace of God. Many of us have unconsciously frustrated God's grace – His goodness, His love, and His mercy extended toward us – because we don't understand who God really is and what He is really like.

Do you know what He made us free from? Some people will say "sin," but what was the strength of sin? It was the law. The whole book of Galatians shows us that Jesus Christ made us free from the bondage of the Old Testament law that condemns us.

THE LAW IS FOR CHILDREN

We saw in 2 Corinthians 3:9 that the Old Testament law was an administration of death and condemnation. Do those sound-like things God wanted to do? God wanted to administer death to us? Did He want to make us feel condemned? That was never God's intention. We saw in Romans 3:19-20 that by the law, we received the knowledge of sin, that all the world could become guilty and every mouth should be stopped before God. The law gave us knowledge of our sin, and it made us feel guilty before God. 1 Corinthians 15:56 says, "The strength of sin is the law." The law gave strength to sin. The Apostle Paul wrote in Romans 7:8-11, *"But sin, taking occasion by the commandment, wrought in me all manners of concupiscence. For without the law, sin was dead. For I was alive without the law once: but when the commandment came, sin revived, and I died. And the commandment, which was ordained to life, I found to be unto death. For sin, taking occasion by the commandment, deceived me, and by it slew me."*

Sin produced negative effects. The law produced negative effects. The law made us knowledgeable of our sin, and it made us hopeless about how we could ever approach God. God didn't want to give the total knowledge of sin, but because He didn't reveal His wrath on sin, people justified their sin. They did not understand how deadly sin was, and therefore they were embracing it. They were just living totally unrestrained lives, and because of that, Satan was dominating the human race. Until Jesus came to earth, God had to put some temporary restraint upon sin to keep it from multiplying, dominating, and destroying humanity. He provided the Old Testament law because of the abundance of transgressions, but only as a temporary measure until Jesus could come. God didn't really want us to know how rotten we were, but He had to use the law to restrain sin, because people had become deceived into thinking sin was all right.

Another bad effect of not having the law in place was that God was not fully judging sin. Lightening wasn't striking people every time they committed sin. Because of what seemed to be a lack of seriousness toward sin, people were thinking, *"Well, I know I should be better, so I'm going to make a new year's resolution. I'm not going to beat my wife anymore. I'm not going to drink anymore."* They would improve their *lives and start trusting in their own goodness, which would cause them to say, "Well I'm pretty good. I'm really very good now. I think I'm going to make it to heaven."* They didn't consider the seriousness of the sin they still had in their lives.

Today we hear the same thing. People are saying, *"How could a loving God send people to hell? God's going to accept people whether they are Muslim, Hindu, Buddhist, or whatever, it doesn't matter. Just as long as they are doing the best they can, God's going to accept them."* That's not the truth. It's a deception.

Without the law, mankind began to think, well, *just do the best you can, and God's going to accept you.* They didn't understand how deadly sin was because God hadn't punished it. So, God began to reveal His standard on sin by giving the law. God's intention in giving us the law is very similar to training a child. You can't get a two-year-old child to obey you by telling him, "Look, Johnny, the reason you are not supposed to take a toy from your sister is because God says we should share. God says we should give and do unto others as you would have them do unto you. So, every time you take a toy from your sister, you are really just stealing it from her. You are obeying the devil. And every time you obey the devil, you are giving him access to your life. You are learning the way of the devil, and if you continue in his ways, when you are twenty years old, that's going to get you fired from your job and mess up your marriage. You are going to have all of these problems, and you'll never amount to anything."

If you start explaining something like that to a two-year-old, he's just going to stare at you. He doesn't understand all those complex thoughts. He doesn't understand God. He doesn't understand devil. He doesn't understand resisting the devil. He doesn't understand demonic spirits. He doesn't understand any of it, so what do you do?

Some people just say, "Well, I'm going to leave them alone until they're old enough to reason with." Well, if you wait that long, you're in trouble! God gave us a temporary measure for dealing with the wrong behavior in young children. The Bible calls it the rod, but most people call it a spanking or getting swats. You can successfully get a two-year-old to obey by saying, "You may not know anything about God or the devil, but you do that again and you are going to get a spanking." The child may not know who the devil is but the next time the devil says, "Steal that toy" or "Hit that child," they'll say, "No!" They'll resist the devil. You can get them to resist sin and conform to a holy standard out of fear of punishment. This is without them even knowing what sin is or who the devil is. You can get them to fear that rod, and I guarantee you, it will get them to comply!

On a temporary basis, the rod is good and useful. But in the long run, if that's the only motivation people have to live holy lives, it is harmful. Fear of getting a spanking is not the proper motivation for adult living. It's a temporary measure we use until a child can reason. When I was a little boy, my mother used to tell me not to cross the street without looking both ways. If I didn't look both ways before I crossed the street, whether or not any cars were coming, I got a spanking.

At that age, I could understand that I would get a spanking if I ran out in front of a car, but I didn't fear getting hit by a car because I couldn't relate to that kind of consequence. What I feared was getting a spanking because I could relate to that! And this fear made me look both ways when I crossed the street. Today I'm a grown adult. Imagine what it would be like if I crossed the street without looking both ways, and when I got to the other side, I just started trembling and said, "Oh, please don't tell my mother. Don't anybody tell my mother what I did. If she found out, she'd spank me." You would think I was strange! You would look at me and say, "Something's wrong with you. The real reason for looking both ways before you cross the street is not because your mother is going to spank you but because you're going to get run over by a truck sooner or later of you don't do it."

As an adult, I'm out from under my mother's dominion. My mother's not going to spank me if I don't look both ways. But it's still wisdom to look both ways because I want to preserve my life. However, until I had enough sense to reason, that physical rod was as a restraint on me to keep me from doing the wrong things. That's why God gave the law. It was only a temporary measure that pointed to the permanent answer. Old Testament people weren't born again. They couldn't receive revelation knowledge as we do.

Incorrect Use of the Law

The purpose of the law was to show us our need for God. But once we correctly recognized our need for God, the law was totally incapable of producing the relationship with Him we need. This is where many people have missed it. After becoming convicted of their sins, they start trying to get right relationship with God by trying to keep the law! The Old Testament law was full of "thou shall not's." People interpreted them to mean "God is telling me what I've got to do to earn a relationship with Him. Now, if I just keep the Sabbath, honor my father and mother, don't murder, don't steal, don't bear false witness, and all these things, then I'll be all right with God."

No, that wasn't what God was teaching. God didn't give the law so we could keep it and earn our way to heaven – because nobody can keep the whole law. Romans 3:23 says, "For all have sinned and come short of the glory of God." No one has been capable of keeping the law except Jesus. God didn't give the law so that by keeping it, we could earn our way to heaven. Rather, God gave the law to show us how hopeless we were. It was to show us how sinful we were so we would quit trusting in ourselves and look to Him for salvation.

Religion preaches the Law. Religion says that unless we go to church and follow an exclusive list of rules, God's not going to answer our prayers and we'll never get to heaven. But if that were true, none of us could have been born again, because we were not living right before we were born again! The Old Testament law wasn't given so that by keeping it, we could earn relationship with God. It was given to show us knowledge of our sin, condemn us and destroy any hope of trusting ourselves for salvation.

The Law Is Not A Red Flag

Imagine an old bull lying in a field, thinking "I've been treating everybody mean. I shouldn't be this way. I shouldn't charge at everybody who comes through this field, so I'm going to change. I'm not going to be mean anymore. I'm going to be loving towards everybody." So, the bull just lays there in the pasture, chewing his cud and thinking he's changed. But just because he thinks he's changed doesn't mean he has. Walk by and that bull just looks at you; he doesn't charge or anything. But pull a red flag out and begin to wave it in front of his face; suddenly that old bull's nature rises up inside of him, and here he comes charging!

Did the red flag make the bull mean? No, all it did was draw out what was in him. If people are deceived, it can be beneficial to draw out the negative stuff on the inside of them. If they think they are all right living sinful lives, pull out the law and wave it in front of them. The law was used by God in the Old Testament to show us our problems -sin-and to reveal the hopelessness of our situation. This is explained to us in the New Testament, and we see how God will still use the law today if He must. It was a terrible burden to live under the Old Testament law, but it was the best God could offer in those days. Some people may say, "Now, wait a minute. You think God wasn't able to introduce the New Testament back then?" That's exactly what I am saying. The Bible says that Jesus was born in the fullness of time (Galatians 4:4).

Jesus was born just as soon as it was possible for Him to come as the Savior of mankind. Many prophecies had to be fulfilled, and certain things had to take place; so, God had to deal with mankind and sin in a temporary way by the law. Unfortunately, that temporary way has been interpreted by many people as the true representation of the way God is. They think the law is the way God really wants to deal with mankind, but that is not true! From the moment Adam and Eve sinned, and long after man was expelled from the Garden of Eden, God showed His mercy toward mankind and sought for them to come to repentance only by His goodness, always pointing to the Savior who would come.

Old Testament people couldn't understand spiritual things, so God gave them a physical strain, something they could understand. They were thinking, "Well sin isn't really very bad." So, God said, "You don't think so? You do this – pick-up sticks on a Sabbath day – and I'll have you stoned to death." God said, "If you don't tithe, you're cursed with a curse." Then people said, "I think God wants us to tithe." God said, "You kill, and you shall be killed. An eye for an eye, a tooth for a tooth, hand for hand and foot for foot." They got a new understanding of how serious sin was!

When God began to reveal His wrath upon sin, suddenly people realized what they had thought was right and wrong was totally off base. Their conscience had been defiled and deadened, so God had to help them realize what right and wrong really were. The law revived their consciences.

Correct Use of the Law

The mistake the old "Church" made (and we are still making) was to use the law incorrectly. The law was not given to bring man justification; the law was not given to make man righteous or to please God and gain eternal life. That's not the purpose of the Mosaic law. Galatians 3:23 reads: "But before faith came, we were kept under the law, shut up unto the faith which should afterwards be revealed." People had been trusting themselves for salvation, thinking, well I'm really pretty good. I haven't done anything terribly wrong in a long time, and surely, I'm all right now. After the law was given, they began to realize, "Even if I never sin again, I can't do anything to atone for my past sins." They began to realize the hopelessness of their situation.

The Apostle Paul wrote to Timothy in 1 Timothy 1:8-10 saying: *"But we know that the law is good, if a man use it lawfully; Knowing this, that the law is not made for a righteous man, but for the lawless and disobedient, for the ungodly and for sinners, for unholy and profane, for murderers of fathers and murderers of mothers, for manslayers, For whoremongers, for them that defile themselves with mankind, for menstealers, for liars, for perjured persons, and if there be any other thing that is contrary to sound doctrine."*

There is a right purpose and use of the law. The correct purpose of the law is to give revelation to people who do not see their need for God. People who do not understand they have transgressed against God have deceived themselves, and the law can be used to show that they are not going to heaven without salvation through Jesus. I was ministering in Tulsa, Oklahoma 2 years ago, when a man stood up in the middle of the services and started yelling at me. I tried to talk to him, but he wasn't even coherent. Finally, I just rebuked him, and told him to sit down, and he did. After the service was over, he came up and sat down on the front row. He was totally spaced out on drugs and could barely talk to me. I told him, "God loves you and wants to change your life. He can set you free and take you out of the bondage you're under."

The man said, "I don't have any problems. I'm not under any bondage. Everything's cool with me. Everything's fine." I could tell by looking at the guy that it wasn't, so I said, "Look, God Himself can come live on the inside of you and set you free." He replied, "I'm God. God's in the ceiling. God's in the cement." He regarded God as a force and a concept, not as a person. He said, "I don't have any sin. Sin is just relative." This man had actually hardened and deceived himself to the point where he didn't understand God's perfect standard. I had started out ministering love, trying to use the goodness of God lead him to repentance. But the man was so deceived that his conscience was disconnected. He couldn't recognize a true standard of right and wrong.

When I saw that, I started using the law on him. I took the Word of God and began to reveal his sin to him. I cut him from one side to the other. "You sorry scum of the earth. You think you're all right, but you're not. You don't have any power. You don't have any joy." I began to reveal every rotten thing on the inside of him: lust, greed, covetousness, and all the other sins God hates. I used the word of God to whittle him down and show him that he needed a Savior, that he was headed straight for hell unless God intervened in his life. And guess what? The law cut through all his deception. The moment the law comes, the conscience will snap back to a proper godly standard.

Have you ever noticed how prone you are to excuse yourself and blame others? This especially comes out for me when I'm driving. The driver who whizzed past me is a maniac. The granny in front of me holding up traffic by her slow driving is a road hazard. But me? Hey, I drive just right! The guy who spends less than I do is a tightwad. The guy who spends more is irresponsible. But me? I'm a careful manager of what the Lord gives me. We chuckle at these examples, but if we go through life justifying ourselves and blaming others, the day will come when we won't be laughing. We'll be standing before God, all our excuses will evaporate, our mouths will be closed, and we will hear the Sovereign Judge pronounce, "Guilty as charged!" At that point, it will be too late to plead for mercy.

The most difficult people to reach with the gospel are relatively "good" people, especially religious "good" people. They go to church. They are outwardly moral. They take pride in their good deeds. They think, "Sure, I've got my faults. Who doesn't? But God knows that I'm a basically good person. Criminals and terrorists may deserve hell, but I'm not like they are." Filled with self-righteousness, they trust in their good works to justify them on judgment day. They don't see their need for a Savior from sin. And so, they never repent of their sins and trust in Jesus Christ.

Paul was like a prosecuting attorney, summing up his case. He was aiming at the self-righteous Jews. In Romans 3:9, he summed up his case, "For we have already charged that all, both Jews and Greeks, are under sin" (ESV). Then, to cinch his case with the Jews, he cited from their own Scriptures to prove that there is none righteous, not even one (Rom 3:10-18). But he wasn't quite done. Paul realized that religious, "good" sinners are very difficult to convince of their sin. He knew that they still may have thought, "The passages you just quoted, Paul, refer only to wicked Jews or to the Gentiles. But I'm a good, law-keeping Jew. Those verses don't describe me!"

So, Paul showed ("we know" appeals to something that is common knowledge, which even the religious Jews would agree with) that the Law speaks to all who are under it. Yes, God's Law condemns the Gentiles, too, so that "the whole world may become accountable to God." But the Law speaks to those who are "in the Law" (literal translation), namely, to the Jews. He showed that their own Law, in which they boasted, condemned them. They would not be justified by the Law unless they kept it perfectly, which no one has.

We can't expect to be justified by a law that we have only kept occasionally and have broken often. That was his closing argument before resting his case. But this raises a question: Then why did God give the Law? Paul showed that God gave the Law to reveal His standard of absolute righteousness to convict us all of our true guilt before Him, so that we would see our need for the gospel. We all need to understand and apply this text personally, so that we abandon any attempt to justify ourselves.

We need to trust in Christ alone. Also, we need to understand these verses and use them to dislodge the propensity of others toward self-righteousness, so that they will see why they need to believe in the gospel. This is by far the most common problem that you will encounter when you talk to others about their need for the Savior. They're blind towards their own sin. They wrongly think, "God will let me into heaven because I'm a good person." They can't imagine how a loving God could damn them eternally for their "few" faults. These verses show God's standard of absolute righteousness and how that standard will convict everyone who trusts in his own righteousness. To be acquitted, we need the perfect righteousness of the Savior credited to our account (Rom 3:21-28)

God gave the Law to reveal His standard of absolute righteousness.

When you tell people that they have sinned against the holy God, you will often hear, "God knows that I've done the best that I could. I believe in the Ten Commandments and the Golden Rule. I try to live by the Sermon on the Mount." They seem to think that if you try to do your best, even if you fail thousands of times, God will let you off on judgment day. He will reward your effort, not penalize your failures. Besides, if He demanded perfection, no one could be saved! Precisely!

But James 2:10 points out, "For whoever keeps the whole law and yet stumbles at just one point is guilty of breaking all of it" (NIV). We don't like to admit this, but if you think about it, you have to admit it. If a man stole your credit card and used it to buy thousands of dollars of purchases, he is guilty of stealing. What would you think if, when he came to trial, he argued, "But judge, I didn't commit adultery with his wife. I didn't steal his car or burn down his house. I didn't lie to him. I didn't molest his children. And, besides, I try to live by the Golden Rule. I do the best that I can."? All of that is irrelevant to the main issue: "Did you steal his credit card and use it to buy thousands of dollars of goods?" If so, he is guilty in spite of all the other bad things he didn't do and in spite of all the good things that he may be doing. He's a law-breaker. Let's look for a moment at the absolute righteousness of God's Law (Paul means the whole Old Testament), which gives us "the knowledge of sin" (Rom 3:20).

The two great Commandments sum up God's absolute standard.

Jesus said in Mathew 22:37-40 that the entire Law rests on the two great commandments: "'You shall love the Lord your God with all your heart, and with all your soul, and with all your mind.' This is the first and great commandment. And the second is like it: 'You shall love your neighbor as yourself.' On these two commandments hang all the Law and the Prophets" (NKJV).

Who can possibly claim even to have come close to keeping the first great commandment? Have you, from your earliest memory, always loved God completely, with all your heart, soul, and mind, every day, all day long? This would mean that you have always obeyed Him, because if you don't obey Him, you don't love Him. It would mean that He always has been the center of your waking thoughts. His will has been at the center of every decision that you have made. His glory has been your supreme desire and aim in whatever you think, say, or do. You begin every day by worshiping Him. You love His Word more than food and meditate on it day and night. Who in his right mind can say, "You've just described me"?

We don't fare any better on the second great commandment, to love our neighbor just as much as we, in fact, love ourselves. Did you always gladly share your toys as a toddler? In school, did you always put others ahead of yourself? Have you given generously and sacrificially to help the needy? Have you always put your mate's needs ahead of your own? Have you always treated your children with love and kindness, even when they were disobedient? At work, did you rejoice when your co-worker got the promotion that you thought you deserved? Again, who in his right mind can say, "You've just described me"? What about the Ten Commandments?

The Ten Commandments Elaborate on the Two Great Commandments.

Surveys have shown that even though many people say that they try to live by the Ten Commandments, few can name them all. So it's hard to imagine how anyone can keep commandments that he doesn't even know! The Ten Commandments are found in Exodus 20:1-17 and Deuteronomy 5:6-21. The first four commandments elaborate on our love for God. (1) "You shall have no other gods before Me;" (2) "You shall not make for yourself an idol;" (3) "You shall not take the name of the Lord your God in vain;" (4) Remember the sabbath day, to keep it holy."

There is a debate about whether Christians under the New Covenant are under the Ten Commandments and especially about how the sabbath command applies to believers in Christ. But all of the Ten Commandments, except for the sabbath command, can be found in the New Testament. So even if we say that you are free to watch a football game on Sunday afternoon, have you perfectly kept the first three commandments? "Yes, I've never had any other gods before the Lord, or made or worshiped any idols." Really? You've never usurped God's rightful lordship over your life? You've never put your money or possessions or some pastime ahead of the place that belongs to God alone? And you didn't mention the third command. Have you never carelessly said, "Oh, my God"? Or "Oh, Jeez"? Most of us have said far worse in a moment of anger!

Skipping how you have violated the Lord's Day, let's move on to the other six, which focus on your love for others: (5) "Honor your father and mother;" (6) "You shall not murder;" (7) "You shall not commit adultery;" (8) "You shall not steal;" (9) You shall not bear false witness;" (10) "You shall not covet." None of us have made it through childhood by always honoring our parents. As for murder and adultery, let's wait until we come to the Sermon on the Mount. But what about stealing? Have you never taken what does not belong to you? Have you always claimed all of your income on your tax forms and never fudged on a deduction? What about lying? Have you always told the truth, even if it made you look bad? And have you never coveted something that belongs to someone else? "But I'm a Christian, Great, and I try to follow Jesus' teaching in the Sermon on the Mount." Really? You just jumped from the frying pan into the fire!

If you are not yet aware, the sermon on the mount reveals that God judges us on the heart level, not just on external obedience. As I just alluded to, Jesus brought up the command about murder. While the self-righteous Pharisees were congratulating themselves that they had never killed anyone, Jesus nailed them (and us!) by saying that if you've ever been angry with your brother, you're guilty of murder in God's sight and deserving of "the fiery hell" (Matthew 5:21-23). He did the same thing regarding the seventh commandment against adultery. He said that if you've ever lusted in your heart after a woman, you're guilty of adultery (Matthew 5:27-29). He sums up the requirement in Matthew 5:48: "Therefore you are to be perfect, as your heavenly Father is perfect" (ESV). How can anyone claim, "I keep the Sermon on the Mount"? The so-called Golden Rule is a part of the Sermon on the Mount. "In everything, therefore, treat people the same way you want them to treat you, for this is the Law and the Prophets" (Matthew 7:12, NASB). Again, it's a noble goal, but who can claim that they've done it perfectly? If you say that you have, you just broke the commandment about lying! So, Paul's point is that God's Law reveals His standard of absolute righteousness. As a result,

God's Law Convicts Us All of Our True Moral Guilt Before Him.

This is Paul's point when he says, "So that every mouth may be closed and all the world may become accountable to God; because by the works of the Law no flesh will be justified in His sight; for through the Law comes the knowledge of sin" (Romans 3:19b-20, NASB). These verses re-emphasize the universality of sin, which verses 10-12 of Romans 3 established so forcefully. Paul makes three points:

The law closes every mouth.

The picture is of an accused person standing before the judge to present his case. But in this case, the judge is the Sovereign, holy God, Creator of heaven and earth! Here comes the proud atheist, who wrote books arguing that God is not great or that He is a delusion. What will he say when he stands before the blinding glory of the holy God? Nothing! His mouth will be stopped. He has no more arguments. Or here is the person who often complained about how unfair God is. "If He were a God of love and power, He would not allow all of the suffering that we see in this world. If He would just run the universe differently (as I would!), it would be a much happier place." Now he stands before the Almighty. What does he say? Nothing! He has no defense.

Even godly men have had their down times when they questioned God. God allowed Satan to attack the righteous Job by taking his possessions, killing his ten children, and then covering his body with painful boils. Job wanted to argue his case before God that he was being dealt with unfairly. But when God appeared and gave Job a glimpse of His power and wisdom, Job's response was to slap his hand over his mouth, to be silent, and to repent in dust and ashes (Job 40:4-5; 42:6). Isaiah, Habakkuk, and the apostle John were also silenced when they got a glimpse of the glory of the Lord (Isaiah 6:1-5, Habakkuk 3:16, and Revelations 1:17, respectively).

It's the straight edge of the Law that shows us how crooked we are.

The point is, when you stand for judgment before God on His throne, you won't have anything to say. Every mouth will be closed. I read about a woman who got a traffic ticket. She was guilty, but she thought that she had some excuses that might get the charges dropped, so she arranged to argue her case before the judge. In her mind, she imagined how the judge would ask if she was guilty. She would say, "Yes, but I want to explain why." She would proceed to convince the judge that what she did could hardly be avoided, and so the ticket should be excused. She had her argument ready. "But," she said, "when I came into that court and stood up there all alone, and the judge was on the bench, dressed in his black robe, and he looked over his glasses at me and said, 'Guilty or not guilty,' all my arguments faded." Her mouth was stopped.

If that happened in a traffic court with a human judge, how much more will we be silenced when we stand before the Sovereign of the universe! Martyn Lloyd-Jones observed, "You are not a Christian unless you have been made speechless! How do you know whether you are a Christian or not? It is that you 'stop talking.' (Romans: Atonement and Justification [Zondervan], p. 19).

The Law Makes Us All Accountable to God.

"Accountable" is a legal term that occurs only in the New Testament. It means that we are guilty and liable for punishment. We are not accountable in a human court, but to God Himself! He knows every evil thought that we've entertained. He knows every secret sin that we've committed. All things are open and laid bare before Him (Hebrews 4:13). We've all broken His holy Law, not just a few times, but thousands and thousands of times. How could we possibly hope that all charges will be dropped?

But you may wonder, how can the whole world be accountable to God through the Law, since it was only given to the Jews? Paul already pointed out that even the Gentiles, who did not have the Law, had the work of the Law written in their hearts and consciences (Romans 2:15). But here, Paul did not seem to be referring to that, but to the Law that God gave in written form to the Jews. He argued from the greater to the lesser: If the Jews, who were God's covenant people, could not even keep His Law, then it follows that no one else could keep it either. The failure of the Gentiles was obvious (Romans 1:18-32), but here Paul was indicting the self-righteous Jews. If they were guilty, then the whole world was also accountable to God. None will escape His judgment.

Keeping the law cannot be the way to justification.

Back in Romans 2:13, Paul said, "It is not the hearers of the Law who are righteous before God, but the doers of the Law will be justified" (ESV). As I explained when we studied that verse, some understand it in a hypothetical sense, that if anyone can keep the Law, he will be justified, but none can. Others (and I lean this way) say that in the context there, Paul was not speaking of hypothetical perfect obedience, but rather to the general obedience that some, by God's saving grace, are able to perform. He was not looking at the front end of how one attains justification, but at the pattern of life of those who have been justified by faith.

But here Paul looked at how one attains justification in the first place. It is not earned by keeping the Law, because no one can keep it perfectly. If we could earn right standing with God by our perfect obedience to God's Law, salvation would not be by grace alone, and we then could boast. Nothing that we do by way of obedience (here called, "the works of the Law") will ever be good enough, because we all have sinned and fall short of God's glory (Romans 3:23). As we've seen, God gave the Law to reveal His standard of absolute righteousness, not to be the way of salvation.

J. B. Phillips, author of *The New Testament in Modern English*, paraphrases the last clause of verse 20 as, "It is the straight-edge of the Law that shows us how crooked we are." Thus, our utter failure to keep God's Law should drive us to the gospel for salvation. Paul has been laying the foundation for this point from 1:18 through 3:20. We will study it in 3:21-28, but briefly notice Romans 3:21-22: "But now apart from the Law the righteousness of God has been manifested, being witnessed by the Law and the Prophets, even the righteousness of God through faith in Jesus Christ for all those who believe" (NASB). He went on to say we are "justified as a gift by His grace through the redemption which is in Christ Jesus." That's the greatest news in the world: Even though we are all guilty of breaking God's Law, He offers a pardon to all who trust in Jesus and His substitutionary death on the cross!

CHAPTER 17
COMMON MISCONCEPTIONS IN THE BODY OF CHRIST

There are lot of misconceptions on numerous issues/subjects in the body of Christ that I feel strongly passionate to address as we come to the last chapter of this awesome book. I believe if we view every issue or doctrine through the lens of Jesus Christ, all of Christendom will be strongly united in knowledge, and there will be little or no room for misconceptions. Jesus is the revelation of the Bible, and until we start reinterpreting Bible doctrines in light of Christ, we will keep having major misconceptions about things that, through the knowledge of God in Christ, should have had uniformity of views across all denominations.

I understand that there is a diversity of views in the Christian faith, and I sincerely think it's a beautiful thing. We come from different cultural backgrounds, have different family up-bringings, and have different life experiences and views about life in general. So, all of this tends to influence our belief system and views about almost everything in the Bible: salvation, tithing, giving, righteousness, leadership, fashion, marriage, and governance itself. People who hold various opinions usually have favorite isolated Scriptures that support their views. Some seem contradictory and can be confusing if we allow them to be. Paul addresses this problem in I Timothy 1:3-7.

How can we call ourselves children of God or brothers and sisters in the Lord while a majority of Christians hate each other? We can't even live in peace with each other. Denomination XYZ has this view about salvation, and denomination XXY has a different view on the same subject. How can we claim to have the same Father but our testimony and knowledge of Him are so different and sometimes opposite? As you move from one church to another, you hear different doctrine and views about God and His dealings with man.

We can have different experiences with our heavenly Father, but when it comes to the nature and character of God and His children and the unbeliever, I believe our views and doctrine should be the same. This can only be made possible if we center our views and knowledge of God on the person of Christ Jesus because Jesus is God revealed to humanity. Jesus is all of God. Let's look at some of the doctrinal misconceptions we have in the body of Christ. I'm going to try to give corrections in light of Jesus Christ. Here are some misconceptions I have seen among Christians. I will throw light into these subjects scripturally and contextually and expose them in light of Jesus Christ, who is the revelation of the Bible and the absolute truth of God.

IS ONCE SAVED ALWAYS SAVED?

The subject of eternal security for the believer has been a major topic of debate for decades, with different Christian denominations having disparate views. In my short years of teaching and pastoring, people have confronted me with this question several times. Can I lose my salvation? Is once saved always saved biblical? Friend, the simple truth is once saved is always saved. To say otherwise, and to preach it, is akin to insulting the Holy Spirit or the finished works of the Cross. You cannot lose your salvation either through future sin or by choosing to say you don't believe in Jesus anymore. Why do I say this? Because it's the same way you can't unfry an egg or decide to go back to jail after a judge has ruled that your case is dismissed, and you have been discharged and acquitted.

The day you acknowledge Jesus as your Lord and Savior, your spiritual life was fried just like the egg, and you can't unfry it or bring it back to where it was before you came to receive Jesus Christ into your life. Yes, once a person is saved, they are always saved. When people come to know Christ as their Savior, they are brought into a relationship with God that guarantees their salvation is eternally secure. To be clear, salvation is more than saying a prayer or "making a decision" for Christ. Salvation is a sovereign act of God whereby an unregenerate sinner is washed, renewed, and born again by the Holy Spirit (John 3:3; Titus 3:5).

When salvation occurs, God gives the forgiven sinner a new heart and puts a new spirit within him (Ezekiel 36:26). The Spirit will cause the saved person to walk in obedience to God's Word (Ezekiel 36:26–

27). Numerous passages of Scripture declare the fact that, as an act of God, salvation is secured. Romans 8:30 declares, "And those He predestined, He also called; those He called, He also justified; those He justified, He also glorified" (NIV). Once a person is justified, his salvation is guaranteed—he is as secure as if he is already glorified in heaven. Paul asks two crucial questions in Romans 8:33-34 "Who will bring any charge against those whom God has chosen? It is God who justifies. Who then is the one that condemns? No one. Christ Jesus, who died—more than that, who was raised to life—is at the right hand of God and is also interceding for us" (NIV). Who will bring a charge against God's elect? No one will because Christ is our advocate. Who will condemn us? We have both the advocate and judge as our Savior.

Believers are born again (regenerated) when they believe (John 3:3; Titus 3:5). For a Christian to lose his salvation, he would have to be un-regenerated. The Bible gives no evidence that the new birth can be taken away. The Holy Spirit indwells all believers (John 14:17; Romans 8:9) and baptizes all believers into the Body of Christ (1 Corinthians 12:13). For a believer to become unsaved, he would have to be "un-indwelt" and detached from the Body of Christ. John 3:15 states that whoever believes in Jesus Christ will "have eternal life." If you believe in Christ today and have eternal life but lose it tomorrow, then it was never "eternal" at all. Hence, if you lose your salvation, the promises of eternal life in the Bible would be in error.

In a conclusive argument, Scripture says, "For I am convinced that neither death nor life, neither angels nor demons, neither the present nor the future, nor any powers, neither height nor depth, nor anything else in all creation, will be able to separate us from the love of God that is in Christ Jesus our Lord" (Romans 8:38-39, NIV). Remember the same God who saved you is the same God who will keep you. Once we are saved, we are always saved. Our salvation is most definitely eternally secure! John 10:28-29 is as solid as one could ever ask for. For that matter, so is John 3:16. In fact, every scripture that calls our salvation "eternal" or "everlasting" is making this claim, that salvation is forever and cannot be undone, that eternal security happens the moment we accept Jesus Christ. (For us to say, "Well, it's eternal so long as I keep up my end of the bargain" is insulting to the Lord.)

But there are plenty of other Scriptures which speak of the eternal and lasting nature of the salvation we have in Christ. The entire Epistle to the Hebrews addresses this in numerous places. For instance, Jesus is a better priest and a superior sacrifice than under the former system because while those priests were forever slaughtering sacrificial animals, "by His own blood He entered the holy place one for all, having obtained eternal salvation" (9:12). One for all. One time for all time. Once saved, always saved. The priests of the temple had no chairs because their work was never done. "But He, having offered one sacrifice for all time, sat down at the right hand of God" (10:12). "For by one offering He has perfected for all time those who are sanctified" (10:14). And then, after saying in 10:17 that our sins would be remembered no more, Scripture says, "Now where there is forgiveness of these things, there is no longer any offering for sin." Get it? No more offering because there's no need. Once saved, forever saved.

But Great, **What about Hebrews 6:4-6?** Doesn't that teach one can lose his salvation? I was listening to a television broadcast in which teachers in a certain denomination were spouting their flawed doctrine in answer to rigged questions (purported to have been called in by listeners). Someone phoned asking about Hebrews 6:4-6. The teacher said, "This passage teaches it's possible to lose your salvation." And he went on to other subjects. Not so fast my friend. That Scripture states that something is impossible. "[In the case of certain things], then if they have fallen away, it is impossible to renew them again to repentance." See that?

I grant you that it's not an easy text for any of us, regardless of the position you take on this issue. If you believe, as I do, that the Bible presents salvation as an irrevocable gift from God which cannot be undone, then you have to admit this passage at least teaches the possibility of "falling away." I answer that a) it does not say someone has done that, only that "if" they did, so the writer is posing a theoretical situation; and b) "if" they did fall away, getting them saved the second time is impossible. For that to happen, it would be necessary for Christ to return to the cross and die all over again.

I find it interesting that a preacher or pastor who teaches one can lose his/her salvation and get it back, lose it again and regain it does not baptize the person each time he/she "gets saved" again. And yet they teach baptism is an essential part of salvation. Anyone looking for consistency in many denominations' doctrines will be endlessly frustrated.

Okay Great, **Can I give back my salvation?** The short answer to this question is no. A true Christian cannot "give back" salvation. Oddly enough, some who agree that a Christian cannot "lose" his salvation still believe that salvation can be "given back" to God. Some who hold this viewpoint will take Romans 8:38-39 and claim that while nothing outside of us can separate us from the love of God, we ourselves can choose, in our free will, to separate ourselves from God. This is not only unbiblical, it defies all logic.

To understand why it is not possible for us to "give back" our salvation, three things are necessary to grasp: the nature of God, the nature of man, and the nature of salvation itself. God is, by nature, a Savior. Thirteen times in the Psalms alone God is referred to as the Savior of man. God alone is our Savior; no one else can save us, and we cannot save ourselves. "I, even I, am the LORD, and apart from me there is no savior" (Isaiah 43:11). Nowhere in Scripture is God ever portrayed as a Savior who depends on those He saves to affect salvation. John 1:13 makes it clear that those who belong to God are not born again by their own will, but by God's will. God saves by His will to save and His power to save. His will is never thwarted, and His power is unlimited (Daniel 4:35).

God's plan of salvation was accomplished by Jesus Christ, God incarnate, who came to earth to "seek and save that which was lost" (Luke 19:10). Jesus made it clear that we did not choose Him, but that He chose us and appointed us to "go and bear fruit" (John 15:16). Salvation is a gift from God through faith in Christ, given to those whom He has, before the foundation of the world, foreordained to receive it and who have been sealed by the Holy Spirit into that salvation (Ephesians 1:11-14). This precludes the idea that man can, by his own will, thwart God's plan to save him. God would not foreordain someone to receive the gift of salvation, only to have His plan destroyed by someone wanting to accept that gift and then return it. God's sovereign omniscience and foreknowledge make such a scenario impossible.

Man is, by nature, a depraved being who does not seek God in any way. Until his heart is changed by the Spirit of God, he will not seek God, nor can he. God's Word is incomprehensible to him. The unregenerate man is unrighteous, worthless, and deceitful. His mouth is full of bitterness and cursing, his heart is inclined toward bloodshed. He has no peace, and there is no "fear of God before his eyes" (Romans 3:10-18). Such a person is incapable of saving himself or even seeing his need for salvation. It is only after he has been made a new creation in Christ that his heart and mind are changed toward God. He now sees truth and understands spiritual things (1 Corinthians 2:14; 2 Corinthians 5:17).

A Christian is one who has been redeemed from sin and placed on the path to heaven. He is a new creation, and his heart has been turned toward God. His old nature is gone, passed away. His new nature would no more desire to give back his salvation and return to his old self, condemned by sin to hell for eternity, than a heart transplant recipient would want to give back his new heart and have his old, diseased one placed back in his chest. The concept of a Christian giving back his salvation is unscriptural and unthinkable.

But Great, **"Is it possible for a believer to unbelieve?"** The question of whether a believer can become an unbeliever usually arises to explain puzzling situations involving people we know. Someone who at one time made a profession of faith denies the faith. By all outward appearances, he was a believer involved in church life and perhaps even in ministry. So, what happened? Is this a case of a believer becoming an unbeliever? There are a number of prominent skeptics who started out as professing believers. There are thousands, perhaps millions of people who have made professions of faith, often as children, but years later maintain no faith in Christ. Whether they call themselves atheistic, agnostic, or simply uninterested, they have left the faith. What are we to make of these people? Were they born-again believers at one time but now are unbelievers?

There are a number of possibilities that are often suggested. The first is to affirm that these people were and still are saved, born again, made part of the Body of Christ, and indwelt and sealed by the Holy Spirit. Since God's salvation is irreversible, once a person has been saved, he will always be saved regardless of any future state of unbelief or disobedience. It seems that parents often take comfort in this idea, for, even though a child may be walking far from the Lord, the parent holds on to a specific time and place where the child "accepted Christ." Second, you can believe that these people were once true believers but that, when they stopped believing, they lost their salvation. All of God's blessings have been reversed. The former believers have become unbelievers and unsaved.

Finally, you can believe that, although these people may have given outward signs of having genuine faith, their subsequent choices and statements reveal that they were never true believers. No matter what they say, they were never born again and sealed by the Spirit. True believers may experience times of doubt, uncertainty, disobedience, and momentary unbelief, but they will never renounce their faith. This idea is known as the perseverance of the saints—all who are truly saved will persevere (continue) in their faith, kept by the power of God. We can only know if a "decision for Christ" was genuine by the fruit that it produced. This is the approach that is most supported by Scripture.

Scripture and history are filled with examples of people who made an initial, positive response to Christ only to fall away later. In the parable of the sower and the seed, some of the seed sprung up quickly, only to wither away or be choked out by weeds. "As for what was sown on rocky ground, this is the one who hears the word and immediately receives it with joy, yet he has no root in himself, but endures for a while, and when tribulation or persecution arises on account of the word, immediately he falls away. As for what was sown among thorns, this is the one who hears the word, but the cares of the world and the deceitfulness of riches choke the word, and it proves unfruitful" (Matthew 13:20-22, ESV). But the seed (the gospel) sown on good soil brings forth fruit for harvest. In the initial stages, it might be very difficult to tell which plants will make it or not. Time reveals the truth.

In John 6, Jesus called himself the Bread from Heaven and makes some statements that were very hard to understand. Verse 66 says, "After this many of his disciples turned back and no longer walked with him" (ESV). There were people who had identified themselves as followers of Jesus, but they turned back when Jesus said something they disliked. It was not that they lost salvation; they never had it to begin with, and this incident is what showed their true colors.

Following this, "Jesus said to the twelve, 'Do you want to go away as well?' Simon Peter answered him, 'Lord, to whom shall we go? You have the words of eternal life, and we have believed, and have come to know, that you are the Holy One of God.' Jesus answered them, 'Did I not choose you, the twelve? And yet one of you is a devil.' He spoke of Judas the son of Simon Iscariot, for he, one of the twelve, was going to betray him" (verses 67-70, ESV). At the time Jesus spoke those words, Peter and Judas looked very much alike—both were disciples. On the night that Jesus was arrested, Peter and Judas looked very much alike—both denied the Lord. A few days later, however, they showed themselves to be very different. Judas, overcome with remorse, did not seek repentance and forgiveness but committed suicide (Matthew 27:5). Peter was filled with shame and wept (Matthew 26:75). Three days later Peter was still with the disciples and became an apostle of the Risen Lord.

Neither Judas nor Peter lost his salvation. Judas' true nature was that of an unbeliever. He liked Jesus well enough and dabbled with faith for a while, but he never really believed—we might say he only pretended to be a believer. Judas was the treasurer for the disciples, and John 12:6 tells us that he was dipping into the money for himself. Peter, on the other hand, for a short period of time, "pretended" to be an unbeliever, but over the course of time his true, redeemed nature showed itself. First John directly addresses the issue of professing believers who seem to become unbelievers. Some false teachers, who had appeared to be true believers at one time, were troubling the church.

First John 2:19 explains, "They went out from us, but they were not of us; for if they had been of us, they would have continued with us. But they went out, that it might become plain that they all are not of us" (ESV). Although those who departed the faith had appeared to be genuine, John makes it clear that they had never actually been "of us." One of the marks of a believer is that he "continues with us." People may be able to "fake it" for a while, but they cannot sustain the part forever. The truth will eventually outlast their fakery. First John 3:9 says, "No one born of God makes a practice of sinning, for God's seed abides in him; and he cannot keep on sinning, because he has been born of God" (ESV). A genuine believer is kept from falling into continuous sin because he has been born of God—God keeps him safe.

A true believer may fall into disobedience and struggle with doubt, but a true believer will never renounce Christ. A person who has renounced Christ by his words or deeds has not lost salvation; rather, he is demonstrating that he never had genuine faith. This is one reason why church discipline is so important. In Matthew 18, Jesus outlined the steps. If a person in the church sins, he should be confronted and given the chance to repent. Once all the steps in the process have been followed and there is still no repentance, then the unrepentant sinner is to be put out of the church and treated as an unbeliever (verses 15–17). This process is designed to get the sinner off the fence. Either he will see the error of his ways and be brought to his senses, or he will decide that the church and the Christian life are not that important and walk away. Either way, church discipline forces a person's true nature to come out.

A genuine believer can never become an unbeliever because he or she has been born again by the Spirit of God. It is not one's faith that keeps one safe but the power of God that enables continual faith. But Great, **"If our salvation is eternally secure, why does the Bible warn so strongly against apostasy?"** The Bible teaches that everyone who is born again by the power of the Holy Spirit is saved forever. We receive the gift of eternal life (John 10:28), not temporary life. Someone who is born again (John 3:3) cannot be "unborn." After being adopted into God's family (Romans 8:15), we will not be kicked out. When God starts a work, He finishes it (Philippians 1:6). So, the child of God—the believer in Jesus Christ—is eternally secure in his salvation.

However, the Bible also contains some strong warnings against apostasy. These warnings have led some to doubt the doctrine of eternal security. After all, if we cannot lose our salvation, why are we warned against falling away from the Lord? This is a good question. First, we must understand what is meant by "apostasy." An apostate is someone who abandons his religious faith. It is clear from the Bible that apostates are people who made professions of faith in Jesus Christ but never genuinely received Him as Savior. They were pretending believers. Those who turn away from Christ never really trusted Him to begin with. As 1 John 2:19 says, "They went out from us, but they did not really belong to us. For if they had belonged to us, they would have remained with us; but their going showed that none of them belonged to us" (NIV). Those who apostatize are simply demonstrating that they are not true believers, and they never were.

The Parable of the Wheat and the Tares (Matthew 13:24-30) provides a simple illustration of apostasy. Wheat and "false wheat" (tares or weeds) were growing in the same field. At first, the difference between the two types of plants was undetectable, but as time went on, the weeds were seen for what they were. In the same way, in any given church today, there may be true, born-again believers' side by side with pretenders—those who enjoy the messages, the music, and the fellowship but have never repented of their sins and accepted Christ by faith. To any human observer, the true believer and the pretender look identical. Only God can see the heart. Matthew 13:1-9 (the Parable of the Sower) is another illustration of apostasy in action.

The Bible's warnings against apostasy exist because there are two types of religious people: believers and unbelievers. In any church there are those who truly know Christ and those who are going through the motions. Wearing the label "Christian" does not guarantee a change of heart. It is possible to hear the Word, and even agree with its truth, without taking it to heart. It is possible to attend church, serve in a ministry, and call yourself a Christian—and still be unsaved (Matthew 7:21-23). As the prophet said, "These people come near to me with their mouth and honor me with their lips, but their hearts are far from me" (Isaiah 29:13, NIV; cf. Mark 7:6). God warns the pretender who sits in the pew and hears the gospel Sunday after Sunday that he is playing with fire. Eventually, a pretender will apostatize—he will "fall away" from the faith he once professed—if he does not repent. Like the tares among the wheat, his true nature will manifest.

The passages warning against apostasy serve two primary purposes. First, they exhort everyone to be sure of their salvation. One's eternal destiny is not a trifling matter. Paul tells us in 2 Corinthians 13:5 to examine ourselves to see whether we are "in the faith." One test of true faith is love for others (1 John 4:7-8). Another is good works. Anyone can claim to be a Christian, but those who are truly saved will bear fruit. A true Christian will show, through words, actions, and doctrine, that he follows the Lord. Christians bear fruit in varying degrees based on their level of obedience and their spiritual gifts, but all Christians bear fruit as the Spirit produces it in them (Galatians 5:22-

23). Just as true followers of Jesus Christ will be able to see evidence of their salvation (see 1 John 4:13), apostates will eventually be made known by their fruit (Matthew 7:16-20) or lack thereof (John 15:2).

The second purpose for the Bible's warnings against apostasy is to equip the church to identify apostates. They can be known by their rejection of Christ, acceptance of heresy, and carnal nature (2 Peter 2:1-3). The biblical warnings against apostasy, therefore, are warnings to those who are under the umbrella of "faith" without ever having truly exercised faith. Scriptures such as Hebrews 6:4-6 and Hebrews 10:26-29 are warnings to "pretend" believers that they need to examine themselves before it's too late. Matthew 7:22-23 indicates that "pretend believers" whom the Lord rejects on Judgment Day are rejected not because they "lost faith" but because the Lord never knew them. They never had a relationship with Him.

There are many people who love religion for religion's sake and are willing to identify themselves with Jesus and the church. Who wouldn't want eternal life and blessing? However, Jesus warns us to "count the cost" of discipleship (Luke 9:23-26; 14:25-33). True believers have counted the cost and made the commitment; apostates fail to do so. Apostates had a profession of faith at one time but not the possession of faith. Their mouths spoke something other than what their hearts believed. Apostasy is not the loss of salvation but evidence of past pretension.

IS DRINKING ALCOHOL OR SMOKING A SIN?

Drinking alcohol is not a sin. Smoking Cigarettes is also not sin. The irresponsible intake of these things is the problem. If you are a believer that loves alcohol, then drink it responsibly, and never be ashamed of doing so. If you are a Christian that likes to smoke, then do it responsibly, and don't be ashamed of it. It's scripturally/medically advised that we apply wisdom and moderation in all we do and eat to avoid unnecessary health problems and addiction. Therefore, when you get drunk and/or drink yourself to a stupor, you are not sinning against God, nor does it make you a bad or evil person. Rather, you are harming your health and may hurt people by your actions or words or even break the law due to that irresponsibility.

When you smoke without moderation and become addicted to it, your health is at risk. God's will for your life is not for you to be sick, but that you be in good health to enjoy the beauty of the world He has given unto you (3 John 1:2). Therefore, it's your responsibility to apply wisdom with everything you put in your body, taking into consideration your unique body chemistry, since what is good for Mr. A's body may not be well received by Mr. B's body. You should also consider your climate, culture, and the nature of your job, which all influence the consumption of anything. To a Cameroon, Italian, Belarus, or Russian citizen, the consumption of alcohol is part of their cultural identity. It all boils down to personal choice and being able to maintain moderation.

Great Igwe doesn't drink alcohol but he is addicted to coffee and Coca-Cola. That doesn't make Great Igwe a more responsible Christian than Damian, who likes to drink Hennessey and other kinds of liquor. Great doesn't smoke but likes to eat a lot of bitter kola because it's medicinal to him, but Peter likes to smoke. That Great doesn't smoke doesn't make him a holier or better Christian than his Christian brother Peter who does. The point to note here is that if Great, Peter, and Damian are not responsible enough to ensure moderation in what they enjoy consuming, they are all putting their health at a higher risk. For Great, too much sugar and nicotine will bring about diabetes, high blood pressure, and/or liver problems. For Damian or Peter, excess smoking and consumption of liquor will cause lung failure, cancer, or other medical conditions. Therefore, moderation is key to an effective and healthy lifestyle as Christians.

Is Smoking a Sin?

The Bible never directly mentions smoking. There are principles, however, that definitely apply to smoking. First, the Bible commands us not to allow our bodies to become "mastered" by anything. "Everything is permissible for me—but not everything is beneficial. Everything is permissible for me—but I will not be mastered by anything" (1 Corinthians 6:12). Smoking is undeniably strongly addictive and very harmful to our health. Later in the same passage we are told, "Do you not know that your bodies are a temple of the Holy Spirit who is in you, whom you have received from God? You are not your own; you were bought at a price. Therefore, honor God with your bodies" (1 Corinthians 6:19-20, NIV).

Smoking is undoubtedly very bad for your health. It has been proven to damage the lungs and the heart, and like I said earlier, this is not the wish of God for your health. Smoking is not a sin, but it sure is dangerous to our health based on medical science. If one can be moderate, fine. But I don't know, nor have I seen any moderate smoker since the substance is very addictive. Can a person honestly smoke "for the glory of God" (1 Corinthians 10:31)? I believe that the answer to these questions is a resounding "no." Now, in stating that smoking is harmful to your health, I'm not stating that smokers are unsaved. There are many true believers in Jesus Christ who smoke. Smoking does not prevent a person from being saved, nor does it cause a person to lose his salvation. Smoking is no less forgivable than any other sin, whether for a person becoming a Christian or a Christian confessing his/her sin to God (1 John 1:9)

Should a Christian Work Where Alcohol and Tobacco are Sold?

This is a question many Christians struggle with because they feel convicted that by working in a store that sells alcohol and tobacco, they are in some way encouraging or enabling others to sin by drinking and smoking. While the Bible is silent on the subject of selling alcohol and tobacco, there are scriptural principles that can be applied to this question. Many people believe smoking cigarettes to be sinful since it is willfully harming one's body. However, overeating, which is much more prevalent than smoking (at least in the U.S.), is just as sinful, if not more so because of the biblical commands to avoid gluttony (Proverbs 23:2, 20). Does this mean that restaurant waiters and fast-food employees are causing others to sin by selling rich, fattening foods to them?

Drinking wine and/or alcohol is not identified in the Bible as sin. The sin is being "drunk with wine, wherein is excess" (Ephesians 5:18).

Consider that Jesus Himself drank of the fruit of the vine, and Paul recommended drinking wine to his student, Timothy (1 Timothy 5:23). It is the responsibility of the individuals to determine for themselves when they need to stop drinking, and so the responsibility for drinking lies with the drinker, not the supplier. To be sure, in some situations, where a person is obviously already intoxicated, or situations that break the law, it would be wrong to sell alcohol to a drunken person or to sell alcohol or tobacco to minors. However, in the day-to-day work environment, selling alcohol is no more sinful than working in a grocery store. But aside from these circumstances, it is the responsibility of the drinker to regulate his/her intake, not the seller. It is also the responsibility of the individual to decide whether smoking or overeating is detrimental to his health and to act accordingly.

As Christians, we should act according to our faith when it comes to matters such as these, relying on our consciences to approve or not approve of our actions. Paul addresses this same principle regarding whether it was proper for believers to eat food sacrificed to idols: "Blessed is the man who does not condemn himself by what he approves. But whoever has doubts is condemned if they eat, because their eating is not from faith; and everything that does not come from faith is sin" (Romans 14:22-23, NIV). Ultimately, the decision should be made with prayer for wisdom, which God promises to grant to all without finding fault (James 1:5).

THE TRUTH ABOUT TITHING

One major avenue for fraud in Christendom, especially in Africa, is this thing called "tithing." Throughout my young Christian life, I have not seen any subject of the Old Testament so wrongly used against believers like this form of giving called Tithing. I grew up in one of the developing sub-Saharan nations where I saw with my own eyes how certain men and women used one verse of the Bible to defraud millions of saints. These clergymen are worth millions and millions of dollars; some have a private jet, while others have two to three jets, each worth millions of dollar.

People have complained that some pastors of today are materialistic. Yes, there are many pastors who are money-oriented, but there are honest men and women of God who are genuinely concerned about the body of Christ. The subject of tithing has recently raised a series of questions. Therefore, I have a burden in my heart to share with you from the Scriptures the truth about this subject, the truth backed up with facts from the Old Testament, the Gospels, and the Epistles, which is the climax of all revelations, and relay it through the lens of Jesus Christ, the sole revelation and theme of the Bible. Many will hate me for writing this to you. I will be called all sorts of names, but I refuse to endure watching this deception go on. Saints, it is time we grow up and start desiring the revelation of the Scriptures, because if we don't, men will continue to take advantage of our ignorance of the Word of God.

Now, I'd like you to know that I have been a faithful tither myself. In fact, I doubt if there was any more faithful in tithing than I was in my local community back then. I was faithful to the point of paying double whenever I missed paying my tithe. I paid tithe from my school fees back in college, paid tithe from every bit of money that came into my hands. Until I encountered revelation through the Scriptures, I was against anyone who rebelled against paying his or her tithe. I have served in churches where tithing was used to measure one's commitment to the church. I have enforced the payment of tithing, and as a pastor, I had often taught wrongly on the subject of tithing, cursing and raining condemnation on those who refused to pay or had financial impediments and were unable to pay their tithes to my church.

In some of the churches where I served, the consistent payment of tithe was a key requirement before any member could be given any leadership position in the church or receive any financial help from the church. Thank God for revelation knowledge of His word. I'm free from being a victim of such fraud. And I hope through this book, you will receive the knowledge you need to break out of this bondage and become the better and cheerful giver that God expects you to be. Now, let's begin!!!

To understand the subject of tithing, we must look at it within the complete context of the Bible: the origin, who paid tithe first, and who asked the first tither in the Bible to pay tithe. We must also consider the reason why tithing was introduced, and the audience being addressed in the Scripture. Further, we must consider every Scripture of the Old

Testament where "tithing" or "tithes" was mentioned, consider what the New Testament (the Gospels, the Epistles) said about tithing, and most importantly, summarize our findings through the lens of Jesus Christ, whom we have seen from the previous chapters is the central message of the Bible and the express revelation of God the Father to Mankind.

The Scriptures, Gospels, and Epistles are not loud on the topic of tithing. Doctrinally, we should be loud on issues the Bible is loud on and silent on issues the Bible is silent on. The Scripture will never mean today what it never meant when it was first spoken. God doesn't change. So, to understand the subject of tithing, we are not just going to look at it as the passage. We will have to subject it to the interpretation of the Gospels and the Epistles. What did Jesus say about tithing? How do the Epistles address the subject of tithing?

It's interesting to note that the word tithe, tithing, or to tithe are words that were not emphasized in the Epistles. In fact, the word was only used once, by the writer of Hebrews, and it was not an instruction but a historical reference. Hebrews 7:5-9 reads, "And verily they that are of the sons of Levi, who receive the priesthood, have a commandment to take tithes from the people according to the law, that is, of their brethren, though they have come out of the loins of Abraham: But he whose descent is not counted from them received tithes from Abraham, and blessed him that had the promises. And without all contradiction the less is blessed of the better. And here men that die receive tithes; but there he received them, of whom it is witnessed that he liveth. And as I may so say, Levi also, who received tithes, paid tithes in Abraham."

The account referred to by the author of the book of Hebrews can be found in Genesis 14:17-23, and we shall look at it shortly. This is the only reference to tithing you will see throughout the Epistles. The writer of the book of Hebrews was not encouraging people to tithe in these verses any more than Hebrews 11:17 was an encouragement to offer your sons just as Abraham did. There are lessons to learn from historical accounts, but some have tried to create a doctrine out of Hebrews' singular mention of the tithe. They claim verse 8 means Jesus received tithe. This is unscriptural and certainly not true. The phrase "he received them" is italicized in the English text. This means that the phrase was not in the original text. Rather, it was added by the translators, in this case the King James translators since we are quoting from the King James Bible. A contextual reading will plainly show the reader he was referring to Melchizedek symbolically. (*See* Hebrews 7:3).

How was Tithing Taught in the New Testament Books of the Bible?

The words "tithe" or "to tithe" or "tithing" were not mentioned at all in the book of Acts, not mentioned in the Pauline Epistles, nor in Peter, John, James, or Jude's Epistles. This pattern of its lack of mention in the New Testament writings is very instructive, as all the Apostles taught giving, but none taught the tithe or tithing. First, let us examine what Jesus Christ said about the tithe. Jesus spoke about the tithe twice: once as rebuke and once in a parable.

AS A REBUKE

Mathew 23:23 reads, *"Woe to you, scribes and Pharisees, hypocrites! For you pay tithe of mint and anise and cummin and have neglected the weightier matters of the law: justice and mercy and faith. These you ought to have done, without leaving the others undone."* Jesus expressly refers to the tithe as a matter of the law, same as mercy, judgment, and faithfulness. So, Jesus was not instructing tithing here, as tithing preceded his incarnation. That is, these customs were already in practice before the advent of Jesus Christ's coming. Just like other practices like Passover, Pentecost, and all the ceremonial sacrifices, they all preceded Jesus Christ's coming. Who was Jesus' audience here? The Pharisees and the scribes (the religious sects).

AS A PARABLE

Luke 18:11-12 reads, *"The Pharisee stood and prayed thus with himself, 'God, I thank You that I am not as other men – extortioners, unjust, adulterers, or even as this tax collector. I fast twice in the week, I give tithes of all that I possess."* It's notable that the speaker is a Pharisee. Thus, on the two occasions when Jesus mentioned the tithe,

He was not commending the tither. In fact, if you read these verses in context (verses 13-14), He talks about the pride of this Pharisee. So, we have two mentions by Jesus, which are rebuking and exposing the hypocrisy of the Pharisees, and one mention in the Epistles, which is historical and not an instruction. The Epistles are the explanation of the Old Testament books of the Bible. Hence being emphatic on tithing would not be consistent with the Epistles concerning giving.

This then leads us to a very important question: Is the nonpayment of tithe robbing God? This ideology has its origin in one of the texts in the Old Testament. Malachi 3:6-10 reads, *"For I am the LORD, I change not; therefore, ye sons of Jacob are not consumed. Even from the days of your fathers ye are gone away from mine ordinances and have not kept them. Return unto me, and I will return unto you, saith the LORD of hosts. But ye said, wherein shall we return? Will a man rob God? Yet ye have robbed me. But ye say, wherein have we robbed thee? In tithes and offerings. Ye are cursed with a curse: for ye have robbed me, even this whole nation. Bring ye all the tithes into the storehouse, that there may be meat in mine house, and prove me now herewith, saith the LORD of hosts, if I will not open you the windows of heaven, and pour you out a blessing, that there shall not be room enough to receive it."*

The prophet Malachi spoke about bringing the tithe into the store house, required under the law of Moses. In Numbers 18:25-32, God told the Levites to take out 10% from whatever they produced or collected from the Israelites. Did you get that? The Levites. So, the people who were to bring the 10%, as seen in the book of Numbers 18, were the Levites. Who were the Levites? The Levites were one of the tribes of Israel who did nothing but attend to the Tabernacle (Temple) and the spiritual needs of the nation of Israel. Because they did not do anything else – they did not farm or do any other job – the entire nation of Israel was asked to pay a tithe to them from their harvest, crops, and livestock. That was considered the Levites' reward or wages since they worked in the Temple.

Moses instructed that the Levites take a tithe from the children of Israel as their inheritance. They were instructed to also offer up a tenth of that tithe unto the Lord as their heave offering. Nehemiah also spoke about the tithe in chapter 13 of his book. The golden question is who then was the prophet Malachi referring to in Malachi 3? I'd like you to

The Misrepresented God

note that Malachi, Zachariah, and Haggai all spoke about the Temple. They came chronologically after Nehemiah, so everything they said was in the same dispensation. This was when they were back from the exile. (*See* Nehemiah 13:4-13). Nehemiah 13:4-13 shows that they were restoring the practice of the Levites and the priesthood after returning from exile because, at that time, the tithe was restricted to the promised land, Canaan.

Now, a basic fact that must be established is who was the book of Malachi written to? In Malachi 1:6, the first audience was the priests, and this is consistent throughout the Book of Malachi (Malachi 2:1 & 3:3). The instructions contained in the book of Malachi were to the Levites. They were the ones that brought the tithe into the storehouse, but in verse 10 of Malachi 3, the audience switched to the people. Now, observe carefully in verses 8-10. *"Will a man rob God? Yet ye have robbed me. But ye say, wherein have we robbed thee? In tithes and offerings. Ye are cursed with a curse: for ye have robbed me, even this whole nation. Bring ye all the tithes into the storehouse, that there may be meat in mine house, and prove me now herewith, saith the Lord of hosts, if I will not open you the door of heaven, and pour you out a blessing, that there may not be room enough to receive it."*

Did you note the phrase "Even this whole nation"? That is indicative that the first audience and the main audience of Malachi was the priests. Why? Because the prophet Malachi introduced the entire nation of Israel as victims of the priests' refusal to bring in their tithe as instructed by Moses. It's evident that the key thing Malachi was addressing here was selfishness: The word "meat" is translated from the word *tereph* in the Hebrew Lexicon. It majorly refers to leaves, more like vegetarian food, though it includes other kinds of foods. Thus "the tithe" was not money but plants and livestock. Meat refers to food. There is no other interpretation. That is what the Scriptures call it, and that is exactly what it says. It's food. Not dollars, pounds, or naira, but food. Plants and livestock.

The word "store" is translated from the Hebrew word *otsar*, which means a treasury, or a safe place (silo) where they stored food. The word storehouse (*otsar*) was also mentioned in Deuteronomy 28:12, Deuteronomy 32:34, and 1 Kings 7:51. The *Ostar* was built in such a way that it could preserve food. It was not Bank of America, Capital

One, Wells Fargo, First Bank, or Zenith Bank. It was a wooden- and mud-built silo. The word "house" is translated from the word *bayeith*. It means a temple. These words were used literally and referred to physical things. The tithes were brought in during the same period the Priests were present to minister on behalf of the nation, and because the Levites were part of the temple ministers and did not farm or labor like the other tribes, they had no food to eat. The Israelites would bring food for the priests in the temple. Everything is physically explained.

The word "rob" is translated from the Hebrew word *qaba*, which means to cheat someone of something that is his/hers. It was the same word used in Proverbs 22:23, translated as "spoil." Thus to "rob" means to spoil, to circumvent, or cheat. It means not to give another what is deserved. It's different from the word used to describe a criminal or a thief. A thief is one that breaks in to steal or takes something not belonging to him/her. These are two different things. In other words, Malachi meant that the Levites were not bringing the tithes, which was food to the store house, since they were the ones that brought the food into the storehouse in the tabernacle. So, robbing God was in reference to the Levites cheating the priests or depriving the priests who served in the temple of what was rightfully theirs. This instruction was therefore not for the believer.

Note that the word "tithe" means to give a tenth (10%) of your income or earnings etc. Hence, since it is yours, then it certainly cannot be wrong. However, the question to ask is this:

Is it mandatory to Tithe your Income?

Obviously, since there are no such instructions in the New Testament, whoever makes people do so is not instructing from the Scriptures. Therefore, the answer is NO. Any Pastor/Bishop who is asking people to tithe mandatorily, however mightly placed he/she is in Christendom, is going against the Scriptures. Notice, however, that a key lesson one might fail to see is that the tithe was done to honor God at different points in people's lives.

Tithing is an Old Testament law requirement, like Pentecost and Passover.

The First Tithers in The Bible: ABRAHAM AND JACOB

ABRAHAM:

Abraham, the friend of God, was the first to ever tithe. Genesis 14:19-20 reads, "And he blessed him, and said, blessed be Abram of the highest God, possessor of heaven and earth: And blessed be the highest God, which hath delivered thine enemies into thy hand. And he gave him tithes of all." Nobody instructed Abraham to pay tithe, not God or any prophet. The patriarch Abraham went to war, and when he came back from a victorious battle, he saw Melchizedek the priest, and the joy of winning the battle provoked Abraham to take 10% of the spoils of war and willingly "give," not "pay." He gave because it was not an obligation. He generously gave out of joy. Nobody preached to him to pay or be cursed; nobody preached to him to pay if he wanted to be blessed, no. Abraham gave voluntarily.

JACOB:

Jacob was the second person to tithe in the scriptures. Genesis 28:20-22 reads, "And Jacob vowed a vow, saying, If God will be with me, and will keep me in this way that I go, and will give me bread to eat, and raiment to put on, So that I come again to my father's house in peace; then shall the LORD be my God: And this stone, which I have set for a pillar, shall be God's house: and of all that thou shalt give me I will surely give the tenth unto thee." Jacob did the same thing as Abraham. Jacob poured oil on a stone in Genesis and said, "God if you take me and bring me back, I will give 10%," not "I will pay." Nobody instructed Jacob to pay or give. God never instructed Jacob or Abraham to pay or give tithe. It was Jacob's choice to do so. Jacob made the vow to tithe if God blessed him.

The two scenarios show tithing as an honor to God from whom all blessings came. Also, it's noteworthy that both Abraham and Jacob did this once. Throughout the Old Testament, there were no other mentions of Abraham or Jacob tithing again.

Are you Cursed if you refuse to Pay Tithe?

Of course, that is a capital NO. "There is therefore now no condemnation to them who are in Christ Jesus." (Romans 8:1a). Jesus Christ has redeemed you from the law being made a curse for you. (*See* Galatians 3:12-14). Let us examine the Old Testament (The Law) on tithing. There are several texts on tithing in the law. However, the following is very instructive. Deuteronomy 14:28-29 reads, *"At the end of three years thou shalt bring forth all the tithe of thine increase the same year, and shalt lay it up within thy gates: And the Levite, (because he hath no part nor inheritance with thee,) and the stranger, and the fatherless, and the widow, which are within thy gates, shall come, and shall eat and be satisfied; that the LORD thy God may bless thee in all the work of thine hand which thou doest."*

You can see from Deuteronomy 14 that the tithes were meant for the following persons:

1. The Levites: Why? The Levites were priests, who were not allowed to have an inheritance in the promised land – no farm, no livestock, no real estate or business. Their job was to serve in the temple of the Lord and attend to the spiritual needs of the Israelites. Hence the need for the Israelites to support them with food. (See Numbers 18:20-21). Since the Levites were to be at the service of the people, they had to be taken care of by the people. In the Epistles, Paul equates this to New Testament ministers, saying: *"Do ye not know that they which minister about holy things live of the things of the temple? and they which wait at the altar are partakers with the altar? Even so hath the Lord ordained that they which preach the gospel should live of the gospel."* (1 Corinthians 9:13-14).

Notice, Paul never asked believers to give them (ministers, pastors, evangelists, bishops or anyone who labors in the church full time) tithes. Rather, the church was to support them materially, and no percentage was given. We are instructed to care for our pastors, ministers, and church leaders generously, but no percentage is given. So, the choice is yours to make, whether it be groceries, 1% or 100%. (*See* 1 Timothy 5:17-18). If a man of God is laboring in the vineyard, he is entitled to double wages. We are expected to care for and give to that man of God handsomely and not just casual handouts. Galatians 6:6 (NASB) reads: *"The one who is taught the word is to share all good things with the one who teaches him."* (The term "good things" implies things of value, not just anything you feel like. In other words, our pastors must be well taken care of.

Again, notice that the word "tithe" was not used, neither was there a percentage for the gifts. Rather, wages, reward, or good things. Why is this so? Paul had taught how to give in his letters. (*See* 2 Corinthians 9:7). From Paul's explanation, you (the believer/church member) are to decide what wages or good things you give to support for your pastors. This must not be done grudgingly, because ministers ought to be well cared for. This refers to support and caring for their needs and not appetites. Owning private jets is an appetite; luxurious mansions are appetites; Ferraris and Lamborghinis are appetites and not needs. Why should you give your money to a church were the pastors own private jets and live in million dollar luxurious mansions while there are servants of God in remote villages and communities who need that help to continue the work of the ministry? Why?

2. Strangers: The widows, fatherless, the poor/needy folks among us (Malachi 3:5). Romans 15:26 reads, *"For it hath pleased them of Macedonia and Achaia to make a certain contribution for the poor saints which are at Jerusalem."* We can see that the church in Macedonia collected a contribution and sent the entire amount to the poor and needy people in Jerusalem. (See 1 Corinthians 16:1-2; James 1:27; Acts 4:32-35; Acts 6:1-4). The tithes of the Old Testament law were meant for this category of brethren. Today, our giving is for pastors, church members who are poor, and those who need support like school fees, medical emergencies, or in times like the global pandemic of Covid-19. This giving is meant to honor God, and our giving should always reflect that. (See Proverbs 3:9).

No Christian should find it difficult to honor God with his or her income or services. However, it must be clear that there is no mandatory percentage foisted on anyone. It's key to note that Paul gave instructions on how to give. 1 Corinthians 16:2 Paul said, "Upon the first day of the week let every one of you lay by him in store, as God hath prospered him, that there be no gatherings when I come." Observe that the word "God" was italicized, which implies it was inserted by the translators. Thus, the text can be better understood as: "Upon the first day of the week let every one of you lay by him in store as he has prospered, that there be no gatherings when I come." In other words, as one prospers, let him/her give. That is, your giving should be proportional to your income. Notice again, Paul did not mention the tithe or any percentage. He need not use percentages for men and women born of the Spirit.

New covenant believers don't give because they want to be blessed; they give because they are already blessed in Jesus, and it's their nature.

So, the idea of one being cursed if he/she refused to pay tithe is a capital NO. No believer is cursed. (*See* Galatians 3:12-14). You are blessed and will always remain blessed. God has blessed you with all you need in life. Do not allow any pastor to tell you different. God doesn't bless you because you tithe and won't curse you because you don't. God doesn't want you to tithe, but God expects us to give to those around us who are poor, sick, and need our help. God expects you to show love to the less privileged, the orphans, the widows, the fatherless, and the older population around us. God expects us to be the good Samaritan to that stranger on our path or in our community. (See Mathew 25:35-40).

Give to support your local churches. Give so your church can continue preaching the gospel to you and to the world, doing the missionary works they do, and paying all the staff working in the church. But let it be a church support offering or pastor support. This is a "voluntarily" obligation to your local church. Don't give because you want God to bless you. Give because God has blessed you and because you want to honor God with your resources.

Religion has given birth to all manner of false doctrines and money grabbing masters who are after people's bank accounts and not the growth of the believers, men who fly private jets and live in mansions at the expense of their ignorant congregation. Any country whose citizens pay more tithes than taxes will always borrow and depend on a country whose citizens pay more tax than tithe. This is the problem facing a lot of African countries. Religion has produced more fraud than politics.

The greatest fraud is being committed in some churches today in broad daylight, and no one is saying anything because these religious Mafias are hiding behind the pulpit and collar to brainwash and extort from the saints. These pastors' own houses all over the world. Some own private universities with tuitions even more expensive than government universities and colleges. There are schools owned by some of these churches that even members of the church cannot afford to attend. Some have five-star hotels, shipping companies, and even hold shares in multi-national corporations all over the world.

How did they make all this money? Was it not from their church members? Many of these pastors had nothing before they went into the ministry. Do you know how much these pastors make from these tithes? Imagine 10% of the income of one hundred members. Now imagine what that figure will be for a church with 10 to 30 thousand members. This is why we have many people rushing to open their own churches and the reason why we have more churches than industries in many African countries, especially my country of birth Nigeria. While other nations are building industries and establishing companies, many African countries are busy opening more and more churches on every corner of the street. Nigeria has the largest church auditorium in the world, big church buildings, and edifices without industries and companies. How can such a country thrive and compete with developed nations of the world? Nigeria is a developing country with a Gross Domestic Product (GDP) of less than 400 billion dollars, but this same country has the richest pastors in the world. Isn't that surprising? I am not against ministers living a good life, far from it. I believe men of God should live decent lives but not amass wealth at the expense of their members.

Church has become a business, and one of the fast avenues to unchecked and untaxed wealth. Gone are the days when men went into ministry for the sake of the gospel of salvation. Now it's for the sake of their bank accounts. Is this the kind of ministry Apostle Paul did? Did the disciples live the kind of lavish lifestyles we see among some pastors of today? Did the Apostle Paul have a private ship, boat, or even donkey? Did Jesus Christ or Apostle Paul live in luxurious mansions while on earth? Somehow, I feel as though "Pentecostalism" have created room for wolves, fraudsters, and Juju priests who are bent on enriching themselves and their families at the expense of the congregation to enter the Church of Jesus Christ. There is a wave of spiritual awakening sweeping through Christendom, and soon these money chasers will go out of business as their devices and ploys are gradually exposed. Their fake prophecies that never comes to pass, their fear driven hell fire and Satan-centered teachings are coming to an end.

The good news of the death, burial, and resurrection of Jesus Christ and His love for the world and the gift of righteousness is gradually taking central stage in many churches as it was meant to be. All over the world, people are awakening to their new life of grace, their rights and privileges in Jesus Christ. The truth is prevailing, and nothing can stop it.

CHRISTIANS LISTENING TO SECULAR MUSIC

Whether Christians should embrace or avoid secular music is a great question, and since there are many differing opinions and views on this topic, it can be a little difficult for some believers to come to a solid conclusion. But is there really anything called Christian songs in the Bible? In the church where I grew up and even the churches I attended six to seven years ago, certain kinds of music were forbidden. My pastors would not even attend the wedding of some church members if they were going to play "secular" songs like Afro pop or anything outside of the gospel. I, for one, think this is wrong.

Since the Bible does not specify what kinds of music Christians should listen to, believers may enjoy a freedom of choice, using biblical principles to give us discernment about those choices. A lot of songs out there go against godly morals or foster animosity, aggression, and hate. Negative principles are not something we want pounded into our minds over and over as we listen to music (1 Corinthians 15:33; Proverbs 22:24-25). Music can be a unique and powerful way to process our emotions—or just to have fun. There's a good chance that some of your favorite memories are tied to the song that was playing at the time. From the radio in the car to the loudspeakers in a grocery store to the Spotify playlists we share with our friends, music follows us wherever we go. But what does the Bible have to say about music and how we should interact with it?

Music weaves its way through the Bible early on. The entire book of Psalms is exactly what you might guess from the sound of the title: songs. About half of these songs were written by King David. Some of the songs recorded here were used in temple worship, while others are personal prayers asking for rescue and praising God when help arrived. But music's presence in the Bible goes back even further than that. Musicians are often referenced in the books of Genesis and Exodus, which tell the earliest stories about creation and God's calling of the nation of Israel. Jubal, "the father of all such as handle the harp and organ," was just the fourth generation descended from Adam and Eve (Genesis 4:21). In Exodus, when God safely led the Israelites out of slavery in Egypt, their first response was to sing. In Exodus 15, we have on record the lyrics to a song that Moses himself sang in praise.

Songs accompany the stories of the great Biblical heroes. After Moses, Joshua led Israel to literally bring the walls of Jericho down with musical instruments in Joshua 6. As mentioned above, King David, Israel's greatest leader, was a passionate musician. His son Solomon followed in his footsteps and is usually credited with two other full books of poetry and song: Ecclesiastes and Song of Solomon. In the New Testament, we don't have any books that are completely made of songs. But we do continue to see music as a key part of the human experience and an immediately present part of how the new church responded to the life, death, and resurrection of Jesus. In Luke 1:46-55, you can read Mary's Magnificat—the song she sang in praise when she found out she had been chosen to be the mother of Jesus, God's Son.

Songs are mentioned throughout Jesus' ministry, maybe most powerfully after the Last Supper when it says that Jesus and His disciple sang a hymn at the end of their Passover meal (Matthew 26, Mark 14). One of the last things the disciples did as a group during Jesus' earthly ministry was worship with music. When the disciples formed the early Church after Jesus' resurrection and ascension into Heaven, music was a part of their gathering and worshipping from day one. We know this because Paul talks about it in his letters to the growing churches in different locations (*see* Ephesians 5:19 & Colossians 3:16). In Paul's letter to the Philippians, he gives us the lyrics for one of the very first hymns ever used by the early church, quoting a very early worship song about Jesus, full of phrases like "though he was in the form of God, did not count equality with God a thing to be grasped, but emptied himself, by taking the form of a servant, being born in the likeness of men" (*See* Philippians 2:5-11).

Music itself is amoral—neither good nor bad. There are no "evil" musical instruments nor "morally good" styles of music. What differentiates the beneficial from the not-so-beneficial comes down to the lyrics. Music affects each of us in some way; specific songs can affect different people in different ways. While a certain song may not affect one person, it may be detrimental to another. (*See* 1 Corinthians 10:23-33). God gave humankind a creative heart; there is no music that has not stemmed from that initial gift. In fact, we can find bands not categorized by the music industry as "Christian," though they have Christian band members and/or their songs carry a message of hope.

For example, Skillet is an all-Christian rock band, but they're primarily played on the hard rock radio stations, alongside Korn and Black Sabbath. Different music styles, types, and genres are equally fine. Biblically, none are forbidden in and of themselves. That said, people resonate with what connects with their own heart and usually prefer listening to a certain kind of music, and that is OK. Some enjoy heavy metal, some classical, some gospel, some rap, and the list go on. It's simply a matter of taste. This reflects the fact that God made us uniquely, with unique tastes in what we enjoy.

There are many Christians who feel that the presence of God comes down in their church whenever they sing praise, but this is wrong. You don't need to sing to bring down the presence of God because the presence of God already resides inside you as a believer. The Holy Spirit lives in you 24/7. Also, you don't need worship songs or gospel songs to stir the spirit inside you. The Holy Spirit in you is God, and He doesn't need stirring. There are those who feel that they need to listen to worship songs in order to be in a spiritual mood or worship God, but in as much as we can worship God with songs, our entire life is a form of worship to God. Whatever you do as a believer is also worshiping God; when you laugh, play, cook, dance, shower, run, walk, go to the beach, or party. When you live with this mindset and knowledge, you will enjoy worship in a different, whole new way.

Not all songs that mention God or Jesus are even gospel songs. We assume that because a song has a particular beat or has the word God or Jesus in it, it's automatically a gospel song. This is not correct.

WHAT IS A GOSPEL SONG? A Gospel/Christian song should be a song that is centered on Jesus Christ, His Death, Burial and Resurrection. A Gospel song should be a song that speaks of the Goodness, Mercy and Loving nature of God. A Gospel song is a song that promotes our unity in Christ, our inheritance and position in Christ. A Gospel song should center on the man Jesus Christ and the awesomeness and power of God above all things. A Gospel song should speak of our restored position in Christ. In summary, a gospel song must be Christ-centered, and Christ-glorifying. Not all Christian songs are Gospel songs, but all Gospel songs are Christian songs. To clarify, when I say Gospel song, I'm not talking about the gospel music genre popularized by African American artists but the message of an individual song – the Gospel is Jesus Christ, and the message is the significance of His death, burial and resurrection to a sinner.

The Gospel is this: that Jesus Christ died for the sins of the world, and by His resurrection, all that acknowledge and receive Him into their hearts are forever saved, have eternal life, are forgiven of their sins (past, present, and future), receive the gift of righteousness, are redeemed and reconciled to the Father, and are blessed with all spiritual gifts from above. Therefore, if any "Christian" song is not written around this premise, such a song should be avoided and not called a Gospel song. But when a song is written and focused on the above, notwithstanding the beat of the song or the character of the artist, such a song should be listened to, sung, and enjoyed to its fullest.

So, I make bold to say that many of the songs we call "Christian songs" are not Gospel songs at all, because they glorify the artist instead of Jesus or, worse still, the songs are in direct opposition to the revealed Word of God, His nature and character. I have listened to "Christian songs" where the artist is either questioning God for why his life is the way it is, blaming God for all the bad things in the world, saying God should free him/her from the generational curses in the family, or even asking God why He would allow Satan to be so mean to him or her. Such songs are nothing but songs of ignorance of the gospel. There are songs asking God to destroy a set of people or kill every evil or bad person on earth, trying to introduce Old Testament laws, or asking God to bless them for being obedient, good children to Him. Again, such kinds of songs can never and should never be called Christian songs because they come from a place of ignorance and even go against the revealed Word of God.

Listening to secular songs or playing them at church events or your home is not a sin, and nothing is wrong about it. Period. Music is a choice. Whatever soothes your ears, enjoy it if you are comfortable with the lyrics and your spirit is okay with it. I don't like songs that use profane words a lot or that promote crime, drugs, or violence, but I do enjoy many songs by numerous artists. There are songs that contain pure knowledge and give very beautiful inspiration and comfort. Growing up, I learnt a great deal from listening to songs by Bob Marley, Lucky Dube, Gregory Isaac, and Culture. These legendary reggae artists sang about injustice, racism, and love. The songs we listen to have nothing to do with our spirit or in any way affect our spiritual position in Christ. It's simply an issue of what you like or don't like.

I personally like a lot of different music—both Christian and secular. A Christian label has nothing to do with how a song will affect a person; it has more to do how it affects you personally and (to an extent) the intention of the artist. Even though I do listen to secular music, I realize some songs affect me negatively, so I avoid them. Of course, a song that affects me badly may not affect another person at all. So, discernment must be done on a case-by-case basis. There is no "blanket" rule about which styles of music are OK. It depends on each song and each person. As a Christian, you aren't limited to Christian music or songs that are sung in church. There is nothing wrong with enjoying different types of music. You may choose what's best for your heart, between you and God. At the same time, do not harshly judge those who choose different music than you. God created us to grow in Him and to glorify His name. Any music, Christian or secular, has the ability to do so.

Not all Christian songs are gospel songs,

but all gospel songs are Christian songs.

Many secular musicians are immensely talented. Secular music can be very entertaining. There are many secular songs that have catchy melodies, thoughtful insights, and positive messages. In determining whether or not to listen to secular music, there are three primary factors to consider: 1) the purpose of music, 2) the style of music, and 3) the content of the lyrics.

1) The purpose of music. Is music designed solely for worship, or did God also intend music to be soothing and/or entertaining? The most famous musician in the Bible, King David, primarily used music for the purpose of worshiping God (see Psalm 4:1; 6:1, 54:1, 55:1; 61:1; 67:1; 76:1). However, when King Saul was tormented by evil spirits, he would call on David to play the harp in order to soothe him (1 Samuel 16:14-23).

The Israelites also used musical instruments to warn of danger (Nehemiah 4:20) and to surprise their enemies (Judges 7:16-22). In the New Testament, the apostle Paul instructs Christians to encourage one another with music: "Speak to one another with psalms, hymns, and spiritual songs" (Ephesians 5:19). So, while the primary purpose of music does seem to be worship, the Bible definitely allows for other uses of music.

2) The Style of Music and Beat. Sadly, the issue of music styles can be very divisive among Christians. There are Christians who adamantly demand that no musical instruments be used. There are Christians who only desire to sing the "old faithful" hymns. There are Christians who want more upbeat and contemporary music. There are Christians who claim to worship best in a "rock concert" type of environment. Instead of recognizing these differences as personal preferences and cultural distinctions, some Christians declare their preferred style of music to be the only "biblical" one and that all other forms of music are unwholesome, ungodly, or even satanic.

The Bible nowhere condemns any style of music. The Bible nowhere declares any musical instrument to be ungodly. The Bible mentions numerous kinds of string instruments and wind instruments. While the Bible does not specifically mention drums, it does mention other percussion instruments (Psalm 68:25; Ezra 3:10). Nearly all the forms of modern music are variations and/or combinations of the same types of musical instruments, played at different speeds or with heightened emphasis. There is no biblical basis for declaring any style of music to be ungodly or outside God's will. I love Afro pop, Reggae, country, and some R&B.

3) The Content of the Lyrics. Since neither the purpose of music nor the style of music determines whether a Christian should listen to secular music, the content of the lyrics must be considered. While not specifically speaking of music, Philippians 4:8 is an excellent guide for musical lyrics: *"Finally, brothers, whatever is true, whatever is noble, whatever is right, whatever is pure, whatever is lovely, whatever is admirable—if anything is excellent or praiseworthy—think about such things"* (NIV). If we should be thinking about such things, surely those are the things we should invite into our minds through music and lyrics. Can the lyrics in a secular song be true, noble, right, pure, lovely, admirable, excellent, and praiseworthy? If so, then there is nothing wrong with a Christian listening to a secular song of that nature.

FASTING AND PRAYER

Fasting is a practice that spans through the whole of Scripture. However, there is fasting as was done in the Old Testament, and there is New Testament fasting. What do I mean? People fasted in the Old Testament for many reasons. They fasted because they wanted to seek God's face. They fasted for forgiveness of sins (e.g., tearing of clothes and putting on sackcloth and ashes in order to seek the forgiveness of God). They fasted when they felt like they were under a curse or they felt like the heavens were shut towards them (e.g. in the Old Testament you see a prophet say: if my people who are called by my name shall humble themselves and fast and pray, and turn from their wicked ways and seek my face, I will hear from heaven. But this was the prophet's opinion.) They also fasted to seek for God's intervention in war between countries and fasted to seek material things.

The reason for fasting in the Old Testament is totally different from that of the New Testament.

We also saw Moses and Elijah, who both fasted for 40 days to seek God's face...but when Jesus fasted for 40 days, it was not for the same reason as Moses and Elijah. Rather He was preparing Himself, through prayer and fellowship with His Father, for His assignment. The New Testament Church begins after Pentecost. In the New Testament we don't fast to seek the face of God because God dwells in us. We don't fast to seek for forgiveness because we are forgiven by the sacrificial work of Christ. We don't fast to seek freedom from curses because Jesus had redeemed us from the curse (Galatians 3:13). We also do not fast to get things because His divine power has granted to us everything pertaining to life and godliness. (2 Peter 1:3).

Why do we fast in the New Testament?

We fast as an act of consecration, to set ourselves apart so we can pray and fellowship with God without interruption. Fasting in the New Testament was also done when there was a need to set people apart for Ministry. In Acts 13, they ministered unto the Lord in fasting, and the Holy Ghost said, "separate unto me Paul and Barnabas." These are the reasons why we fast in the New Testament.

Fasting doesn't have to be 6am to 6pm. It can be 6pm to 6am. The important thing is that you spend time fellowshipping and enjoying your Father's presence, through prayer, worship, and/or studying the Word of God. Fasting without these activities is simply a hunger strike. It is not the punishing of our bodies that is the fasting, but the time spent praying and studying or just simply fellowshipping with the Father, away from all distractions. If you have a serious problem, you can also take a fast. It is not the fast as an act that solves your problem, but as you fast, pray, and fellowship, God gives you wisdom and direction on how to overcome the problem.

New Testament Pattern of Prayer

It's important that you understand the concept of prayer and how to make effective use of it in order to maximize its benefits in your life. Prayer is a very profound means of relationship and intimacy with God. Prayer is not the means for you to ask God for anything, but rather it's a way through which you receive by faith those things that have been made available to you. Through prayer, a believer enforces spiritual power against the enemy. Through prayer, we get to go into a spiritual intercourse with God. The New Testament pattern of prayer is done with gratitude in one's heart. You go into prayer with gratitude that what you need has been made available for you.

We don't fast to receive from God, but rather,

we fast as a means of consecration and fellowship with God.

Grace doesn't exclude a believer from praying because prayer is a way to exercise sonship or your rights in the kingdom. We don't pray to ask; we go to prayer to receive what has been provided to us through Jesus Christ. The errors I have seen in many of the prayers we offer today in churches and in our homes is that we pray outside of the knowledge of the significance of the new covenant and lack of understanding of the Scriptures. The prayer is the receiving. The moment you start praying, that is the same moment you start receiving or taking delivery of your answers. God doesn't hold back; He has provided all you need. Remember that your prayer doesn't move God, nor does God react to your prayer. God acted before you prayed.

It's also imperative that you are aware that you don't have a faith problem as a believer. When you feel like you lack faith, and as a result, your prayers are not answered, you are acting/judging from a point of ignorance. No believer has a lack of faith problem. What some believers lack is ability to exercise their faith. Why? Faith is a gift, one of the contents of the package of redemption. Romans 12:3 reads; "For by the grace given me I say to every one of you: Do not think of yourself more highly than you ought, but rather think of yourself with sober judgment, in accordance with the faith God has distributed to each of you." (NIV). Faith has already been given unto you, so exercise it. The finished work of Jesus Christ was a complete package. It comes with all the believer needs to fully enjoy his or her new life. The new covenant life was designed in such a way that Man has no part in its achievement but is instead a beneficiary of it.

In Jesus Christ, all your prayers/needs

have been answered and provided.

It's your duty to receive or enforce it.

As a new covenant believer, there is no role you played in the attainment of your redemption. The new covenant closed all avenues that would give you the opportunity to boast. In this new covenant living, our boasting or pride is not in ourselves but in the person of Jesus Christ, His triumph through His death and resurrection on our behalf. We have been wrongly taught that until we pray, God doesn't answer or that it's when we pray that God answers. I'd like you to know that in Jesus Christ, all prayers have been answered. In Jesus Christ, all needs of Man have been provided. The day you became born again; you also received the answers for all you will ever need. So, through prayers you collect those things or take possession of them.

Prayer is reasoning with God on the platform of His Word. It's a medium through which you exercise your authority and dominion on earth as was given to you at creation. (*See* Genesis 1:26-28). Prayer must be done around the character and nature of God. What do I mean by this? When you pray and ask God to kill someone who did you wrong or you pray to ask God to hurt or punish someone who hurt you, such prayer is not in line with the character and nature of God. Asking God to kill someone or hurt them is a foolish prayer point. God doesn't kill or hurt people. It's not in His nature. Certain kinds of prayers Christians pray, especially in developing nations like my country of birth Nigeria, are a result of corrupt government and incompetent leadership, mismanagement of the economy and government. When you live in a developed nation where the economy is good and the government is making efficient use of taxpayer's money and country resources, certain kinds of prayer requests will leave your mouth.

You don't need Jesus or prayer to make money or have certain material things. If you did, then people of other religions who do not believe in Jesus Christ would all be poor and helpless, but you and I know that is not the case. When you have a thriving economy, and low unemployment rate, and the good skills/education needed, you get job offers easily. If there are good roads all through your country, you are more confident as long as you obey all traffic rules and regulations. You don't necessarily start panicking and speaking in tongues and praying for safety on the road when the road is, to a large extent, safe. But if you are living in a corrupt country where the roads are bad and dangerous, of course your instinct as a Christian is to always pray consistently out of fear each time you are travelling.

For example, a job candidate in the United States or any Western country is different from a job candidate in Nigeria or Cameroon. Why? Because the environment is different. A job applicant in Cameroon can have to have a good University degree and graduate with first class or second class and do well in the interview. Even when this job applicant is qualified, there is the problem of corruption which manifests in various ways. For a man, he must know someone to get the job. For the ladies, they are asked for sex or some form of relationship. So if you're a Christian living in a country where experience and qualification are, for the most part, second to connection, seeing that you don't have any political connection or know someone who can help speak on your behalf to get the job, all you can do is to go into seven days of fasting and prayer, blaming all the witches in your community, your grandparents or a family curse as the reason for your predicament or the reason for not getting the job. Whereas it's the result of a failed and corrupt government. Note, this is not to say that prayer is not necessary in such situation.

Not everything is resolved through prayer. You must differentiate between those things that are happening or affecting you as a result of a failed economy and corrupt government from those that are spiritual. Being a Christian or believer doesn't exclude you from the effects of a poor economy or bad and corrupt government. Therefore, you need sound spiritual and physical knowledge. In many African countries,

Christians pray about everything, and we think it's right or normal, but it's not. We pray about money as though money falls from heaven. They pray for a visa to travel abroad. I myself made this same mistake. I remember how I was fasting and praying just because I wanted to get a visa to travel to a Western country many years ago. A prayer of foolishness and ignorance.

Does a British citizen pray and fast for visa to travel to any African country, or any European, Asian, or American country? I don't think so. I have never gone to any church in the United States or the United Kingdom and heard members give testimony of how God answered their prayers and gave him/her a visa to an African or European nation. That's is not something you testify about or treasure like a golden egg. If not for business or tourism and experiencing the world, there is no reason for an American, German, or British citizen, even citizens of UAE, to travel to any country for anything. Why do I say so? Because all he or she needs is available in his/her country. There is good education, job opportunities with good salaries, security, good roads, a good healthcare system, and a working government.

If you go to many churches in Nigeria, there is no Sunday service where people don't give testimony for visas or where the pastor doesn't include getting visas to travel to a Western nation as the favor and rare blessing of God for those who are faithful and pays their tithes. Some pastors even have special anointing service for people looking for visas to travel abroad as though it's a divine achievement or benefit. If these countries were as successful as the United States or other developed nations like the UK, Germany, or Canada, why would their citizens, including my humble self, leave our motherland for greener pastures elsewhere?

A country with high unemployment rate, low wages, poor healthcare facilities, and no constant electricity supply... Why wouldn't people pray about virtually everything? Why wouldn't people be afraid of armed robbers and kidnappers while traveling? The same kidnappers and armed robbers are citizens who are acting out of frustration due to lack of employment and means to survive. To pray effectively, one must have a sound knowledge of the nature and personality of God, the significance of the finished works of Jesus Christ, and most importantly, one must be conscious of his restored identity in Christ. Effective and fervent prayer is not in the loudness of your voice or the use of large vocabularies, tongue speaking, or the duration you pray. A prayer is effective when it's done in knowledge and backed up by faith.

In Jesus Christ, all your prayers/needs have been answered and provided. It's your duty to receive or enforce it. This is where prayer comes in. This knowledge is very important if you want to pray effectively. Do you need healing? Then go into prayer and receive it by faith. Note, I said receive not ask. Do you need wisdom in any area of your life? Then go into prayer and receive it by faith. Do you need the fruit of the womb? Then go into prayer and receive it by faith. Do you need ideas for financial breakthroughs? Then go into prayer and receive it by faith. Do you need protection over your life and that of your loved ones? Then go into prayer and receive it by faith. Faith is the tool through which we receive what grace has provided. Our prayer must come out of a heart of gratitude first. Gratitude for what? Gratitude for the gift of salvation, gratitude for the forgiveness of sins, gratitude for eternal life, and gratitude for what you are about to receive.

In the New Testament, unlike the Old, we show gratitude before we receive, not after we had received. Why? Because we are conscious of the fact that it was provided even before we came to know and confess Jesus as our only Lord and Savior.

FAITH AND FASHION

There is a lot of doctrinal divergence in the body of Christ concerning a believer's faith-walk and his fashion life. This has affected their approach to fashion purely from self-imposed religion/regulations and moral modification in deliberate defiance of what the Scripture explains in the light of Christ. Let's be thorough with our understanding and not quick to pervert the image of Christ because of religious over-zealousness and ignorance that stems from being unskilled in the word of truth. Fashion does not define our relationship with God, but it came into existence the moment man realized they were naked. They made coverings for themselves from fig leaves according to the account in Genesis 3:7: *"Then the eyes of them were opened, and they knew that they were naked; and they sewed fig leaves together and made themselves coverings."*

God never saw man in his mortality state naked, and He still doesn't. Accordingly, God does not deal with us based on our fashion sense and physical appearance. In His image we are made; in His image we are seen. Genesis 1:27 reads, "So God created man in His own image; in the image of God, He created him; male and female He created them." Our mode of fashion has nothing to do with our relationship with God, which entails our faith-walk and how He sees us.

So, let's look at jewelry and tattoos. After the fall of man, men were at liberty in their sense of fashion as governed by their culture before God As recorded in Exodus 35:22-23: *"They came, both men and women, as many as had a willing heart and brought earrings and nose rings, rings and necklaces, all jewelry of gold, that is, every man who made an offering of gold to the LORD. And every man, with whom was found blue, purple, and scarlet thread, fine linen, goats' hair, red skins of rams, and badger skins, brought them"* (NKJV). Fashion has never been a barrier between God and man, they came to God with all the ornaments you can think of as an offering of gold to God.

Has God changed toward our sense of fashion? Well let's consider another interesting Scripture: Numbers 31:50 reads; *"Therefore we have brought an offering for the LORD, what every man found of ornaments of Gold: Armlets and Bracelets and Signet Rings and Earrings and Necklaces, to make atonement for ourselves together before the LORD."* Ornaments (earrings, rings, nose rings, bracelets, ankle chains necklaces) were used to make atonements before the Lord. Men and women, boys and girls wore earrings from the beginning. These ornaments were mostly used for outer adornment or we can say body decoration in the Old Testament.

It was also recorded in the Scripture that prophet Ezekiel of the old testament was outwardly decorated by God in fine linen and ornaments. Ezekiel 16:10-12 makes this clear: *"I clothed you in embroidered cloth and gave you sandals of badger skin; I clothed you with fine linen and covered you with silk. I adorned you with ornaments, put bracelets on your wrists, and a chain on your neck."* God decorating Ezekiel with ornaments is a clear proof that He does not see such adornment as something that should affect our walk with Him. Furthermore, the Mosaic law in the Old Testament concerning fashion was one of the 623 laws given to Moses to be kept by men. Deuteronomy 22:5,11 reads: *"A woman shall not wear anything that pertain to a man, nor shall a man put on a woman's garment, for all who do so are an abomination to the LORD your God. You shall not wear a garment of different sorts, such as wool and linen mixed together."*

What about Tattoos?

Tattooing your skin as a man or a woman has nothing to do with your faith walk. Though some persons find it immoral for personal reasons, the Scripture is the only answer to this, not men's personal opinions. Scripture has nothing clear to say about the practice of tattooing as a New Testament believer. Tattoos were forbidden under the old covenant: "You shall not make any cuttings in your flesh for the dead, nor tattoo any marks on you: I am the LORD" (Leviticus 19:28, NKJV). However, the law also said men shouldn't have their beards shaved or trimmed or have a stylish haircut, according to Leviticus 19:27. Therefore, if we go by the entire law then, the men having their beards or head shaved are sinning.

Now we are in the dispensation of Grace, which was given to us through faith in Christ. We are no more under the law but at liberty, liberty to our choices of fashion included. There are no two sides to liberty. The liberty which Christ gave us covers everything in its totality, that which we can ever think of or imagine. "Stand fast therefore in the liberty by which Christ has made us free and be not entangled again with the yoke of bondage" (Galatians 5:1). Why then do we choose to be entangled again with a yoke of men self-imposed regulations on what to wear and what not to wear? Our choice of dress does not in any way affect our faith-walk or stand in our way of imitating Christ.

In Colossians 2:20-23 Paul says: *"Therefore, if you died with Christ from the basic principles of the world, why, as though living in the world, do you subject yourselves to regulations—'Do not touch, do not taste, do not handle,' which all concern things which perish with the using—according to the commandments and doctrines of men? These things indeed have an appearance of wisdom in self-imposed religion, false humility, and neglect of the body, but are of no value against the indulgence of the flesh."* If our faith-walk is tied to our fashion sense or style, then Christ came and died as a fashion designer, which is an insult to the cross and the finished work of Christ. If He doesn't see it as an abomination before Him or highlight it as a sin, then we shouldn't. Who are we imitating, Christ or man-made doctrine/regulations? God's only concern is our faith-walk and relationship with Him as a Father.

We are so caught up in mundane things and men's philosophy/regulations that we let go of our spiritual reality. 1 Peter 1:18-19 reads: *"Knowing that you were not redeemed with corruptible things, like silver or gold, from your aimless conduct received by tradition from your fathers, but with the precious blood of Christ, as a Lamb without blemish and without spot."* Is God not seeing what Christ did because of your earrings, nose rings, tattoos, rag jeans, trousers, necklaces etc.? It is not wrong for a Man/woman to dress in clothing that is best comfortable for them both in church and outside the church. Colossians 2:16-17 reads, "So let no one judge you in food or in drink, or regarding a festival or a new moon or Sabbath, which are a shadow of things to come, but the substance is of Christ."

It is not a sin or irresponsible for a man to wear ornaments such as earrings, nose rings, necklaces, rings, bracelets, dreadlocks, tattoos, rag jeans, long hair, braided hair, rag shirts, hair beads, etc. The scriptures nowhere condemn an earring in men, and there were men in the Bible who wore earrings. It was never a sin problem to God in the Old Testament, and I don't expect that it should be now. God is not bipolar.

There are verses about fashion in the New Testament, but they must be taken in context. I once heard someone say that a man was sinning because he said a prayer while wearing a hat. Is your hat strong enough to stop your prayers from reaching God? This religious thought comes from 1 Corinthians 11:4 *"Every man praying or prophesying, having his head covered, dishonors his head."* OUCH! But...is there more to this verse? Yes, and it will take a little while to walk through. Translated accurately, the phrase is rendered "Having something down from his head." What the something is, is neither implied nor stated in this verse.

Similarly, 1 Corinthians 11:5 and 14 says, *"But every woman who prays or prophesies with her head uncovered dishonors her head, for that is one and the same as if her head were shaved. Does not even nature itself teach you that if a man has long hair, it is a dishonor to him. But if a woman has long hair, it is a glory to her; for her hair is given to her for a covering."* The covering here was referring to hair. The covering will be "cut off" or "shaved." How often do we "cut" or "shave"?. Conclusively, 1 Corinthians chapter 11 was one of Apostle Paul's letters to the church in Corinth addressing and making known in clear terms the authorities in the body of Christ as shown in 1 Corinthians 11:3 "But I want you to know that the head of every man is Christ, the head of woman is man, and the head of Christ is God."

Paul addressed the church in Corinth based on their cultural beliefs and practices. In the Jewish culture it is wrong for men not to wear a hat, or yamaka, while praying, which emanates from the Jewish custom of wearing yamaka in the tabernacle. Are they all sinning because of this act? Of course not! This is their culture. The Gospel (the finished work of Christ) is our tradition. It is the way of our people, the people we have now become. It is the saying of our ancestor and progenitor, Christ Jesus. The Gospel is our culture. It supersedes every culture and tradition. Apostle Paul had this to say in Colossians 2:8: *"Beware lest anyone cheat you through philosophy and empty deceit, according to the tradition of men, according to the basic principles of the world, and not according to Christ."*

If you choose certain clothing to be worn to Church and others elsewhere, then you are championing hypocrisy. Does God see us only when we are in church? Of course not! Every man born (again) in Christ is Righteous, Justified, Redeemed, Sanctified, Glorified, Holy, Free, Qualified, not by his own act but by the one act of Christ. 1 Corinthians 1:30 reads: *"But of Him you are in Christ Jesus, who became for us wisdom from God—and Righteousness and sanctification and Redemption."* The earlier we renew our minds towards the ideology of fashion and our faith-walk in the light of Christ and the liberty that we have been brought into, the better for us.

WHITE WEDDING/CHURCH MARRIAGE IS NOT SCRIPTURAL.

Is a white wedding or Church wedding scriptural?

Did the Bible give Pastors/Bishops the authority to pronounce or join a marriage?

Is there a special blessing in getting married or wed in the Church?

Who in the Bible is authorized to join marriage?

Beloved brothers and sisters, the answers to these questions are very important and need to be resolved in light of the Scriptures. Doctrinal issues must be rightly interpreted and explained. Eph: 5:31 and Gen 2:24 says a man shall leave his father and mother and be joined to his wife and they two shall become one flesh. The scriptures did not say in Church or mention pastors. In the year 1164, the church established marriage as a sacrament. Once this happened, the involvement of clergy mushroomed. The Catholic Church did not require marriages to be officiated by a priest until 1563, and the Anglican Church did not get around to making this requirement until 1753. So, for the past five hundred years there have been, in the European tradition, three kinds of marriage: legal, religious, and social. But social marriage, strictly speaking, is the most biblical.

There is nowhere in the Scriptures from Genesis to Revelation, or from the words of the prophets, Apostles or even Jesus, who is the revealed God, that said that Church marriage is scriptural. Marriage is purely a family/Social affair. Marriage is between two families. It has nothing to do with the Church. But why have we made something that's purely unscriptural so mainstream that it has caused so much pain for many couples? No pastor or bishop is authorized in the Bible to join any marriage. That responsibility is given to the two fathers or the elders of the two intending families and also the government of the land via registry.

Why have we made a cultural/family centered function into a religious doctrine that has no biblical grounds. Did the bible ever say that if we don't get wedded in Church that God blessings is not with us?

So many young ladies are single today because their Pastor, Bishop or Prophet told them that the man they are dating is not their spouse. Did the Bible ever give pastors such right? In America/Europe, people get married in Court or Church. This is purely a cultural tradition. In fact, on these two continents and Asia, the bride's family takes the responsibility of the wedding. In Nigeria, people take 3 years just planning for a white wedding even after a traditional marriage or court wedding. Some churches in Nigeria forbid couples to know each other sexually after traditional marriage until they have done with Church wedding. Who gave us this instruction? Jesus Christ or who? Please I need to know.

In Africa, we have our own cultural form of marriage called the traditional marriage. Once a man pays the bride price/dowry of the woman, he is officially married. But why have we decided to make the white wedding in Africa such a huge thing? Why have we decided to adopt a culture that's not ours and make it a law and cross for people? Many people have gone into huge debt in the name of a white wedding. Couples have separated because of white weddings. In some African churches if you are not wedded in the church, your marriage is not even considered legal. In Nigeria, people celebrate the white wedding even more than the traditional wedding. I will say this emphatically here: There is no special blessing attached to a church marriage. In fact, there is nothing spiritual about marriage in and of itself. Some churches will say you have to go through a series of counseling before some marriage committee before you will be wed.

I know of ladies who have brought their intended husbands first to their Pastors even before their parents or family elders. Where did we get this idea from, people? The average young couple of today take time to prepare for their white wedding - the type of white gown/suit they will buy, the number in their bridal party, the entrance music, the dance, the kind of food, the cake - but they don't take time to plan and prepare for the marriage itself. The duty of the Church or pastor is to preach Jesus Christ and not to be holding marriage ceremonies. The Bible has not given the Church any such duties. If you are a Westerner, then do your white wedding/ court marriage because that's your culture. If you are an African, have your traditional marriage and be okay with it. That's your culture. Yesterday, a brother sent me a very long email saying his fiancée says if he doesn't give her a white wedding, she is not interested in the marriage. Do you see what we have unconsciously caused for ourselves as Africans? Now, if you choose to have Church Marriage, it's your choice to make. But never attach any special spiritual blessing or importance to that, for there is none. Many young men are still single today, not because they don't want to marry their girlfriends but because they don't have the money yet to finance a white wedding. Africans no longer even fancy or celebrate their traditional marriage ceremony like they do the white wedding. All in the name of wearing Brazilian/Italian wedding gowns and an Italian Suit.

DOCTRINAL DIFFERENCES AMONG CHRISTIANS

There's a story of a man marooned on a deserted island. When a ship came to his rescue, the captain learned that the man had lived alone on this island for five years. There were three huts, so he asked about them. The man said that he lived in the first one. "Then what's that second hut?" the captain asked. The man said, "That's where I go to church." "What about that third hut?" the captain asked. The man replied, "Oh, that's where I used to go to church." I think he was a Baptist! While that story is funny, actual church splits are not so funny. When churches divide, people get hurt. Some get so disgusted that they drop out of church altogether. Some may be so disillusioned that they leave the faith. Many, if not most, of you have been through church splits. In the New Testament, the churches in Corinth, Galatia, Ephesus, Philippi, and Colossae were all in danger of divisions.

Unity among believers is particularly important to our Lord. He died to secure it (Ephesians 2:12-14) and it's a major part of our witness to the world (John 13:34-35; 17:20-23). So, we must diligently preserve the unity of the Spirit in the bond of peace and to grow to maturity in Christ, so that we may attain to the unity of the faith (Ephesians 4:3,13). But how do we preserve the unity of the Spirit and attain to the unity of the faith? Obviously, it doesn't happen automatically! There are at least four kinds of differences in the modern church which threaten church unity: doctrinal difference, personal difference, personality difference, and methodological difference.

Resolving doctrinal differences from a Christocentric point of view is crucial for the sake of the Gospel.

You may be inclined to think that doctrine is not important or that theological controversies are for theologians to argue about and don't affect you. But I would remind you that this year is the 503rd anniversary of the Protestant Reformation, which centered on several important doctrinal disputes that the Roman Catholic Church refused to correct. And although some are now calling for an end to the division that happened then, the doctrinal division between the Catholic Church and the Reformers was and still is primarily over the gospel.

Doctrinal differences are crucial because truth matters. Think about this: What is the difference between a Jehovah's Witness who is trying to work his way into heaven but is actually on his way to hell, and you, a believer in Jesus Christ, bound for heaven? The main difference is theological. You may object, "No, the difference is that I believe in Jesus Christ, but he doesn't." But every Jehovah's Witness I've talked to claims to believe in Jesus Christ as Savior and Lord. The problem is that the "Jesus" he believes in is not the Jesus of the Bible. The Jehovah's Witness "Jesus" is a created being, not the eternal Son of God.

Perhaps someone would still object, "Isn't doctrine divisive? Isn't love the most important thing?" What if someone you love was about to drink a glass of water containing deadly poison because he believed it was pure water? You know that if he drank that contaminated water, he would die. Love would not ignore the truth that that drink would kill him. Even if he sincerely believed that that poisoned water was good for him, it still would kill him. Faith is only as good as its object. Faith in a contaminated glass of water is deadly. Faith in a contaminated gospel is eternally deadly! Spiritual truth is not relative to every person's opinion of God or the gospel! To be saved, our faith must be in God's only revealed way of salvation: the eternal Son of God, crucified for our sins, and risen for our justification.

In the early church, a doctrinal controversy arose as the gospel spread from its Jewish origins to the Gentiles. In Jerusalem, the early church consisted mostly of Jews who had come to faith in Jesus as their crucified and risen Messiah. But when the gospel spread north to Antioch and beyond (through the first missionary journey of Paul and Barnabas), many Gentiles came to faith in Christ (Acts 11:20-21). After Paul and Barnabas returned to Antioch, some Jews who professed to believe in Jesus, called Judaizers, began going to the largely Gentile churches that Paul and Barnabas had established, teaching that in addition to believing in Christ for salvation, the Gentiles must also be circumcised and follow the Jewish ceremonial laws. Paul wrote the letter to the Galatians to refute their spiritually deadly error.

Eventually, the Judaizers went to Antioch and were teaching, "Unless you are circumcised according to the custom of Moses, you cannot be saved" (Acts 15:1). After Paul and Barnabas had great dissension with them, the church sent them with a delegation to Jerusalem to get this matter cleared up with the apostles and elders there. The Jerusalem Council affirmed the same gospel that Paul preached but asked the Gentile converts to abstain from some things that would needlessly alienate unbelieving Jews. Doctrinal differences must be resolved to preserve unity without compromising the truth of the Gospel.

The point is that Paul didn't see this as an unimportant doctrinal dispute that should be overlooked in love. He saw it as poisoned water that threatened the truth of the gospel itself. Doctrinal differences are crucial when the truth of the gospel is at stake. Even though the Judaizers were probably sincere and only wanted to preserve the Law of Moses, they were sincerely wrong! Paul didn't just shrug it off, saying, "Unity must prevail! Let's set aside our differences and come together where we agree!" Rather, he fought vigorously for the truth of the gospel, pronouncing eternal judgment on these false teachers (Galatians 1:6-9)! He saw that people's eternal destinies were at stake. Correct doctrine can make an eternal difference!

Doctrinal differences must be resolved to preserve unity without compromising the truth of the Gospel.

While unity is extremely important, it cannot trump the truth of the Gospel. If the Gospel is compromised, the resulting "unity" is not the unity of the Spirit. It would be a superficial "unity" of some who believe in Jesus and some who do not. Jesus prayed for the love and unity of His disciples, but it was love and unity based on the truth (John 17:17). Jesus claimed to speak the truth (John 8:45) and to be the truth (John 14:6). He told Pilate, "For this I have been born, and for this I have come into the world, to testify to the truth. Everyone who is of the truth hears My voice" (John 18:37, NASB). He promised that He would send to His disciples "the Spirit of truth" (John 14:17; 15:26). So, to argue that Jesus set love above truth is false. He knew that tolerating a false gospel is not love, because it would lead the person believing it to damnation, not to eternal life.

The Apostle Paul also knew that to preserve peace while compromising the truth of the Gospel was not true love and unity. He risked disunity with Peter and Barnabas over a situation that occurred in Antioch (I think before the Jerusalem Council, although scholars debate the timing of this incident). Peter visited the Antioch church and ate with the Gentiles, something strict Jews would never do, and realized that the Gentiles who believed were true brothers and sisters in Christ (Acts 10:28). But when the Judaizers visited Antioch, Peter and even Barnabas feared their disapproval and withdrew from eating with the Gentiles. Paul boldly confronted Peter and Barnabas in front of the entire church (Galatians 2:11-14). He knew that to preserve unity while compromising the Gospel would have been spiritually fatal.

All of this is directly relevant to our day when many influential Christian leaders are calling for Protestants to be unified with the Roman Catholic Church. They argue that we should come together because of the many beliefs we share and agree to disagree over the doctrine of justification by faith alone. The Catholic Church teaches that we must not only believe in Jesus, but also add our good works and merit to be saved. It's the same error the Galatian Judaizers were teaching: Believe in Jesus plus add your good works (such as getting circumcised and following Jewish traditions). Rome still affirms the canons of the Councils of Trent that condemn those who believe that we are justified by faith alone.

Even the famous evangelist Billy Graham for many years played down any differences between evangelicals and Roman Catholics. He said, "I have no quarrel with the Catholic Church" (Iain Murray, Evangelicalism Divided [Banner of Truth], p. 68). Speaking of the difference between evangelicalism and Roman Catholicism, he said, "I don't think the differences are important as far as personal salvation is concerned" (Ibid.). He also often said, "The one badge of Christian discipleship is not orthodoxy, but love" (Ibid. at 33). I readily admit that there have been many shameful divisions among Christians over petty issues, which is a sin. But the Bible shows that there are times when it is sinful not to divide over doctrine. When the doctrine concerns how a person gets saved, there can be no compromise. So then, how should we attempt to resolve doctrinal differences in a biblical manner, while trying to preserve the unity of the Spirit in the bond of peace?

Doctrinal differences should be resolved from a Christocentric standpoint and not be brushed aside, especially subjects regarding very fundamental areas of our Christian faith. Why is it important we do this? Because these subjects affect how we live as Christians, the way we relate and fellowship with God and Man, our salvation, and the Christian life in general. Thank you for reading and I hope it was worth your time and effort. You are blessed.

Recent Titles from Pastor **Great Igwe** available online at
www.greatigwe.com

Forward: Bishop Harry Jackson Jr.

WALKING TALL IN TOUGH TIMES

AN EVERYDAY GUIDE TO DEALING WITH EVERYDAY CHALLENGES

GREAT IGWE

GETTING IN TOUCH WITH Great...

Hey, like to contact Great Igwe, for Bookings, Mentorship, Counselling or questions and clarity on any topic in this book, you can do so by:

Email: greatigwe28@gmail.com

Website: www.greatigwe.com

OR

Follow Pastor Great on:

 *@Greatigwe2*

@Greatigwe

@Greatigwe

NOTES

Great Igwe

The Misrepresented God

Great Igwe

www.ingramcontent.com/pod-product-compliance
Lightning Source LLC
Chambersburg PA
CBHW031135160426
43193CB00008B/150